sex
-planations

sex
-planations

A guide to discussing
Sex & Sexuality in the Caribbean

Dr. Alverston Bailey

PELICAN PUBLISHERS LIMITED
Kingston, Jamaica W.I.

First Published in Jamaica, 2014 by Pelican Publishers Limited

44 Lady Musgrave Road
Kingston 10, Jamaica, W.I
Tel: (876) 978-8377 Fax: (876) 978-0048
Email: pelicanpublishers@gmail.com
Website: www.pelicanpublishers.com.jm
   www.pelicandigitalbooks.com

© 2014, Alverston Bailey

ISBN 978-976-8240-04-0

All rights reserved. No part of this publication may be reproduced or transmitted in any form or by any means electronic, mechanical, photocopying, recording or otherwise; or stored in any retrieval system of any nature without the written permission of the copyright holder.

Cover design by Pelican Publishers Limited
Illustrations provided by Courtney Robinson

Table of Contents

Preface	vii
Foreword	x
Acknowledgements	xi

PART 1 - FOREPLAY — 1

The Chemistry Of Love	2
What Turns You On?	12
Sexual Fantasies	26
The Sexual Response Cycle	34
Sex Dreams	44

PART 2 - THE MAIN EVENT — 51

Flirting	52
Dating	58
Scentsational Sex	64
Erogenous Zones	78
Aphrodisiacs	86
The Art Of Kissing	112
Sex Toys	118
The Top 20 Sexual Positions	130
Tantric Sex	146

PART 3 - AFTER PLAY   151

Overcoming Emotional Barriers To Sex   152

Sexual Healing   158

Sexercise   168

Rekindling Desire   176

Coping Skills For The Frustrated Woman   182

The Joys Of Solo Sex   188

PART 4 - SEXUAL DISORDERS   195

Penis Stress   196

Erectile Dysfunction   202

When Love Hurts   210

Premature Ejaculation   216

Sexual Desire Disorders   222

The Elusive Female Orgasm   230

PART 5 - SEXUAL TABOO   237

Sex In The Elderly   238

Sex In The Disabled   250

Voyeurism   264

Sexual Fetishism Exposed   270

Kinky Sex   278

Pornography   288

PART 6 - SAFER SEX — 295

How To Keep It Sexy and Safe — 296

The Mysterious Condom — 304

PART 7 - SEX THERAPY — 311

Sex Therapy – A New Beginning — 312

GLOSSARY — 318

Preface

My chosen career as a family physician has afforded me the opportunity over the years to interact and care for patients with a variety of sexual concerns. I have been intrigued and perturbed by the high level of anxiety, anger, fear, ignorance and dysfunctional relationships caused by sexual disorders. I therefore launched a journey of discovery about human sexuality which I have called *Sexplanations*. This book chronicles the pearls of wisdom I have picked up along the way. This journey, in fact, began as a young medical student in the 1970s, when I read *The Naked Ape,* a controversial and provocative text at the time written by Desmond Morris.

Since then, I have read many of the great masters, whose pioneering works have helped to demystify human sexuality such as Masters and Johnson, Alfred Kinsey, Helen Fisher, Alex Comfort, Ethel Person, Alan Hirsch, Ernest Grafenberg, *Kama Sutra* Vatsayama, Winnifred Cutler, Tracy Cox, Betty Dobson and others. With the knowledge gleaned I was well on my way. When I was asked by *The Gleaner* to write a series of articles on sex in 2008, I embarked on an in depth review of the literature to find answers to questions which had been swirling in my mind for years such as: What turns us on? Why do people fall in love and just as quickly fall out of love? Why do men and women have such a serious desire discrepancy? Is sex primarily for procreation and pleasure or are there health benefits to sex? Why are men so obsessed with penis size and women quite indifferent?

I am pleased to use this medium to share my findings with you. The other perplexing question that I sought to clarify, is the perceived inadequacy of our sexual appendages and the vast array of paraphernalia euphemistically called marital aids that are available to enhance the sexual experience. The chapter on this subject should be a real eye opener.

Many of my male patients are overwhelmed by performance anxiety and yearn for that sexual elixir, that potent aphrodisiac, that will enable him to meet all his sexual expectations. So, I have unearthed a plethora of exotic herbs, spices and foods, used all around the world, that are said to enhance a man's virility — a must read for men plagued with doubts about their potency.

Many books have been written on sexual positions, but I have often questioned their usefulness since most people lack either the agility, the stamina or the capability to even consider most of these positions. This book will walk you through the basic positions and help you to decide which options are best for you.

Sexual taboos are rife in our society and I hope the section that addresses this issue will enhance your understanding and promote tolerance for those whose sexual mores and tastes differ from yours. A book on sex would not be complete without a section on safe sex practices in this era of HIV. Therefore, I have provided you with an in depth potpourri of options you can consider, to minimize your risks of contracting sexually transmitted diseases and I am sure you will enjoy the section on the humble little condom.

Well, readers, as you turn the pages of this book and join me in this *Sexplanation*, you will be exposed to some compelling evidence that love is a matter of chemistry and sex is a matter of physics. And if the flames of your love have grown dim, I hope this book will enable you to rekindle the fires. Readers who would like to gain more in depth information on any of the issues raised are invited to peruse the extensive references and bibliographies at the end of each chapter.

Happy reading.

Foreword

Dr. Karen Carpenter PhD; CST; PGCHE Research fellow UWI

Dr. Alverston Bailey's *Sexplanation* is very aptly titled, taking the reader on a sexual journey that begins with the gentlest of flirtations in foreplay, to a satisfying release in the main event and the ever so important after play. The book is a first of its kind in that it encompasses the medical, practical and therapeutic approaches to sexuality. Readers will find *Sexplanations* a wonderful resource book; full of useful information about various aspects of human sexuality.

Dr. Bailey gives us good insights into sexual chemistry between men and women and the pleasures of attraction. He very carefully takes us through the stages of physical attraction and falling in love. The book explores and debunks a variety of sexual myths that have hampered sexual expression over time. Some of the less understood sexual conditions are also unpacked in clear language that will help readers to gain insight into their own issues and challenges. *Sexplanations* takes us through the intricacies of good sex, as well as providing a foundation for understanding sexual dysfunctions.

For those readers who are shy about broaching the subjects of safe sex and the use of sex toys; both topics are covered in some detail. The chapter on Kinky Sex is an interesting and informative look at sado-masochism, which cautions readers as to acceptable rules of engagement for these practices. This is an enjoyable and well thought out book on love, life and the enjoyment of human interaction. Dr. Alverston Bailey is a trail blazer in the area of sexual health literature and has provided us with a well researched book that is certainly food for thought and discussion.

Acknowledgements

This book has been for me a labour of love, but this dream could not have been realized without the encouragement and unstinting assistance of many persons. First let me thank my family for their support throughout the production of this manuscript. The genesis of this book really was born from a series of articles that I wrote for *The Gleaner* in 2008, and I must express my deep appreciation to the editor of *The Gleaner* who afforded me the opportunity to share my thoughts with their readers.

Special thanks must be given to Ms. Petrina Francis formerly of *The Gleaner*, who invited me to write these articles. I thank her also for her rigorous editorial advice. I must express deep gratitude to Dr. Henry I. C. Lowe for encouraging me to publish this book, and of course to Pelican Publishers Ltd.

I must also thank Mr. Cliff Hughes and Ms. Elizabeth Bennett of Nationwide News Network for the wealth of experience I gained while hosting the show '*People, Relationship and Sex*' and of course the many callers to the show who shared their experience with me and enhanced my understanding of matters of the heart. Thanks to my friend and mentor Dr. Karen Carpenter for her support and contribution to the foreword. Finally, you would all agree that the book would not have achieved its Caribbean flavour without the high quality cartoons drawn by Courtney Robinson.

Part 1 - FOREPLAY

" The psychological turmoil evoked by sexual passion often leaves the unwary quite befuddled as they are swept away on the crest of love into unknown emotional territories. Part one (foreplay) will enable you to navigate safely through these turbulent times "

The Chemistry of Love:
The Experience of Being in Love

"Love is a matter of chemistry but, sex is a matter of physics"
- Author unknown

This opening chapter will prove to you that love is indeed a matter of chemistry.

Are we at the mercy of our biochemistry?

Have you ever been in love, does your heart ache for that someone? Would you die for him or her? Why are we consumed with passion for our love object? Does the feeling haunt, startle and waylay? This introductory chapter will shed some light on this most perplexing of life's emotions.

In the early seventies a fellow medical student revealed to me that he was having a life changing experience, he had actually fallen in love, but at that time he had no idea what malady had affected him. All he knew was that he had met this girl and she had blown him away. He could neither eat nor sleep, he had tremors, he felt dizzy; he was devastated. At the time I was unable to help him because I had no idea what was wrong. But, now I know.

In the mid 1960s, Dorothy Tennov surveyed four hundred people. She wanted to know what it's like to be in love and surprisingly the respondents said the emotions they felt were "fear, shaking, flushing, weakness and stammering". When we are attracted to each other, a cascade of events occur in our bodies resulting in flushed cheeks, racing hearts and clammy hands. Dr. Tennov concluded that 'when it comes to love we are at the mercy of our biochemistry.' [1]

It appears that being in love causes some type of mental aberration and many of you, like me, can attest to having had this experience at some time in your life. It is now known that people who have recently fallen in love have some of the symptoms of a mental disorder called Obsessive Compulsive Disorder or OCD. This startling fact was revealed in a study done in Pisa, Italy in 1999. The study included twenty students who had recently fallen in love, and who had obsessed about their new love for at least four hours every day, but had not yet consummated the relationship with sex. Seventeen women and three men volunteered. A separate group of twenty people with OCD was studied at the same time, as was a control group of twenty people not in love.

Members of all three groups were tested for a serotonin transporter protein in their blood platelets. The subjects who claimed they had recently fallen in love were found to have serotonin levels forty per cent lower than their peers (Low levels of serotonin are associated with obsession, compulsion, anxiety and depression). However, serotonin levels measured in those same students once their relationships were one year old were back to normal. The scientific conclusion here, is that new love can actually trigger feelings of depression, anxiety and obsession. Donatella Marazziti won an Ig Nobel Prize for this work in 2000. One author of the study even suggested that we require this chemical response for relationships to survive. After all, infatuation is called 'a little madness.'

Another interesting finding proved that some men have a particular version of the 'Serotonin transporter' gene and therefore have lower levels of serotonin in their brains. This makes them more anxious and sexually active than other men. This may in fact be the harbinger of sexual addiction. [2]

The elegant research conducted by Helen Fisher and Lucy Brown summarises this phenomenon quite well. Fisher opines that 'When you fall in love, exactly the same system becomes active as when you take cocaine. You can feel intense elation when you're in love or when you're high on cocaine.' A surprising statement indeed, but this was proven when functional Magnetic Resonance Images (fMRI) of the brain of people who were in the throes of love, revealed that the cognitive area of the brain actually loses blood when they were in love. [3] [4]

Lucy Brown validated this claim when she asked college students to look at the photos of their lovers while undergoing an fMRI scan and discovered that the caudate area of the brain (which is involved in cravings) became active. Another area that became active was the ventral tegmental area which produces dopamine. This is thought to be the pleasure chemical that produces a feeling of bliss. [4]

Men are particularly susceptible to female charm

Now, we all know that men get weak kneed when they are in the presence of the fairer sex; but why? A study done in 2003, showed that even a casual chat with a female stranger can cause a man's testosterone level to spike by over thirty per cent. This spike can cause intense sexual allure and have propelled many men into irrational acts of indiscretion. Testosterone is the hormone that drives men's desire and initiates the mating dance. Interestingly, the author contends that high testosterone levels cause some men to act reckless and dangerous. [5] [6]

The stages of love

So, what is love? Is there such a thing as love at first sight? Is love conditional or should real love last forever? My favourite anthropologist Helen Fisher proposed that we fall in love in three stages and that there are different hormones driving each stage.

The stages of love according to Helen are: lust or erotic passion, attraction or romantic passion and attachment or commitment. When all three of these happen with the same person, you have a very strong bond. Sometimes, however, the one we lust after isn't the one we're actually in love with. She concludes that love is not an emotion but a physiological drive as powerful as hunger. Romantic love is actually a basic drive that has evolved for the purposes of mating and reproduction.[7]

Lust/erotic passion

Oestrogen and testosterone become active in our bodies just after puberty for the first time and create the desire to experience love. These desires called lust play a big role both during puberty and throughout our lives. Lust is driven by the sex hormones testosterone and oestrogen. Testosterone is a libido-enhancing, energy producing chemical secreted in the testes of males and ovaries of females. On average, men produce about twenty times more testosterone than women. These hormones, as Helen Fisher says, 'get you out looking for anything.'

According to Lisa Diamond from the Department of Psychology at the University of Utah, 'lust and romantic love are two different things caused by different underlying substrates. Lust evolved for the purpose of sexual mating, while romantic love evolved because of the need for infant/child bonding. So, even though we often experience lust for our romantic partner, sometimes we don't, but we might also lust after someone else,' states Dr. Diamond. [8] [9] Sexologist John Money draws the line between love and lust in this way: 'Love exists above the belt, lust below. Love is lyrical; lust is lewd.' [10] We can therefore conclude that pheromones, looks and our own learned predispositions for what we look for in a mate play an important role in whom we lust after. The truth is, without lust, we might never find that special someone. But while lust keeps us looking around, it is our desire for romance that leads us to attraction.

Romantic love/attraction

While the initial feelings may or may not come from lust, what happens next if the relationship is to progress is attraction. When attraction or romantic passion comes into play, we often lose our ability to think rationally. The old cliché 'love is blind' is really accurate in this stage. We are often oblivious to any flaws our partner might have. We idealize them and can't get them off our minds. This is the truly love-struck phase. When people fall in love they can't think of anything else. They lose their appetite, need less sleep and spend hours at a time daydreaming about their new lover. This overwhelming preoccupation and drive is part of our biological make up.

That euphoric surge that comes when we're first falling in love, researchers say, is due to the dopamine, nor epinephrine and phenyl ethylamine being released. Dopamine is thought to be the pleasure chemical, producing a feeling of bliss. It stimulates the production of oxytocin, sometimes known as the cuddle chemical.

According to Dr. Fisher, another euphoria-inducing chemical in your brain, nor epinephrine, makes your blood pressure soar, produces the racing heart, elation, intense energy, sleeplessness, craving, loss of appetite and focused attention when near the person you're attracted to. She posits the argument that the human body releases this cocktail of love only when certain conditions are met and men more readily produce it than women because of their more visual state. The above research has therefore shown that in romantic love, when two people have sex, oxytocin is released which helps bond the relationship.

A closer look at oxytocin

In 1999, researchers at the University of California, San Francisco, concluded that the hormone oxytocin is associated with the ability to maintain healthy interpersonal relationships and healthy psychological boundaries with other people. They also posited that when it is released during orgasm, it begins creating an emotional bond. The more sex you have, the greater the bond. Oxytocin is also associated with mother/infant bonding, uterine contractions during labour in childbirth and the let down reflex necessary for breastfeeding. [11] [12] [13] [14]

Interestingly, many scientists now think that both genders release this nurturing hormone when touching and cuddling, with the oxytocin level peaking during orgasm. Elevated oxytocin in a father when he cuddles his offspring is also recognized as a key component in initiating and maintaining his nurturing instincts. [15]

Regretfully, those feelings of passionate love do lose their strength over time. Studies have shown that passionate love fades quickly and is nearly gone after two or three years. The chemicals responsible for that loving feeling of adrenaline, dopamine, nor-epinephrine, phenyl ethylamine or others, tend to dwindle. Suddenly your lover has faults. "Why has he or she changed?", you wonder. Actually, your partner probably hasn't changed at all; it's just that you're now able to see him or her rationally, rather than through the blinding hormones of infatuation and passionate love.

At this stage, the relationship is either strong enough to endure or it ends. In this stage, couples spend many hours getting to know each other. If this attraction remains strong and is felt by both of them, then they usually enter the third stage, attachment.

Attachment/commitment

Some scientists believe that after a certain period from eighteen months to 4 years, one's body gets accustomed to the hormones of passion. After building up a tolerance to uppers like PEA, passionate romance can morph into what Helen Fisher, author of *Anatomy of Love* calls attachment. In this phase of the relationship, your brain produces endorphins, which resemble the opiates such as morphine in their abilities to produce analgesia and a feeling of well-being. 'Unlike PEA,' says Fisher, 'they calm the mind, kill pain and reduce anxiety.' So what some people call separation anxiety might actually be a form of drug withdrawal. Have you ever wondered why some marriages fail and others succeed? There are many variables that inform marital success and one of them is the length of the courtship period. It appears that the speed at which courtship progresses often determines the ultimate success of the relationship. In other words the longer the courtship, the stronger the long-term relationship.

According to Ted Huston, 'Those who divorce after many years (Action Divorcer) tend to rush into marriage after a short, romantic courtship, only to become quickly disappointed. Those who divorce soon (Early Exiters) are involved in troubled courtships, and consequently fall out of love soon after the wedding, perhaps as they lose hope of improving an unpromising marriage.' It appears that the wise thing to do is to spend some time and get to know each other before you take that final plunge. [16] [17] [18] [19]

The attachment or commitment stage is long term love. You've passed fantasy love and are entering into real love. This stage has to be strong enough to withstand many problems and distractions such as children, sicknesses, financial woes, sexual slumps and so on.

Studies by University of Minnesota researcher, Ellen Berscheid and others have shown that the more we idealize the one we love, the stronger the relationship during the attachment stage.

In a study done in 1998, she asked a group of young men and women to make four lists: of all their friends, of the people they loved, of everyone they thought sexually attractive, and finally of those with whom they were in love. As you would expect, the last list was the shortest, usually with just one name.

Surprisingly, that same person appeared on all the lists. 'It's this combination of friendship, affection and lust,' Berscheid said, 'that makes it so powerful.' This power is enough to warp judgment in otherwise sensible people. Many psychologists have demonstrated in several studies, that new lovers often idealize their partner, magnifying the other's virtues and explaining away their flaws: This behaviour, sometimes called the pink lens effect, often contrasts sharply with the perceptions of friends and family. New couples also exalt the relationship itself. 'It's very common for them to think they have a relationship that's more special, closer, than anyone else's,' said Berscheid. [20] [21]

'Some idealization may be crucial to building a longer-term relationship,' said Pamela Regan, a researcher at California State University in Los Angeles and author of *The Mating Game*, a book about relationships. She continued, 'If you don't sweep away the person's flaws to some extent, then you're just as likely to end a relationship or not even try; this at least gives you a chance. If you think of romantic attraction as a kind of drug that alters how you think, then in this case it's allowing you to take some risks you wouldn't otherwise.' [22]

Attachment is a longer lasting commitment and is the bond that keeps couples together when they go on to have children. Important in this stage are two hormones released by the nervous system, which are thought to play a role in social attachments: oxytocin and vasopressin. Oxytocin is thought to promote bonding when adults are intimate. The theory states that the more sex a couple has, the deeper their bond becomes.

Vasopressin is another important chemical in the long-term commitment stage. It is an important controller of the kidney and its role in long-term relationships was discovered when scientists looked at the prairie vole. Dr. Fisher believes that oxytocin and vasopressin interfere with the dopamine and nor epinephrine pathways, which might explain why passionate love fades as attachment grows. [3] So, we have seen that falling in love floods your bloodstream with a plethora of powerful chemicals: dopamine, nor epinephrine, phenyl ethylamine (PEA) and other natural cousins of amphetamines, stimulants and painkillers. In fact, falling in love is like being on drugs. But it's a natural high far more satisfying than anything you could inject, snort, smoke, drink or swallow.

What happens when you fall out of love?

From the compelling evidence given above, it is clear that hot love is transient, but warm love can last forever and is quite habit-forming. That's why breaking up is so hard to do. Even when you really don't like someone anymore, and you know you should move on, it often feels like you can't. Why? Because you're chemically addicted to oxytocin – the cuddling hormone – and you fear the pain of separation In fact fMRI-based studies done in 2004, on nine right-handed women whose romantic relationship ended within the preceding four months, demonstrated that the insular cortex, in charge of experiencing pain, became active when subjects viewed photos of former loved ones. So at least we can sympathize with our friends and relatives who can't let go. [23] [24]

As one anonymous writer said: 'Love strikes you like a mystical gift from God, then it stirs up that euphoric, chemical soup that permeates your cells, creating a place within you where hormones meet holiness, wildflowers bloom, angels dance and the city never sleeps.'

References

1. Tennov, D. (1979). *Love and Limerance: the Experience of Being in Love.* New York: Stein and Day.

2. Marazziti, D., Akiskal, H. S., Rossi, A. & Cassano, G. B. (1999). A*lterations of the Platelet Serotonin Transporter in Romantic Love. Psychological Medicine*, *29*, 741 – 745.

3. Fisher, H. (2004). *Why We Love: The Nature and Chemistry of Romantic Love.* New York: Henry Holt.

4. Aron, A., Fisher, H., Mashek, D., Strong, G., Li, H., & Brown, L. L. (2005). *Reward, Motivation, and Emotion Systems Associated with Early-Stage Intense Romantic Love. Journal of Neurophysiology, 94*, 327 – 337.

5. Roney, J.R., Mahler, S.V. & Maestripieri, D., (2003). *Behavioral and Hormonal Responses of Men to Brief Interactions with Women. Evol. Hum. Behav., 24*, 365–375.

6. Roney, J.R., Lukaszewski, A.W., Simmons, Z.L (2007).Rapid endocrine responses of young men to social interactions with young women. *Hormones and Behavior,* 52,326– 333.

7. Fisher, H. (2004). *Why We Love: The Nature and Chemistry of Romantic Love.* New York: Henry Holt.

8. Diamond, L. M. (2004). *Emerging Perspectives on Distinctions Between Romantic Love and Sexual Desire. Current Directions in Psychological Science*, *13*, 116-119.

9. Diamond, L. M. & Aspinwall, L. G. (2003). *Emotion Regulation Across the Life Span: An Integrative Perspective Emphasizing Self-regulation, Positive Affect, and Dyadic Processes. Motivation and Emotion, 27* (2), 125-1.

10. Money, J. (1993) *The Adam Principle: Genes, Genitals, Hormones, & Gender. Selected Readings in Sexology.* Buffalo, NY: Prometheus Book.

11. Turner, R. A., Altemus, M., Enos, T., Cooper, B. & McGuinness, T. (1999). *Preliminary Research on Plasma Oxytocin in Normal Cycling Women: Investigating Emotion and Interpersonal Distress. Psychiatry: Interpersonal & Biological Processes, 62*, 97-113.

12. Turner, R. A., Altemus, M., Yip, D. N., Kupferman, E., Fletcher, D., Bostrom, A. & Amico, J. A. (2002). *Effects of Emotion on Oxytocin, Prolactin, and ACTH in Women. Stress: The International Journal on the Biology of Stress, 5*(4), 269 276.

13. Feldman, R. (2007). *Evidence for a Neuroendocrinological Foundation of Human Affiliation: Plasma Oxytocin Levels Across Pregnancy and the Postpartum Period Predict Mother-Infant Bonding. Psychological Science*, 18 (11), 965-970.

14. Carmichael, M.S., Humber, R. et al. (1987). *Plasma Oxytocin Increases in the Human Sexual Response.* J. Clin. Endocrinol. Metab. 64: 27.

15. Birth Psychology - *The Science of Father Love.* Retrieved January 23, 2013, from http://www.birthpsychology.com/birthscene/fathers1.html

16. Huston, T. L. (2000). *The social ecology of marriage and other intimate unions. Journal of Marriage and the Family,* 62 (2), 298-320.

17. Huston, T. L. & Levinger, G. (1978). *Interpersonal attraction and relationships. Annual Review of Psychology, 29,* 115-156.

18. Huston, T. L. (2000). *The social ecology of marriage and other intimate unions. Journal of Marriage and the Family,* 62(2), 298-320.

19. Huston, T. L., Caughlin, J. P., Houts, R. M., Smith, S. E. & George, L. J. (2001). *The Connubial Crucible: Newlywed Years as Predictors of Marital Delight, Distress, and Divorce. Journal of Personality and Social Psychology,* 80 (2), 237-252.

20. Berscheid, E. & Reis, H. T. (1998). *Attraction and Close Relationships. The Handbook of Social Psychology,* 2, 193-281.

21. Berscheid, E. & Campbell,B.. (1981). T*he Changing Longevity of Heterosexual Close Relationships: A Commentary and Forecast.* Pp. 209-234 in Lerner, M. J. & Lerner, S. C. (Eds.), *The Justice Motive in Social Behavior.* New York: Plenum.

22. Regan, P. C. (2008). *The Mating Game: A Primer on Love, Sex, and Marriage.* Thousand Oaks, CA:Sage Publications, Incorporated.

23. Najib, A., Lorberbaum, J. P., Kose, S., Bohning, D. E. & George, M. S. (2004). *Regional Brain Activity in Women Grieving a Romantic Relationship Breakup. American Journal of Psychiatry,* 161 (12), 2245-2256.

24. Kendler, K. S., Karkowski, L. M. & Prescott, C. A. (1999). *Causal Relationship Between Stressful Life Events and the Onset of Major Depression. American Journal of Psychiatry,* 156 (6), 837-841.

What Turns You On?
The Science of Attraction

So, what really turns you on? What actually initiates this cascade of events called love? Anthropologists and psychologists believe they have the answer to why we fancy someone.

The inexplicable attraction we feel

As humans, we are often perturbed by the inexplicable attraction we feel for someone, but cannot really fathom the cause for such intense allure. However, anthropologists and psychologists believe they have the answer to why we fancy someone. Physical attractiveness serves as a biological signal to members of the opposite sex and is a key element of successful mating and reproduction. It is the perception of the physical traits of an individual as pleasing, attractive, cute or beautiful. The criteria you use to determine attraction is usually informed by your culture or individual taste. Interestingly, attractive people are assumed to be extroverts, popular, and happy and they do tend to have these characteristics. However, this is probably due to a self-fulfilling prophecy, since from a young age, attractive people receive more attention which helps them develop these characteristics.

Which men do women find attractive?

Men, have from time immemorial pondered this question. So pay careful attention as I reveal to you the mystery of the female mind, which seems to ascribe significant importance to facial features, a V-shaped torso, height, penis size and hirsutism (hairiness),

Faces with masculine traits

Women prefer faces with masculine traits associated with increased testosterone; such as prominent chins, heavy brows, broad cheekbones and chiselled jaw lines. The masculinity of male faces - and the femininity of female faces - are described as a sexual dimorphism. A woman's preference for male facial symmetry seems to correlate with her probability of conception, since symmetrical faces and bodies are perceived to be signs of good inheritance to women of child-bearing age, desirous of producing healthy offspring. It has also been noted that females tend to prefer masculine facial traits more for short-term partners, than for long-term partners. [1] [2] [3] [4] [5] [6] [7]

Many women have been noted to like masculine faces during the middle of their cycle but prefer more feminine features later in their cycles or during their menses. Experts who study this phenomenon is of the firm belief that when conception is most likely, females prefer testosterone-related facial characteristics that suggest an healthy immune system. [8] [9] [10]

Does a man's scent affect women?

Many studies have shown that women have a preference for the scent of men with more symmetrical faces, and that women's preference for the scent of more symmetrical men is strongest during the most fertile period of their menstrual cycle. [11]

Are attractive women turned on by a special type of guy?

Studies have found that women who perceive themselves as physically attractive are more likely to choose men with masculine facial dimorphism, than are women who perceive themselves as physically unattractive. Therefore, to use an age old cliché 'some guys have all the luck.' [12]

V-shaped torso

Recent research has found that male physiques with slim waists and broad shoulders; a high shoulder-to-hip ratio (SHR) of 0.75 or lower, are rated as considerably more attractive than men with more even waists and shoulders. Chest muscularity was also given higher rating by some women. Horvath, in a paper published in 1981, in the *Archives of Sexual Behaviour*, concluded that broad shoulders were seen as attractive by both sexes.[13]

How sexy is muscle?

Researchers at Harvard Medical School affiliated McLean Hospital think Taiwanese men have a more accurate view of what women see as ideal male bodies. The research team was led by Chi-Fu Jeffrey Yang. They administered a computerized test to fifty five male university students in Taiwan, who were asked to choose pictures corresponding to their own bodies, the body they would like to have, the body of an average Taiwanese male and the body that Taiwanese women would prefer. They then compared these results to those previously obtained in an identical study in the U.S. and Europe.

The Western men estimated that women preferred a male body with twenty to thirty pounds more muscle than an average man. However, when actual western women were asked to choose the male body that they liked, they selected an ordinary male body without all of the added muscle. By contrast, the Taiwanese men did not show this distortion; they correctly recognized that women did not prefer a bulked-up male body. Senior author Harrison Pope Jr., Director of McLean Hospital's Biological Psychiatry Laboratory concluded that 'our findings suggest that Western men may have a much distorted view of what they ideally should look like, whereas men in Taiwan don't seem to have this problem.'[14]

My take on this study is that women prefer reasonably well muscled guys, but are wary of the incredible hulk types. A man's physique is actually determined by his male hormones; primarily testosterone. A normal level of testosterone is a possible indicator of good sexual health. In the absence of normal testosterone levels, a man may exhibit physical symptoms of less muscle development reduced physical height and low sexual prowess. So men have a strong incentive to start pumping iron to impress the ladies.

Confidence, physical strength and a powerful bearing

Females' sexual attraction towards males is also determined by the height of the man. One study conducted of women's personal ads support the existence of this preference. The study found that in ads requesting height in a mate, 80 percent requested a height of 6 feet or taller. Women universally prefer males who demonstrate confidence, physical strength, and a powerful bearing. This preference can be explained by evolutionary psychology, since ancestral women who were attracted to tall, physically powerful men benefited from better protection and therefore gained evolutionary fitness. It is also well known that the height in men is associated with status in nearly all cultures, which is beneficial to women who cohabit with them. [15] [16]

In 2005, *Cosmopolitan* magazine published an article suggesting that 'women are most attracted to men who are one point one times their own height'. The article also concluded that women are statistically more likely to be attracted to men of average height when looking for long-term commitment, while the opposite is true when a short-term relationship is intended. In addition, the article claimed that women may have these different preferences for height depending on the phase of their menstrual cycle at the time. [17]

The power of smells

We like the look and smell of people who are most like our parents! This was proven in 1995, when researchers asked a group of women to smell some unwashed T-shirts worn by different men. They discovered that women consistently preferred the smell of men whose immune systems were different from their own.

It has also been shown in another sweaty T-shirt study that what women want most is a man whose smell is similar to her father, rather strange indeed!.

The scientists suggested that a woman being attracted to her father's genes made sense. A man with these genes would be similar enough that her offspring would get a tried and tested immune system. On the other hand, he would be different enough to ensure a wide range of genes for immunity. This compares favourably with what happens with rodents, who determine how resistant their partners are to disease by sniffing their pheromones. Human pheromones are odourless chemicals detected by an organ in the nose. Some scientists believe they could be the key to choosing a suitable lover. [18] [19]

Well endowed men

Studies based in China, The United Kingdom, The United States, Italy, New Zealand, Sweden, Spain, and France have shown that women consider men with a longer and wider penis as more attractive.[20]

Hairiness

Many studies based in The United States, New Zealand, and China have shown that women rate men with no body hair as most attractive, and that attractiveness ratings decline as hirsutism increases. Another study found a moderate amount of trunk hair was most attractive, to British and Sri Lankan women.[21]

Which women do men find attractive?

Now that we know what women think, it's time to find out what gets men hot and bothered. The characteristics that men use to deem a woman as attractive include those aspects that display health and fitness for reproduction and sustenance such as youth, waist-hip ratio, mid upper arm circumference, body mass proportion and facial symmetry.

Young and fertile

Men are attracted to signs of youthfulness in a mate, but a woman's reproductive value declines steadily after age twenty one. One study done by David Buss in 1989, across thirty seven cultures, showed men desire, on average, a woman who is two and a half years younger than themselves for a wife; with men in Nigeria and Zambia at the far extreme, desiring their wives to be six and a half to seven and a half years younger. As men age, they also desire a larger age gap from their mates. [22]

In a study by University of Louisville psychologist, Michael Cunningham conducted in 1986, dimensions and proportions of what were regarded as attractive were identified by men with remarkable consistency. The desired traits were large female eyes, small chins and small straight noses. (People with straight noses are considered to be very clever and helpful in nature). It is believed these infant like features induce in men a strong paternal response like a baby would; they make a woman seem cute and adorable. 'High wide cheekbones and narrow cheeks are signs that a woman has reached puberty and high eyebrows, dilated pupils and a wide smile signal excitement and sociability' Cunningham said. Other attractive features are high, firm breasts, blonde or long and lustrous hair, full red lips, clear smooth skin and clear eyes. [23]

Interestingly, some of these changes occur in many women when ovulating, in that, a woman's face becomes more attractive during this time with fuller more sensuous lips and dilated pupils. The author of this study, Craig Roberts, in 2004 posited that 'these changes are very subtle, but they could mean that more men will be interested at the very time of the cycle when the chances of conception are highest.' [24]

Full breasts

In western societies and Jamaica in particular, full breasts may be attractive to some men, because women with higher breast to under-breast ratios typically have higher levels of the sex hormone estradiol, which promotes fertility. Larger breasts also display the aging process more noticeably, hence they are deemed to be relatively reliable indicators of long-term fertility. [25]

Slim and slender

The Body Mass Index (BMI), which refers to the proportion of the body mass to the body structure is another important factor which influences a man's perception of beauty. However, the ideal body proportion is interpreted differently in various cultures. In the West, most men consider a slim and slender body mass as ideal while many Jamaican men consider a plump body-mass as appealing. [26]

To assess current attitudes to body weight and shape in the South Pacific, a region characterised by relatively high levels of obesity and traditionally positive views of large bodies, Swami V, et al in 2007 conducted a study titled '*Preferences for Female Body Size in Britain and the South Pacific*.' They concluded that — participants from both high and low socioeconomic statuses (SES), preferred women with a slender figure as did a comparison group in Britain, suggesting that the traditional adoration of large bodies is no longer apparent in Samoa. However, the results also showed that low SES adolescents were more likely to view overweight figures as attractive, which suggests that the admiration of slim figures may be associated with increasing SES. [27]

Low waist-hip ratio

We now know that secondary sexual characteristics convey information about reproductive potential in the same way that facial symmetry and masculinity, and shoulder-to-hip ratio convey information about reproductive/genetic quality in males. Scientists have discovered that the waist-hip ratio (WHR) of any build is very strongly related to attractiveness across all cultures. It is associated with a higher oestrogen-to-androgen ratio and is a phenotypic cue to fertility, fecundity, neuro-developmental resources in offspring, and overall health and is indicative of good genes in women.

The concept and significance of WHR as an indicator of attractiveness was first postulated by evolutionary psychologist, Devendra Singh in 1993, at the University of Texas. [28] [29] [30] Singh argued that the WHR was a more consistent oestrogen marker than the bust-waist ratio (BWR) studied at King's College, London by Dr Glenn Wilson in the 1970s.[31] [32]

It was always believed that women become more attractive to men as their waist becomes smaller in relation to the hip, with the ideal ratio in healthy premenopausal women being between 0.67 and 0.80. Singh, et al in February 2010 confirmed this postulate using fMRI studies. They found that males show activation in brain reward centres in response to naked female bodies when surgically altered to express optimal 0.7 WHR with redistributed body fat, but relatively unaffected body mass index (BMI).

Relative to presurgical bodies, brain activation related to neural activity in the brain to postsurgical bodies was observed in the bilateral orbital frontal cortex (which is involved in the cognitive processing of decision making and is thought to regulate planning, behaviour and anticipation of reward or pleasure). While changes in BMI only revealed activation in the visual part of the brain, they concluded that these findings suggest that an hourglass figure activates brain centres that drive appetitive sociality; attention toward females that represent the highest-quality reproductive partners. [33] In other words men get turned-on by an hour glass figure.

Some studies have shown that men's preferences vary with the geographic variation and social status in the shape of women who have wider hips in some populations as in Europe and more protruding buttocks in women of African origin.[34] [35] [36]

It is interesting to note that in addition to being a sexual attractant, the high stores of fat in the buttocks are used during the last stages of pregnancy and during breast-feeding to support the baby and those women with low waist-hip ratios also have a lower risk of heart disease and diabetes. Many women have an intuitive awareness of this reality and to enhance their perceived attractiveness, some women may artificially alter their apparent WHR. The methods used, include the use of a corset to reduce the waist size and hip and buttock padding to increase the apparent size of the hips and buttocks.

Short physical stature

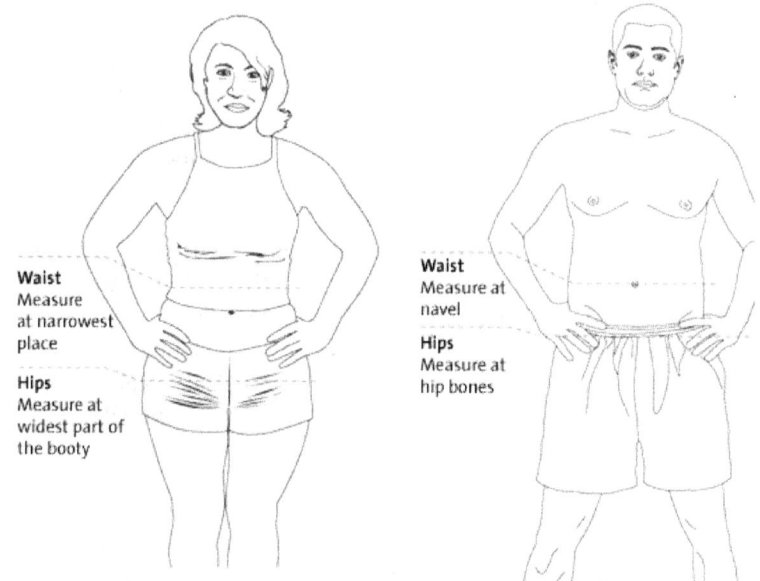

Most males exhibit a preference for females of shorter physical stature than themselves, and a study done by Daniel Nettle in 2002, indicated that women of below average height have greater reproductive success. They claimed that the affinity to smaller size may be that smaller size is seen as more youthful, and males find pedomorphic characteristics (the retention by an adult of juvenile features) in females attractive. Another possible explanation is that shorter females may reach sexual maturity earlier than their taller counterparts.[37]

Another finding by Hensley in 1994, confirmed that height is used as a mate selection characteristic by women, but not men. [38]

Women with symmetrical faces

Factors aside from biology and culture determine physical attractiveness. The more familiar a face seems, the more highly it is usually judged to be attractive; this is called 'mere exposure effect'. Numerous studies in humans have shown that men go for women with symmetrical faces as mentioned above. It is thought that asymmetrical features are a sign of underlying genetic problems. Interestingly, we are often attracted to people who look like our opposite-sex parent. Women tend to choose men with the same hair and eye colour as their fathers, while men tend to prefer women with their mother's colouring. Also, when many faces are combined into a composite image through computer morphing, people usually view the resulting image as more familiar, attractive and beautiful than the faces that were combined to make the composite. [39] [40] [41] [42]

The social impact of attractiveness

Many of us have bemoaned the fact that we might have had some difficulty climbing the ladder of success due to the absence of what was deemed to be charming physical attributes. So, Barry Harper of the department of Economics at London Guildhall University set out to prove this. He investigated a sample of over eleven thousand people born in Britain in 1958, examining the effects of looks, height and obesity on hourly pay, employment, and on a person's marriage prospects. He found that unattractive people earned substantially less than their colleagues. The penalty for unattractiveness is around fifteen per cent for men and eleven per cent for women. If average male earnings are twenty thousand pounds, then an otherwise identical male who is unattractive will earn just seventeen thousand pounds sterling, a penalty of three thousand pounds sterling. Tall people earn more than short people. This pay gap is ten per cent for men and five per cent for women. Only men benefit from being tall. They earn around five per cent more than others. Women who are obese are penalized, earning five per cent less than obese men. Physical attractiveness also has a profound effect on how people are judged, in terms of social opportunities, friendship, sexual behaviour, and marriage. "In many cases we attribute positive characteristics, such as intelligence and honesty to attractive people without even realizing it" Harper says. [43]

So there you have it. If you are good-looking you might have an unfair advantage over your less endowed colleagues.

References

1. Rhodes, G. (2006). *Evolutionary Psychology of Facial Beauty. Annu Rev Psychol.* 57:199-226.

2. Glassenberg, A. N., Feinberg, D. R., Jones, B. C., Little, A. C. & DeBruine, L. M. (2010). *Sex-dimorphic Face Shape Preference in Heterosexual and Homosexual Men and Women. Archives of Sexual Behavior,* 39(6), 1289-1296.

3. Perrett, D. I., Lee, K. J., Penton-Voak, I. S., Rowland, D. R., Yoshikawa, S., Burt, D. M., Henzi, S. P., Castles, D. L. & Akamatsu, S. (1998). *Effects of Sexual Dimorphism on Facial Attractiveness. Nature,* 394, 884-887.

4. Cellerino, A. (2003). *Psychobiology of Facial Attractiveness. J Endocrinol Invest., 26 (3 Suppl)*:45-8.

5. Fink B, Neave N, Seydel H. (2007) *Male Facial Appearance Signals Physical Strength to Women. Am J Hum Biol.,* 19(1),82-7.

6. Cunningham, M. R., Barbee, A. P. & Pike, C. L. (1990). *What do Women Want? Facialmetric Assessment of Multiple Motives in the Perception of Male Facial Physical Attractiveness. Journal of Personality and Social Psychology,* 59(1), 61.

7 Khan, S. & Dobson,R. (2005). *"A Symmetrical Face Isn't Just Prettier - It's Healthier Too".* London: The Independent: Science. Retrieved April 2012, from http://www.independent.co.uk/news/science/a-symmetrical-face-isnt-just-prettier--its-healthier-too-509285.html.

8. Penton-Voak, I. S., & Perrett, D. I. (2000). *Female Preference for Male Faces Changes Cyclically: Further Evidence. Evolution and Human Behavior,* 21(1), 39-48.

9. Gangestad, S. W., & Thornhill, R. (1998). *Menstrual Cycle Variation in Women's Preferences for the Scent of Symmetrical Men.* Proceedings of the Royal Society of London. Series B: Biological Sciences, 265(1399), 927-933.

10. Gangestad, S. W. & Cousins, A. J. (2001). *Adaptive Design, Female Mate Preferences, and Shifts Across the Menstrual Cycle. Annual Review of Sex Research; Annual Review of Sex Research.* 12:145–185.

11. Gangestad, S. W., Garver-Apgar, C. E., Simpson, J. A., & Cousins, A. J. (2007). *Changes in Women's Mate Preferences Across the Ovulatory Cycle. Journal of Personality and Social Psychology,* 92(1), 151-163.

12. Little, A. C., Burt, D. M., Penton-Voak, I. S. & Perrett, D. I. (2001). *Self-perceived Attractiveness Influences Human Female Preferences for Sexual Dimorphism and Symmetry in Male Faces. Proceedings of the Royal Society of London. Series*

B: *Biological Sciences*, 268(1462), 39-44.

13. Horvath, T. (1981). *Physical Attractiveness: The Influence of Selected Torso Parameters*. Archives of Sexual Behavior, 10(1), 21-24.

14. Yang, C. F. J., Gray, P. & Pope, H. G. (2005). *Male Body Image in Taiwan Versus the West: Yanggang Zhiqi Meets the Adonis Complex*. American Journal of Psychiatry, 162(2), 263-269.

15. Pierce, C. A. (1996). *Body Height and Romantic Attraction: A Meta-analytic Test of the Male-taller Norm*. Social Behavior and Personality: an International Journal, 24(2), 143-149.

16. Pawlowski, B., Dunbar, R. I. M. & Lipowicz, A. (2000). *Tall Men Have More Reproductive Success*. Nature, 403(6766), 156.

17. Sohn, E. "*Health*", Nov 2005, Vol. 19 Issue 9

18. Wedekind, C., & Füri, S. (1997). *Body Odour Preferences in Men and Women: Do They Aim for Specific MHC Combinations or Simply Heterozygosity?* Proceedings of the Royal Society of London. Series B: Biological Sciences, 264(1387), 1471-1479.

19. McClintock, M. K. (1971). *Menstrual Synchrony and Suppression*. Nature, 229, 244-245.

20. Paley, M (2000). *The Book of the Penis*. New York: Grove Press. pp. 232, 16–19. and Eisenman, R. (2001). *Penis Size: Survey of Female Perceptions of Sexual Satisfaction*. BMC women's health, 1(1), 1.

21. Dixson, A. F., Halliwell, G., East, R., Wignarajah, P., & Anderson, M. J. (2003). *Masculine Somatotype and Hirsuteness as Determinants of Sexual Attractiveness to Women*. Archives of Sexual Behavior, 32, 29–39.

22. Buss, D. M. (1989). *Sex Differences in Human Mate Preferences: Evolutionary Hypotheses tested in 37 cultures*. Behavioral and Brain Sciences, 12(1), 1-49.

23. Cunningham, M. R. (1986). *Measuring the Physical in Physical Attractiveness: Quasi-experiments on the Sociobiology of Female Facial Beauty*. Journal of Personality and Social Psychology; *Journal of Personality and Social Psychology*, 50(5), 925-935.

24. Roberts, S. C., Havlicek, J., Flegr, J., Hruskova, M., Little, A. C., Jones, B. C., & Petrie, M. (2004). *Female Facial Attractiveness Increases During the Fertile Phase of the Menstrual Cycle*. Proceedings of the Royal Society of London. Series B: Biological Sciences, 271(Suppl 5), S270-S272.

25. Sugiyama, L. S. (2005). *Physical Attractiveness in Adaptationist Perspective. The Handbook of Evolutionary Psychology*, 1, 292-343.

26. Tovée, M. J., & Cornelissen, P. L. (2001). *Female and Male Perceptions of Female Physical Attractiveness in Front-view and Profile*. British Journal of Psychology, 92(2), 391-402.

27. Swami, V., Knight, D., Tovée, M. J., Davies, P. & Furnham, A. (2007). *Preferences for Female Body Size in Britain and the South Pacific*. Body Image, 4(2), 219-223.

28. Singh, D. (1993). *Adaptive Significance of Female Physical Attractiveness: Role of Waist-to-hip Ratio*. Journal of Personality and Social Psychology, 65(2), 293-307.

29. Singh, D., & Young, R. K. (1995). *Body Weight, Waist-to-hip ratio, Breasts, and Hips: Role in Judgments of Female Attractiveness and Desirability for Relationships*. Ethology and Sociobiology, 16(6), 483-507.

30. Singh, D. (2002). *Female Mate Value at a Glance: Relationship of Waist-to-hip Ratio to Health, Fecundity and Attractiveness*. Neuroendocrinology Letters, 23 (Suppl 4), 81-91.

31. Wilson, G. D. & Brazendale, A. H. (1974). *Psychological Correlates of Sexual Attractiveness: An Empirical Demonstration of Denial and Fantasy Gratification Phenomena*. Social Behavior and Personality: an International Journal, 2(1), 30-34.

32. Wilson, G. D., Nias, D. K. & Brazendale, A. H. (1975). *Vital Statistics, Perceived Sexual Attractiveness, and Response to Risque Humor*. The Journal of Social Psychology, 95(2), 201-205.

33. Platek, S. M. & Singh, D. (2010). *Optimal Waist-to-hip Ratios in Women Activate Neural Reward Centers in Men*. PloS one, 5(2), e9042.

34. Marlowe, F., Apicella, C., & Reed, D. (2005). *Men's Preferences for Women's Profile Waist-to-hip Ratio in Two Societies*. Evolution and Human Behavior, 26(6), 458-468.

35. Furnham, A., Moutafi, J., & Baguma, P. (2002). *A Cross-cultural Study on the Role of Weight and Waist-to-hip Ratio on Female Attractiveness*. Personality and Individual Differences, 32(4), 729-745.

36. Swami, V., Miller, R., Furnham, A., Penke, L., & Tovée, M. J. (2008). *The Influence of Men's Sexual Strategies on Perceptions of Women's Bodily Attractiveness, Health and Fertility*. Personality and Individual Differences, 44(1), 98-107.

37. Nettle, D. (2002). *Women's Height, Reproductive Success and the Evolution*

of Sexual Dimorphism in Modern Humans. Proceedings of the Royal Society of London. Series B: Biological Sciences, 269(1503), 1919-1923.

38. Hensley, W. E. (1994). *Height As a Basis for Interpersonal Attraction. Adolescence*, 29: 469-474.

39. Little, A. C., Jones, B. C. & DeBruine, L. M. (2008). *Preferences for Variation in Masculinity in Real Male Faces Change Across the Menstrual Cycle: Women Prefer More Masculine Faces When They Are More Fertile. Personality and Individual Differences*, 45(6), 478-482.

40. Berscheid, E., & Reis, H. T. (1998). *Attraction and Close Relationships. The Handbook of Social Psychology*, 2, 193-281. New York/London: Oxford University Press.

41. Fink, B. & Penton-Voak, I. (2002). *Evolutionary Psychology of Facial Attractiveness. Current Directions in Psychological Science*, 11(5), 154-158.

42. Thornhill, R., & Grammer, K. (1999). *The Body and Face of Woman: One Ornament that Signals Quality. Evolution and Human Behavior*, 20(2), 105-120.

43. Harper, B. (2000). *Beauty, Statute and the Labour Market: A British Cohort Study. Oxford Bulletin of Economics and Statistics*, 62, 773-802.

Sexual Fantasies
Illusion and Eroticism in Your Daily Life

It is obvious that the reason why we fancy someone is buried deep in our genes and is primarily driven by the need to propagate our species and to maximize the chance of a long and satisfying relationship.
Follow me on this journey of discovery as we explore the mystery of sexual fantasies in the next section.

Do you experience flights of fantasy when you have sex, followed by intense guilt that you might have betrayed your partner? You might be surprised to know that sexual fantasies are far more common than you think, and can in fact, add value to your relationship.

Below is an overview of sexual fantasies extracted from a ground breaking book written by Brett Kahr in 2007, called *Sex and the Psyche: Revealing the True Nature of Our Secret Fantasies from the Largest Ever Survey of Its Kind* [1] and the elegant research done by The Kinsey Institute on sexual fantasies.

What is a sexual fantasy?

A sexual fantasy, also called an erotic fantasy, may be defined as a mental imagery, a thought or long, drawn-out story which passes through our mind principally during sexual activity either coital or masturbatory, often resulting in orgasm. Sexual fantasies should be distinguished from sexual daydreams or transient sexual thoughts. They may be very simple or highly complex, tender or sadistic and may cause psychological pleasure or pain. The misconceptions about sexual fantasies began with Freud, who in 1908, declared that 'a happy person never fantasizes, only a dissatisfied one.' Later, thinkers expanded on this theme and called it the deficiency theory.

Many people believe that fantasies are compensation for lack of sexual opportunity; that if your sex life was adequate, you wouldn't have to fantasize. However, Leitenberg in his treatise, *Sexual Fantasy*, informs us that frequent fantasizers have very satisfying sex lives; they have sex more often, engage in a wider variety of erotic activities and have more partners than infrequent fantasizers. The association between fantasies and a healthy sex life is so strong in fact, that it's now considered abnormal not to have them. [2]

Why do we have sexual fantasies?

The origin of sexual fantasies remains obscure. Evolutionary psychologists have suggested that sexual fantasies contribute to the facilitation of sexual arousal, which in turn facilitates procreation. Thus, sexual fantasies may play an important role in the propagation of the human species. Freudian psychotherapists and psychoanalysts on the other hand, have postulated that our fantasies may have developed as a means both of gratifying wishes and of conquering intrusive memories of early traumatic experiences.

What purpose does our sexual fantasies serve?

Sex generally starts in the brain. So an active imagination can mean you're ready for sex before anything physical has happened. Therefore, desire is heightened and arousal is much quicker. There are many reasons why we might fantasise: to fulfil a wish, to overcome an old traumatic experience, to suppress pain, to relive playful childhood experiences and so on. For many, fantasies remain a continuous source of fun and enjoyment. For others, they are a constant reminder of early childhood stressors. Some fantasies even provide pleasure and pain simultaneously, or may be used for just passing time or helping one to fall asleep. They also allow people to imagine themselves in roles they do not normally play. Many couples share their fantasies to feel closer and gain more intimacy and trust or simply to become more aroused or induce a more powerful physical response.

Some people find an active fantasy life can add novelty to a long-standing sexual relationship. This can be particularly helpful if your partner is not as sexually adventurous as you are.

The late Alex Comfort, M.D., in his bestseller *The Joy of Sex,* reminds us that 'our thoughts during sex are not a reflection of our real-life mindset. Rather, sex offers the opportunity to experience things you can't possibly act out. These fantasies can be heterosexual, homosexual, incestuous, tender, wild or bloodthirsty. Don't block and don't be afraid of your partner's fantasy; this is a dream you are in.' [3]

How prevalent are fantasies?

According to psychoanalytical experts, everyone has unconscious fantasy structures. In other words, subliminal tendencies to have certain preferences, or to act in certain predictable ways, sadistically, masochistically, depressively and so on. In most adults, these unconscious fantasy structures will find representation in our conscious sexual fantasies, which occur during masturbation or during intercourse with a partner. A study conducted in the United States in 1994, revealed that fifty four per cent of men think about sex everyday or several times a day, forty three per cent a few times per month or a few times per week, and four per cent less than once a week. On the other hand, nineteen per cent of women think about sex everyday or several times a day, sixty seven per cent a few times per month or a few times per week, and fourteen per cent, less than once a month. [4] Leitenberg in 1995, in a paper published in *Psychological Bulletin* pointed out that the onset of first sexual fantasy is generally between eleven to thirteen years with men recalling earlier onset of fantasy than women. He also stated interestingly, that one in four people feel guilty about their fantasies; this usually 'involves people who feel guilty about fantasizing while making love to their partners.' Even among sexually adventurous groups like college students, twenty two per cent of women and eight per cent of men said they usually try to repress the feelings associated with fantasy, he concluded. [2]

As a rule, we keep our sexual fantasies hidden from our partners and our friends. Ethel Person in her book, *By Force of Fantasy* informs us that 'we tell each other almost everything; our sexual habits, who we lust for, how much money we make; but I do not know the sexual fantasies of my closest friends. We regard fantasies as too revealing; they're treasured possessions, yet we're ashamed of them.' [5]

Gender differences in the content of sexual fantasies

There are significant differences in the content of sexual fantasies of men and women. Men's fantasies focus more on the woman's body and on what he wants to do with it. They also focus more on explicit sexual acts, nude bodies and physical gratification. They are also more likely to fantasize about multiple partners and group sex than women. As a rule, women's fantasies are more passive and focus more on men's interest in their bodies. They are more emotional and romantic. [6]

Flavours of fantasy

Leitenberg and Henning in 1995 described an interesting concept called primary flavours of fantasy; they are:

- **Novel or forbidden imagery** — this includes unconventional settings, questionable partners like strangers or relatives, and exotic sexual positions.

- **Scenes of sexual irresistibility** — here, the emphasis is on seductive power: overcoming the reluctance of an initially indifferent man or woman through sheer animal magnetism. The irresistibility might also take numerical form in fantasies involving multiple partners.

- **Dominance and submission fantasies** — in these, sexual power is expressed either ritualistically, in sadomasochistic activities or through physical force as in rape fantasies. Such fantasies are surprisingly quite common.

Persons report that forty four per cent of men have had fantasies of dominating a partner. Other studies found that fifty one per cent of women fantasized about being forced to have sex, while a third imagined: 'I'm a slave who must obey a man's every wish.' However, 'women who find submission fantasies sexually arousing are very clear that they have no wish to be raped in reality,' says Leitenberg.[2]

The most common female fantasies are:

- Having sex with an existing partner
- Giving and receiving oral sex
- Having sex with a new partner
- Romantic or exotic locations
- Doing something forbidden
- Being submissive
- Reliving a previous experience
- Being found irresistible
- Trying new exotic sexual positions
- Having sex with a co-worker
- Being watched by a voyeur. Many women are excited with the idea of being watched and lusted after by unknown persons through a window
- Having sex with multiple people
- Having sex with a celebrity
- Seducing a younger man or boy
- Having sex with an older man
- Having random sex with a stranger. In this fantasy, she's walking down the street and randomly stops to willingly have sex with a tall, dark, unknown man
- Being tied up/tying someone else up

- Being videotaped. Like the voyeur fantasy, she may visualize being caught naked on camera, either knowingly or unknowingly

- Having intercourse in rooms other than the bedroom

- Having sex on a carpeted floor

The most common male fantasies are:

- Having sex with an existing partner

- Giving and receiving oral sex

- Having sex with more than one person

- Being dominant

- Being passive and submissive

- Reliving a previous experience

- Watching others make love

- Trying exotic sexual position

- Image of a nude or semi nude female

- Sex with a new female partner

- Sex on the beach

If your fantasies enhance your sense of well-being and add colour and excitement to your love life, go for it. I firmly endorse Leitenberg's conclusion which reminds us that "fantasies are an essential part of our sexual repertoire.
It is not a sign of sexual inadequacy or deprivation; they are healthy, occurring most often in people showing the fewest sexual problems and least sexual dissatisfaction". [2]

References

1. Kahr, B. (2007). *Sex and the Psyche: Revealing the True Nature of Our Secret Fantasies from the Largest Ever Survey of Its Kind.* London: Allen Lane Publishers.

2. Leitenberg, H. & Henning, K. (1995). *Sexual Fantasy. Psychological Bulletin*, 117(3), 469-496.

3. Comfort, A. (1991). *More Joy of Sex.* New York, NY: Pocket.

4. Laumann, E. O., Gagnon, J. H., Michael, R. T. & Michaels, S. (1994). *The Social Organization of Sexuality: Sexual Practices in the United States.* Chicago: University of Chicago Press.

5. Person, E. S., & Berry, G. W. (1996). *By Force of Fantasy: How We Make Our Lives. Journal of the American Academy of Psychoanalysis*, 24(3), 571.

6. Zurbriggen, E. L. & Yost, M. R. (2004). *Power, Desire, and Pleasure in Sexual Fantasies. Journal of Sex Research*, 41(3), 288-300.

The Sexual Response Cycle
The Biology of Love

Have you ever wondered about the changes that take place in the body during sexual arousal and orgasm? This section takes you on a guided tour of the sexual response cycle.

The sequence of physical and emotional events during sex

Many of us have been sexually aroused and are totally unaware of the sequence of events which occur to produce this erotic state. Let me therefore walk you through the sexual response cycle. The sexual response cycle describes the sequence of physical and emotional events that occur as a person becomes sexually aroused and participates in sexually stimulating experiences such as intercourse or masturbation. If you know how your body responds during each phase of this cycle, the knowledge will enable you to improve your sex life and identify a specific disorder if you have one.

Phases of the sexual response cycle

The sexual response cycle has four phases: excitement, plateau, orgasm, and resolution. These phases are experienced by both men and women, but the timing usually differs. Contrary to popular belief, it is unlikely that both partners will reach orgasm at the same time. It is also important to note that the intensity of the response and the time spent in each phase varies from person to person. Understanding these differences will better enable you to appreciate each other's body and improve the sexual experience.

Phase 1: Excitement

This phase may last from a few minutes to several hours and includes the following:

- Increased muscle tension

- Increased heart rate and rapid breathing

- The skin may become flushed (a red rash appears on the chest and back)

- The nipples become erect

- There is increased blood flow to the genitals, and both the clitoris and the labia minora (inner lips) become swollen and the man gets an erection

- Vaginal lubrication begins

- The woman's breasts become full and the vaginal walls begin to swell

- The man's testicles swell, his scrotum tightens and he begins secreting a lubricating liquid

See diagrams below:

THE MALE GENITAL TRACT-UNAROUSED

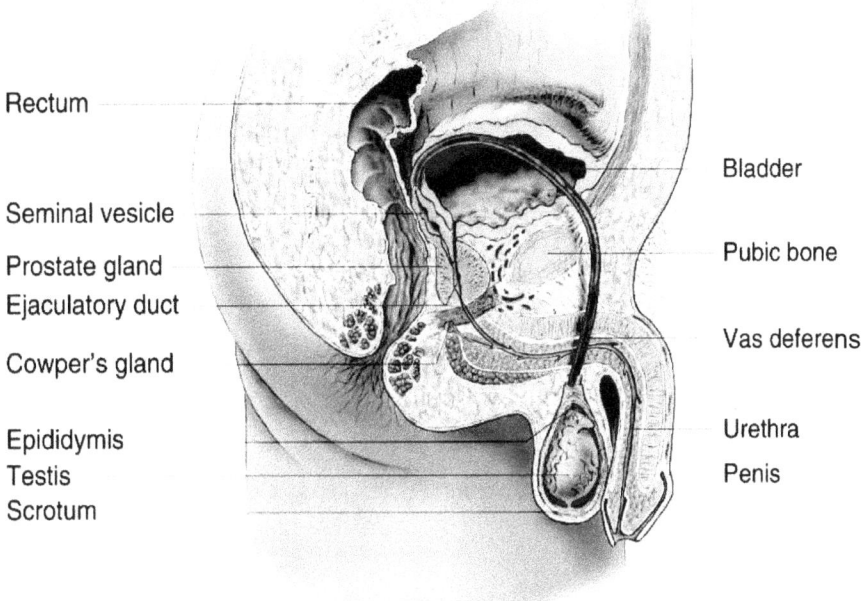

Rectum
Seminal vesicle
Prostate gland
Ejaculatory duct
Cowper's gland
Epididymis
Testis
Scrotum

Bladder
Pubic bone
Vas deferens
Urethra
Penis

THE MALE GENITAL TRACT -AROUSED

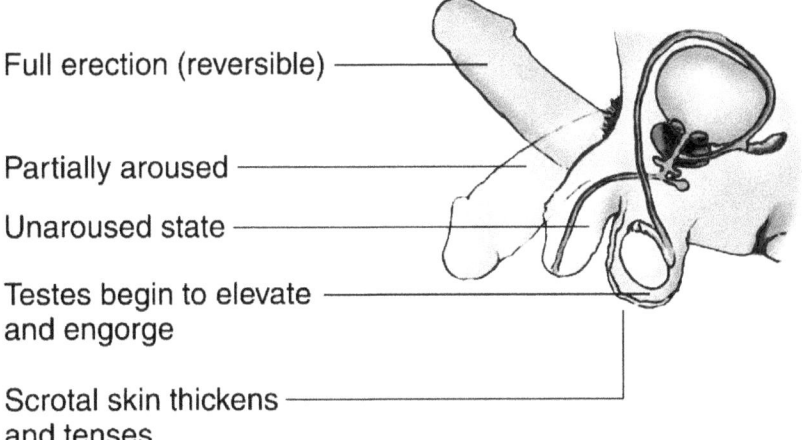

Full erection (reversible)
Partially aroused
Unaroused state
Testes begin to elevate and engorge
Scrotal skin thickens and tenses

THE SEXUAL RESPONSE CYCLE

THE FEMALE GENITAL TRACT–UNAROUSED

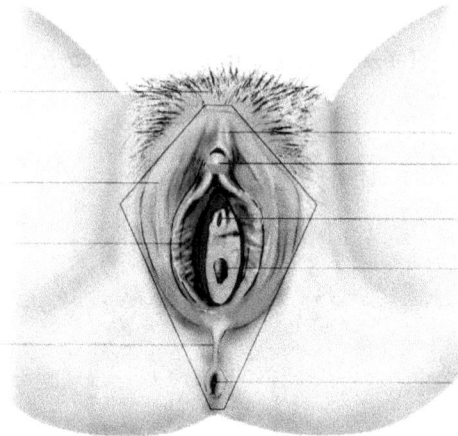

- Mons pubis
- Labia majora (outer lips)
- Labia minora (inner lips)
- Perineum
- Prepuce of clitoris
- Clitoris (glans)
- Urethral opening
- Vaginal opening
- Anus

THE FEMALE GENITAL TRACT–AROUSED

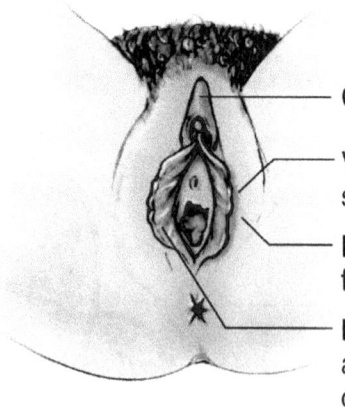

- Clitoral shaft increases in size
- Vestibular bulbs increase in size
- Labia majora separates away from vaginal opening
- Labia minora increases in size and becomes more deeply colored

FOREPLAY

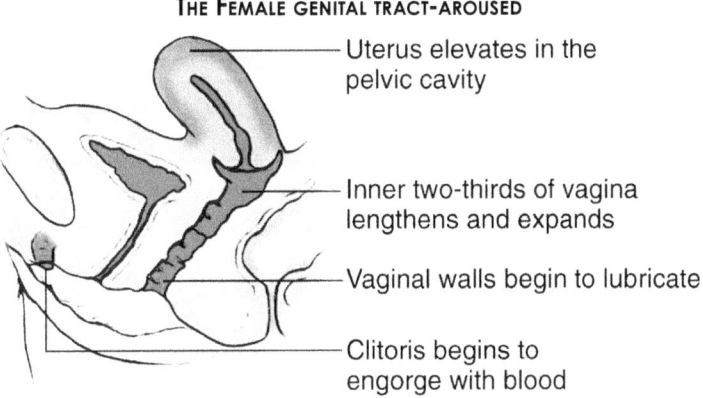

THE FEMALE GENITAL TRACT-AROUSED
- Uterus elevates in the pelvic cavity
- Inner two-thirds of vagina lengthens and expands
- Vaginal walls begin to lubricate
- Clitoris begins to engorge with blood

Phase 2: Plateau

The plateau phase which could also be described as the pre-orgasmic phase is characterized by the following:

- The vagina continues to swell, due to increased blood flow, and the vaginal walls become dark purple

- The woman's clitoris becomes very sensitive and retracts under the clitoral hood to avoid direct stimulation from the penis

- The man's testes are withdrawn into the scrotum

- The breathing, heart rate and blood pressure continue to increase

- Muscle spasms occur in the feet, face and hands

See diagrams below:

PLATEAU - MALE
- Cowper's gland secretion
- Corona may become further engorged
- Cowper's gland becomes active
- Testes become completely engorged and elevated
- Scrotum maintains its thickened and tensed state
- Loss of erection unlikely

THE SEXUAL RESPONSE CYCLE

PLATEAU - FEMALE

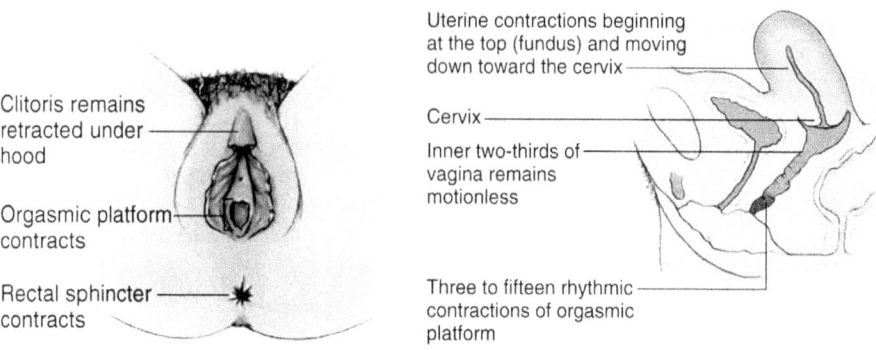

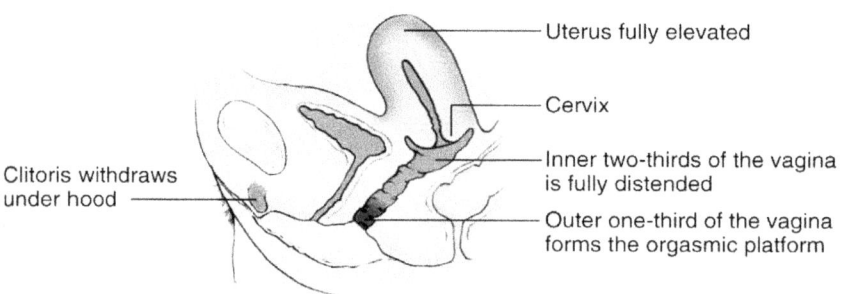

Phase 3: Orgasm

This phase is the climax of the sexual response cycle. It is the shortest of the phases and usually lasts a few seconds. The characteristics of this phase are described below.

- The muscles begin to contract involuntarily

- The blood pressure, heart rate and breathing reach their maximum, with a rapid intake of oxygen

- The muscles in the feet go into spasm

- There is then a sudden, forceful release of sexual tension

- In women, the muscles of the vagina and the uterus contract rhythmically

- In men, rhythmic contractions of the muscles at the base of the penis result in the ejaculation of semen

- A rash or sex flush may appear over the entire body

See diagrams below:

Orgasm - Male

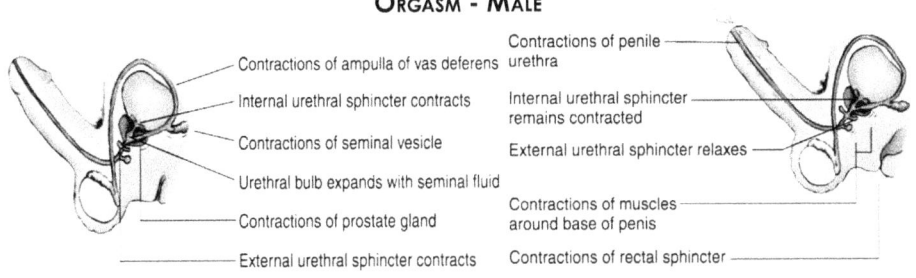

Orgasm - Female

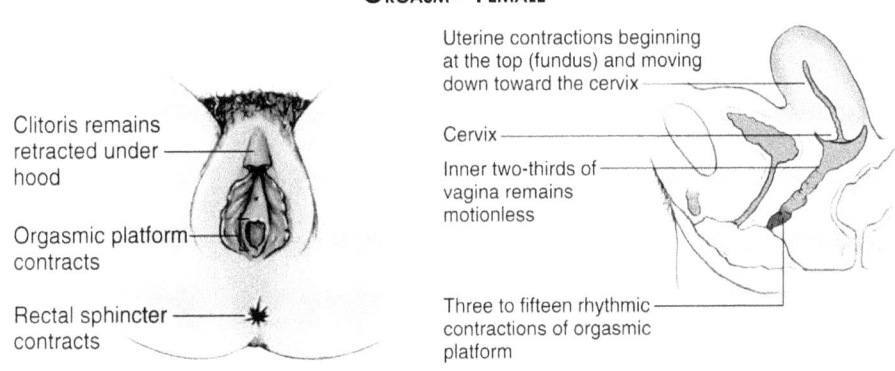

Phase 4: Resolution

During this phase, the body slowly returns to its normal state. As blood empties from the engorged sexual organs, the penis and the vagina assume their original colour and size. This phase is usually associated with a feeling of well being due to the release of endorphin and oxytocin and women feel the urge to cuddle while men tend to feel sleepy. Some women are capable of returning rapidly to the orgasmic phase with further sexual stimulation and may experience multiple orgasms. Most men need time out after an orgasm, called a refractory period and are unable to have an orgasm again. The older the man, the longer the refractory period.

THE SEXUAL RESPONSE CYCLE

RESOLUTION: MALE AND FEMALE

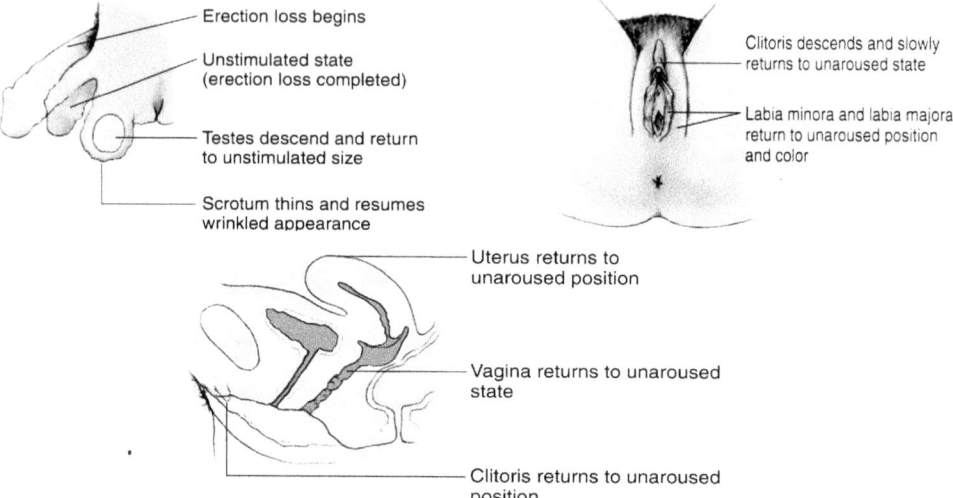

I hope your understanding of this sequence of events will enable you to have a better appreciation of the sex cycle and thus equip you with the knowledge to identify sexual disorders of desire, arousal, orgasm and pain, which we will discuss in the ensuing sections.

Bibliography

1. *Human Sexual Response Cycle*. Retrieved April 20, 2011, from http://www.csupomona.edu/~gdbrum/bio301/sexualresponsecycle.html

2. Masters, W. H. & Johnson, V. E. (1966). *Human Sexual Response*. Boston: Little, Brown & Co, 189-191.

3. *Male and Female Sexual Response-cartoons*. Retrieved April 20, 2011, from http://www.usu.edu/~openshaw/3110/

4. *Sexual Dysfunction in Males*. Retrieved January 23, 2013, from http://my.clevelandclinic.org/disorders/sexual_dysfunction/hic_sexual_dysfunction_in_males.aspx

Sex Dreams
A Guide to Nocturnal Emissions

Let us now reflect on a sexual enigma, sex dreams, its causes and manifestations.

What is a nocturnal emission?

Many parents have come to me and expressed concern about an odd event which they have observed in their teenage sons at nights. 'Why is he wetting the bed at this age,' they ask? Or 'could he possibly have a sexually transmitted disease?' If you have observed this phenomenon in your child, relax, he is just having a nocturnal emission.

A nocturnal emission is an ejaculation of semen experienced by a male during sleep. It is also called a wet dream, a sex dream, an involuntary orgasm or simply an orgasm during sleep.

Medieval legend claims that nocturnal emissions were caused by Succubus; a female demon who takes the form of a human woman in order to seduce men and copulate with them at night. On the other hand, an Incubus is a demon in male form, who, according to a number of mythological traditions copulates with women at nights.

The *Bible* tells us that, among the ancient Hebrews, a man who had an orgasm in his sleep was required to take a ritual bath for purification. His involuntary ejaculation of semen was called a pollution which made him unclean; (Leviticus chapter fifteen and Deuteronomy chapter twenty three). Saint Augustine opined that nocturnal emissions, unlike masturbation, did not pollute the conscience of a man, because they were not voluntary carnal acts, and were therefore not to be considered a sin. He did however, pray that 'he may be released from the glue of lust and thus recommended the beseechment of God's assistance in clearing one's soul of all such carnal affections'. [1] In the eighteenth and nineteenth century, if a patient had involuntary orgasms frequently or released more semen than is typical, he was diagnosed with a disease called spermatorrhoea or seminal weakness. A variety of drugs and other treatments, including circumcision and castration, were recommended to treat this disease.

Sex dreams in men

Kinsey points out that "during puberty, thirteen percent of males experience their first ejaculation as a result of a nocturnal emission and those experiencing their first ejaculation through a nocturnal emission are older than those experiencing their first ejaculation by means of masturbation".[2]

However, nocturnal emissions may happen any time after puberty. They may be accompanied by erotic dreams, and the emission may happen without erection. Whereas an ejaculation normally terminates an erection, in the case of nocturnal emission, the man often still has a functional erection afterward. It is possible to wake up during, or to simply sleep through the ejaculation.

The frequency of nocturnal emissions is quite variable. Some men experience large numbers of nocturnal emissions as teenagers, while others have never experienced one. In the United States it is estimated that eighty three per cent of men will eventually experience nocturnal emissions at some time in their lives. [3]

Do men in non-western countries where masturbation is culturally suppressed have nocturnal emissions? Badan Pusat Statistik (BPS-Statistics Indonesia) between 2002-2004, revealed that ninety eight per cent or more of the men in Indonesia eventually experience nocturnal emissions. [4]

For males who have experienced nocturnal emissions, the mean frequency ranges from 0.36 times per week for single fifteen year old males to 0.18 times per week for forty year old single males. The mean ranges from 0.23 times per week for nineteen year old married males to 0.15 times per week for fifty year old married males.[5] Some have the dreams only at a certain age, while others have them throughout their lives following puberty. The frequency of nocturnal emissions has not been conclusively linked to the frequency of masturbation. Kinsey found that; 'there may be some correlation between the frequencies of masturbation and the frequencies of nocturnal dreams. In general the males who have the highest frequencies of nocturnal emissions may have somewhat lower rates of masturbation. Some of these males credit the frequent emissions to the fact that they do not masturbate, but it is just as likely that the reverse relationship is true, namely, that they do not masturbate because they have frequent emissions.' [6] One factor that can affect the number of nocturnal emissions a person has, is whether he takes testosterone-based drugs.

In a 1998 study, the number of boys reporting nocturnal emissions drastically increased, as their testosterone doses were increased from seventeen per cent of subjects with no treatment, to ninety per cent of subjects at a high dose. [7]

Sex dreams in women (sleep related female orgasms)

In 1953, Kinsey found that "37% of the 5,940 women he interviewed, experienced at least one nocturnal orgasm during sleep by the age of 45". Kinsey and his colleagues defined female nocturnal orgasm as 'sexual arousal during sleep that awakens one to perceive the experience of orgasm.' He also observed that women who suddenly lose the opportunity for several coital orgasms per week have only a few more orgasms in their sleep per year. The obvious conclusion that is derived from this study, is that an orgasm during sleep is a possible natural function of the human body, but it is not a substitute for conscious sexual activity.[8]

Another study by Barbara Wells in 1986, published in the *Journal of Sex Research*, found that eighty five per cent of women who have experienced orgasms during sleep, first did so at a young age, usually before the age of twenty one and some before thirteen. [9]

The content of sex dreams

Sex dreams may conjure up unusual and forbidden behaviour, such as sexual intercourse with close relatives, children or animals, group sex, exhibitionism, and many other activities that the individual would never contemplate in his waking hours. However, during sleep our normal inhibitions and learned controls are suppressed, and many of our unconscious wishes may be brought to the fore in a harmless, symbolic way.

The lack of conscious restraints also accounts for another phenomenon, in that many people, particularly women, reach orgasm much faster in their sleep than while they are awake. Your sexual mores can also influence the character of your dreams. A man with strict sexual morals may have a deep, unconscious desire to have sex with beautiful women and instead of dreaming about vaginas, he dreams of tunnels and subways. Instead of dreaming about breasts he dreams about beautiful hillocks and mounds and so on. Similarly, a woman whose sexual morality is very strict, doesn't actually dream of penises. Instead, she dreams of phallic symbols such as church spires (a tapering conical or pyramidal structure on the top of a building) rockets, cigars, tall chimneys, high rise buildings, baseball bats, snakes etc.

What causes sex dreams?

The cause of sex dreams is not entirely known, but it is associated with the fact that males typically get an erection, often during sleep (this is called nocturnal penile tumescence).

A common theory proposed by some researchers, is that they are the direct result of the stimulation caused by either erotic dreams, or memories of waking sexual activities. However, there has been limited experimental evidence to support this theory, and many men claim to have had nocturnal emissions without having erotic dreams. Another common theory is that wet dreams are the way the body disposes of built-up semen. However, such a theory is unclear, as studies have not shown any significant difference observed in wet dream frequency between men who ejaculated frequently while awake and those who never did. Furthermore, according to the Singapore Science Centre, 'sperm cells degenerate and are reabsorbed (broken down and absorbed by the body) in the seminiferous tubules if they are not ejaculated.' [10]

If you are having sex dreams and are experiencing anxiety qualms, please remember that:

- Wet dreams are normal
- Girls also get wet dreams, but they are more common in boys
- Masturbation can, but will not necessarily stop frequent wet dreams
- Some experts believe that wet dreams are one of the many sub-conscious ways that the body handles stress - they seem to happen more frequently in teens and young adults because this age group is thought to be prone to stress
- Wet dreams are not induced by drugs
- Wet dreams do not suggest a sexual abnormality or mean you are sexually deviant
- The type of wet dreams you have does not reflect your sexual orientation

If you have been guilt ridden about your sex dreams, I am sure that you will now have more restful sleep.

References

1. Augustine, S. (1961). Bishop of Hyppo, *Confessions*, A. C. Outler (Ed.). Mineola, NY: Dover Publications.

2. Kinsey, A. C., Pomeroy, W. B. & Martin, C. E. (1948). *Sexual Behavior in the Human Male*. Philadelphia:Saunders,. p. 190.

3. Kinsey, A. C., Pomeroy, W. B. & Martin, C. E. (1948). *Sexual Behavior in the Human Male*. Philadelphia: Saunders,.p. 519.

4. Badan Pusat Statistik (BPS-Statistics Indonesia) and ORC Macro. (2004). *Indonesia Young Adult Reproductive Health Survey 2002-2003*. (p. 27) Calverton, Maryland, USA: BPS-Statistics Indonesia and ORC.

5. Kinsey, A. C., Pomeroy, W. B. & Martin, C. E. (1948). *Sexual Behavior in the Human Male*. Philadelphia: Saunders,.p. 275).

6. Kinsey, A. C., Pomeroy, W. B. & Martin, C. E. (1948). *Sexual Behavior in the Human Male*. Philadelphia: Saunders. p. 511.

7. Finkelstein, J. W., Susman, E. J., Chinchilli, V. M., D'Arcangelo, M. R., Kunselman, S. J., Schwab, J. & Kulin, H. E. (1998). *Effects of Estrogen or Testosterone on Self-reported Sexual Responses and Behaviors in Hypogonadal Adolescents. Journal of Clinical Endocrinology & Metabolism*, 83(7), 2281-2285.

8. Kinsey, A. C., Pomeroy, W. B., Martin, C. E. & Gebhard, P. H. (1953). *Sexual Behavior in the Human Female*. Philadelphia: Saunders.

9. Wells, B. L. (1986). Predictors of Female Nocturnal Orgasms: A Multivariate Analysis. *Journal of Sex Research, 22*(4), 421-437.

10. *Science Net - Life Sciences - Genetics/Reproduction*. Question No. 18967. Retrieved January 23, 2013, from http://www.science.edu.sg/ssc/detailed.jsp?artid

Part 2 - THE MAIN EVENT

Do you sigh for the love of a woman but feel trapped
by doubts and fears about your mating skills?
This section will provide you with the requisite skills to
break the ice.

Flirting
The Art of Seduction

It's the song of a merryman moping mum, whose soul was sad, whose glance was glum. Who sipped no sup, and who craved no crumb, as he sighed for the love of a lady!

- Sir William Gilbert

An evolutionary process of mate selection

If you see someone you admire you might experience an irresistible urge to approach your object of desire and get to know the person, but do you really know the rules of the game? Are you ready for flirting? If you fail to follow these time honoured rules you will be sorely disappointed.

Flirting is an intriguing behaviour which humans use to initiate what is called the courtship dance; a term which describes the gestures and mannerisms we employ to attract the attention of someone we are interested in and to determine if they are also interested in us.

Some experts describe it as an evolutionary process of mate selection.

The origin of the word flirt has been attributed to the old French conter *fleurette* which means to (try to) seduce by the dropping of flower leaves or to speak sweet nothings.

Flirting signals

When we identify someone in whom we are interested, both men and women display a complex array of behaviours called flirting signals.

Women

- Adopt postures which make them look small and petite by drawing the knees towards the body when seated
- Arch the back to display their breasts, and show off their hips to indicate fertility
- Cross and re-cross the legs to draw attention to them
- Shrug the shoulders, signifying helplessness
- Tilt the head and expose the neck as a sign of vulnerability and submission
- Sway the hips, or emphasize them in a form-fitting dress thus drawing attention to their pelvis, suggesting its capacity for child bearing
- Arch their brows and exaggerate their gaze, their eyes then appear larger than normal, advertising, along with giggles, their youth and submissiveness
- Twirl their hair and toss their head in the direction of their object of interest

- Draw their tongues along her lips thus focusing your attention on what many biologists believe are facial echoes of vaginal lips

Men
- Adopt postures which make them appear taller, larger, dominant, resourceful and non-threatening
- Place their hands in their pockets with elbows akimbo to enlarge their chest or lean against a wall with one hand elevated above shoulder height
- Exaggerate gestures while lighting a cigarette or pouring drinks
- Arch their backs, sway the hips, swagger, laugh loudly and jut out the chin, smile, and flash money

The rules of engagement

If the object of your attention appears to notice these signals, the male almost always initiates what is poetically called the courtship dance which requires him to display tact, wit, charm and maturity. Across all cultures, couples follow four rules of engagement for successful courting as outlined below:

The copulatory gaze

The man usually signals his interest in someone by making eye contact and attempts to hold his target's gaze for more than one second. If the target maintains eye contact with him for more than one second, the chances are that she finds him interesting.

He then approaches this attractive stranger, having established at least an indication of mutual interest through eye contact and tries to make eye contact again at about 4ft away, before moving any closer. If he receives a positive response at 4ft, he then moves in to 'arm's length' (about 2ft 6in), but instinctively refrains from crossing the 18in 'personal zone/intimate zone' border, which could make his object of affection uncomfortable.

The stage of conversation

Having approached the woman, the man must initiate what is the most critical part of the dance; namely conversation. He must aim for moderation in volume and tone, with enough variation in pitch and pace to hold her interest. It is best if he makes a general, impersonal comment on some aspect of the event or activity they are attending. He can also comment on circumstances or surroundings, with a rising intonation or 'isn't it?' type of ending such as 'lovely weather, isn't it?' Your target will recognize this as a conversation-starter, and her response will tell you immediately whether or not it is welcomed. Both parties must avoid negative comments and make suitable compliments with appropriate interjections of humour. A good conversation involves giving, taking, and sharing with both parties contributing equally as talkers and as listeners.

The stage of synchronization

If both parties find each other attractive and are obviously enjoying the conversation, it has been shown by relationship experts that the couple begin to mirror each other's actions such as drinking at the same time, leaning forward together, crossing and uncrossing legs simultaneously and so on.

The stage of touching

At the height of synchronization, a most intriguing event unfolds; the woman leans forward and gently touches her companion, usually in a playful titillating way on his hand, or pat him on his head, nudge his foot with hers and so on. This act of light touching is universally regarded as a sign of camaraderie, bonding and affection. [1] [2]

Words of Caution

It is advisable that you initiate flirting with people of roughly the same level of attractiveness as yourself

Don't flirt with someone who you are really not interested in

Use flirting that is appropriate for the setting: avoid libraries, formal social occasions, funerals and the workplace

Though humour is often a good way to flirt with people, avoid dirty jokes that might make your flirting recipient uncomfortable [2]

Now, close the deal!

This requires tact and subtlety, but be brave. Why not ask if you can meet her again or request a contact number to continue the conversation.

References

1. Fisher, H. (1994). *Anatomy of Love: A Natural History of Mating, Marriage, and Why We Stray.* New York, NY:Ballantine Books.

2. The Social Issues Research Centre (SIRC). *Guide to Flirting*. Retrieved January 23, 2013, from http:// www.sirc.org/publik/flirt.html

Dating
The Joys and Pains

Let's face it; flirting is really a courtship ritual, a way to meet potential life mates. If she is not really interested, well; there will be other times. But, if she is enamoured by your charm, go for it and arrange a date. Let me now guide you through this delicate process.

The tools for successful dating

There are many lonesome people who yearn to meet someone with whom they are compatible, and establish either a short term or long term relationship. Someone to have fun, start a family, experience good sex and have stimulating verbal intercourse with, but they might be hampered by their location, the nature of their jobs, shyness and low self esteem.

We all can recall a few failed dates or an exciting evening that just fizzed out when your date just turned out to be a gross disappointment. However, the biggest challenge women in particular face, is when their dates presume that sex is a given if a date is accepted; in other words dating for many men is a synonym for sex.

This section will provide you with the knowledge to survive the dating game.

What is dating?

Dating is any social activity undertaken by two or more persons, with the aim of each assessing the other's suitability as their partner in an intimate relationship or as a spouse.

There are many types of dates, namely:

- Regular or traditional dates: couples meet for an activity
- Double dates: two couples meet for an activity
- Group dating: an activity shared by more than two couples
- Blind dates: dates where the participants have not previously met each other
- Long distance/holidating: a long distance relationship, in which dating occurs when one, or both parties are on holiday
- Exclusive dating (going steady): the partners in the relationship are committed to each other and date no one else

How are dates organized?

Dates are classified as online, speed, group, virtual or singles events.

What is internet or online dating?

Internet dating or online dating is an activity in which you go to a site on the internet that's specifically for finding a mate.

What is speed dating?

This is a quick way to find a suitable date. This is how it works: a group of like-minded individuals meet and arrange to interview each other at a specific location. At the end of the session everyone would have met each other, shared thoughts and exchanged addresses, phone numbers, e-mail addresses and other personal information. You, as a participant will then mull over all the persons you have met then contact the one who piqued your curiosity and arrange a date

What is mobile/cell phone dating?

In this instance text messages are sent to and from a mobile phone to the party you are interested in and a date can be arranged subsequently.

What is virtual dating ?

This is a combination of video game playing and dating. The participants use avatars (a computer user's representation of himself/herself) to interact with each other. This creates a kind of virtual experience where you meet potential dates

What are singles events?

In this instance, a group of singles are brought together to take part in various events such as parties, games, workshops and voluntary activities for the purpose of meeting new people.

Where can you find a date?

You can find a potential date anywhere if you're friendly, warm and engaging. While strolling down the street, at school, church functions, social occasions, fairs, libraries, on the beach, or at the park.

The rules of dating

- **Have an exit plan** — have an exit plan arranged, and work out how you are going to get home in advance. Set up a buddy system with a friend and arrange for him or her to call you while on your date.

- **Learn how to flirt** — to attract new people, you'll need to show them you are interested; make eye contact and send the right signals with your posture. Learn how to read and interpret facial expressions and most of all, be humorous.

- **Be confident** — timidity and shyness are guaranteed to minimize your chances of successful dating.

- **Enjoy the occasion** — having decided on a date, relax and enjoy the moment; be your most charming self; be witty and engaging, remember first impression lasts.

- **Fine tune your communication skills** — the bed rock of a good relationship is effective communication, so share your thoughts frankly with your date and encourage him/her to reciprocate. Don't divulge all your innermost secrets of course, but remember you need to know what is in your date's head space.

- **Spend conservatively** — a first date is simply that - a primary interaction to get to know someone better. Spend wisely, don't exhaust your resources.

- **Choose a safe venue** — don't go to lonely secluded locations. Choose a venue that you know well; meet somewhere busy and public.

- **Dress conservatively** — please avoid seductive and provocative clothing; remember this is an exploratory date not a committed relationship.

- **Ensure a non-alcohol based first date** — on your first date avoid alcoholic drinks; the best bet is bottled water. Avoid drinks in cups, glasses or opened bottles. Remember drinks can be spiked! Alcohol and drugs dull your awareness, loosen your inhibitions and reduce your ability to make safe choices.

What are some warning signs of a bad date?

Watch your potential dates verbal and non verbal clues to determine if the attraction is mutual; if you sense that the chemistry is wrong, move on.

Date rape

Regretfully, some dates go sour, and I must tell you about the phenomenon called date rape, which is coerced sex between dates, friends or general acquaintances. The rape can be coerced either physically or emotionally. In some cases, date rape drugs are used. These drugs have sedative, hypnotic and amnesic effects and when used to facilitate rape, are usually added to a food or drink without the victim's knowledge.

Alcohol is the most commonly used date rape drug, since victims are encouraged to imbibe large amounts to loosen inhibitions.

Rophypnol benzodiazepine is the drug most commonly used for date rape because it is readily soluble in alcohol. It can incapacitate victims and prevent them from resisting sexual assault and produces anterograde amnesia, which means that the individual may not remember events they experienced while under the influence of the drug. The effects appear in 15 to 20 minutes and may last four to eight hours.

GHB (Gamma Hydroxy Butyrate) has effects similar to alcohol; the victims may not be aware that they have ingested the drug since it is invisible in water and is odourless. It is often used to spike soft drinks, liquor or beer.

Chloral hydrate produces a sedative hypnotic effect similar to benzodiazepines. A drink that has been spiked with chloral hydrate is called a mickey flinn.

Enjoy your dates, but just use your intuition and common sense when choosing a date.

Bibliography

1. *Dating Rules and Etiquette*. Retrieved April 2012, from http://www.dating.about.com/od/rulesetiquette/.html

2. Cloud, H. & Townsend, J. (2000). *Boundaries in Dating: How Healthy Choices Grow Healthy Relationships*. Grand Rapids MI: Zondervan.

3. Glanz, L. & Phillips, R. H. (2003). *Guy Gets Girl, Girl Gets Guy: Where to Find Romance and What to Say When You Find It*. Garden City Park, NY: Square One Publishers Inc.

4. Havelin, K. & Erickson, M. F. (2000). *Dating: What is a Healthy Relationship?* Mankato, MN: LifeMatters.

'Scentsational' Sex
The Mystery of Body Odour and Aromas in Human Sexuality

So, you have wined and dined your date and you are now in the throes of love, but, you are overcome by the complexity of emotions and inexplicable experiences. I will now unravel for you the mystery of odour in sexuality.

It is not uncommon for you to be in the presence of someone and find his/her body odour particularly alluring and you realize that the person has a kind of magnetic appeal, which can't be defined. You might be surprised to know that you may have been blown over by a subtle odour all humans emit called pheromones.

What are pheromones?

The German physician and hygienist Gustav Jäger was probably the first to formalize the concept of human pheromones, which he named anthropines. He correctly identified them as lipophilic compounds that are associated with skin and follicles that determine the individual signature of human odours.[1] The term pheromone was introduced by Peter Karlson and Adolf Butenandt in 1959, based on the Greek pherein (to transport) and hormon (to stimulate). It is a substance that acts as a molecular messenger, transmitting information from one member of a species to another member of the same species. Pheromones among animals are largely transported through the sense of smell. In mammals and reptiles, pheromones may be detected by the vomeronasal organ or Jacobson's organ, which lies between the nose and mouth, although some are detected by regular olfactory (nasal) membranes.

Whereas animals release pheromones from their skin, urine, faeces and to some extent their breath, most research on pheromones in humans indicate that the main odour-producing organ is the skin. These odours are largely produced by the skin's apocrine glands, which develop during puberty and are usually associated with sweat glands and tufts of hair. These glands are located everywhere on the body surface, but tend to concentrate in six areas namely the axillae (underarms), the nipples of both sexes, the pubic (genital and perianal regions), the circumoral region and lips, the eyelids and the outer ear. The first four of these regions are generally associated with varying amounts of hair growth.

The extremely large surface area of a tuft of hair is a very effective means of spreading an odour by evaporation.

The substances produced by these glands cannot be detected easily by the human nose; in reality what we smell when we detect skin odour is not the fresh glandular secretions, but rather the bacterial breakdown products of these secretions. In humans, the pheromone so far discovered is a complex and large molecule. It is chemically related to the hormone testosterone and is called androsterone (androstadienone). This has been identified as the human pheromone present in urine. Androsterone's presence is perceived differently by different people, some detect it as a fruity/grapey character, some as a camphoraceous or aromatic type, others as a urine-like or sexy/musky aroma. Some can detect it in very low concentrations and still others cannot perceive it at all.

Types of pheromones

The main classes of pheromones are territorial, trail, releaser, signaler, primer, sex and modulators. There is good evidence to support the presence of signaler, primer, sex and modulators in humans, but limited evidence for territorial, trail and releaser effects in adult humans.

Territorial pheromones — mark the boundaries of an organism's territory. In cats and dogs, these hormones are present in the urine, which they deposit on landmarks serving to mark the perimeter of the claimed territory.

Trail pheromones — secreted by ants (hydrocarbons) enable these social insects to return to their nest with food and also serve as a guide for other ants.

Releaser pheromones — are pheromones that cause an alteration in the behaviour of the recipient. For example, some organisms use powerful attractant molecules to attract mates from a distance of two miles or more. This type of pheromone generally elicits a rapid response, but is quickly degraded.

Signaler pheromones — serve to bond mothers with their own babies through substances in both breast secretions and the baby's skin that signal to the baby and its mother that they belong to each other.

Primer pheromones — trigger a change of developmental events. They affect the endocrine system and induce a change in behaviour, for example they serve to synchronize the fertile cycles of a close-proximity groups such as college students and office workers.

Sex pheromones in animals — indicate the availability of the female for mating. Male animals may also emit pheromones that convey information about their species, health and genetic constitution and may promote the sexual attractiveness of the animal and elicit attention from the opposite sex.

Modulator pheromones — may cause individuals to exude different odours based on mood. [2] [3]

How does pheromones influence behaviour?

Although humans appear to have lost much of the olfactory sensitivity of their mammalian ancestors, recent research suggests that body odours; even if not consciously perceived, play an important role in social interaction common with other animals. This may be involved in endocrine (hormone) regulation, behavioural responses and in determining when, how and with whom we choose to reproduce. [4]

Below, I will describe the various roles that pheromones seem to play in our lives:

Body odour is related to sexual identification in young children

Michael Kalogerakis and Irving Bieber proposed a theory, that olfaction is related to sexual identification in young children. They performed a study on young boys, two to four years of age, which strongly indicated that at some point in early childhood, a boy will begin to show an aversion to the odours of their father, and will simultaneously feel attracted to the odour of their mothers. [5]

Mothers unconsciously mark their baby with a distinctive scent

Michael J. Russell, in his study, concluded that mothers unconsciously mark their baby with a distinctive scent; a phenomenon observed in many other primates. This possibility is supported by the common parental observation that a child will reject their favourite blanket or stuffed animal after it has been washed, presumably because it has lost specific odours acquired in previous contacts with the mother. [6]

The age of onset of menstruation for girls has had a direct correlation with the amount of time that young girls spend with boys.

Dr. Alex Comfort noticed that in the past three centuries, the age of onset of menstruation for girls has had a direct correlation with the amount of time that young girls spend with boys. It is Comfort's opinion, that this is due to the exposure to odours of the opposite sex. In fact, this phenomenon has been documented in mice and is called the Vandenbergh effect. [7]

Women are very sensitive to male musk exaltolide (pentadecalactone) during their fertile period

There are variations in odour perception between human adult males and females. Le Magnen and Doty found that this is most evident in the case of women's acute ability to smell musk, which are steroids very similar to the male sex hormone testosterone. Women's sensitivity to these substances varies depending on the phase of her cycle. During menstruation, women are no more sensitive to musks than men, but about ten days after menstruation - a woman's peak fertility period - women reach their maximum sensitivity. In addition, women on the pill, those who have had ovarectomies, or if they are either pregnant or post-menopausal are relatively insensitive to these substances. He concluded that men secrete abundant amounts of musky odorants in: the urine, smegma, and from the apocrine glands in the underarms and pubic areas. Bacterial action may be necessary for the release of these odorants. According to Le Magnen, the fact that men's bodies secrete these substances and that women are maximally sensitive to them when they are most fertile, indicates that, 'there may be a olfactory-sexual role for these substances in human sexuality.' [8] [9] [10]

A woman's sexuality and sense of smell peaks during mid-cycle

A study performed by J. Richard Udry at the University of North Carolina, attempted to delineate the relationship between coitus, orgasm and position in the menstrual cycle. He found that women do indeed engage in sexual intercourse about six times more frequently at about the time of ovulation, when women's sensitivity to the male musk odour is highest. In addition, women are much more likely to have an orgasm at these times. Further, the women Udry studied were several times less likely to have sexual intercourse or have an orgasm during and two to three days after menstruation, which is when women's sensitivity to the musky smell of men is lowest. Coupled with women's odour sensitivity, these results also indicate a possible pheromonal trigger for sexual behaviour. [11] Furthermore, there are variations in the sensitivity of females versus males to masculine odorants: women can smell the musk-like compound exaltolide at a concentration 1000 times lower than men, some men may be unable to smell it at all and the sensitivity is highest in the pre-ovulatory or ovulatory phases of the menstrual cycle. [12] [13] [14]

The odour of vaginal secretions is most pleasant at the time of ovulation

Men and women estimated the pleasantness and intensity of the odours of vaginal secretions sampled from consecutive phases of 15 ovulatory menstrual cycles of four women. On the average, secretions from pre-ovulatory and ovulatory phases were slightly weaker and less unpleasant in odour than those from menstrual, early luteal, and late luteal phases. [15]

Human vaginal secretions contain a sexual trigger!

There have been many studies on whether or not human vaginal secretions might contain some kind of sex pheromone or copulin, as one researcher calls them. Several researchers have found that human vaginal secretions contain various small C2 to C6 fatty acids, with acetic acid (vinegar) predominating. Richard P. Michael found that about 30 per cent of the women (he called them producers) produced a significant amount of those small fatty acids (not including acetic acid) that induce copulatory behaviour in rhesus monkeys. In addition, these copulins increased up until ovulation, and then decreased as menstruation approached. Michael also noted that women on birth-control pills did not show this mid-cycle increase, and had a lower overall fatty acid content. Michael theorized that these fatty acids or copulins were a sexual trigger in humans. [16]

The synchronization of menstrual cycles among women based on unconscious odour

Martha McClintock, of the University of Chicago, in a study exposed a group of women to a whiff of perspiration from other women. It was found that it caused their menstrual cycles to speed up or slow down depending on the time in the month the sweat was collected; before, during, or after ovulation. Therefore, this study proposed that there are two types of pheromone involved. One, produced prior to ovulation, shortens the ovarian cycle; and the second, produced just at ovulation, lengthens the cycle. It was evident from the study that girls who lived in the same dormitory and spent a lot of time together, developed closer menstrual cycles, even though their cycles were randomly scattered when they first arrived at the dormitory. This phenomenon has been referred to as menstrual synchronization or the McClintock effect. [17] [18] [19]

The time of menstrual onset may be modified by olfactory cues

Michael Russell provided more insight on the phenomenon of menstrual synchrony. Two groups of women were compared for the timing of the onset of their menstrual cycles. One group was rubbed on the upper lip (directly beneath the nose) with a mixture of alcohol and underarm perspiration collected from a single female donor. The other group was rubbed with plain alcohol. The group which received the perspiration showed a significant shift in the timing of their menstrual cycles which conformed closely with the donor's monthly cycle. This study supports the hypothesis that the time of menstrual onset may be modified by olfactory cues. [20]

Women who have sex with men at least once a week are more likely to have normal-length menstrual cycles

In 1986, Dr. Winifred Cutler conducted a study which also suggested that the human body produces pheromones. Underarm secretions from seven men and women were collected to test the effects of pheromones. A soup of aromatic essences was taken from underarm pads worn by the volunteers for 18 to 27 hours a week over a three-month period. Male essence (male under arm sweat) mixed with alcohol, was applied three times a week to the upper lips of six women with abnormal menstrual cycles and no current sexual relationship. The cycles of these women speeded up or slowed down toward 29.5 days.

The irregular cycles of six women in a control group, dabbed with only pure alcohol, remained the same. In a second group, ten women who received female essence (female underarm sweat) showed a significant trend toward synchronized menstrual periods, having periods around the same time after only a few cycles. It was also found that women who have sex with men at least once a week are more likely to have normal-length menstrual cycles, fewer infertility problems and a milder menopause than women who are celibate or who have sex in an irregular feast or famine pattern. The investigators concluded that an essential factor, aside from sexual intercourse itself, is exposure to specific aromatic chemicals exuded in a man's normal body odours - pheromones. When a woman receives these chemicals, by smell or skin absorption, even though she may not consciously notice them, they automatically improve her physiological functioning. [21]

Human sweat proven to be a potent aphrodisiac

How potent is sweat? Well, many studies have been done to prove that this ubiquitous substance is quite powerful. Dr. Michael Russell in 1976, performed an experiment to determine whether young adults could discriminate between their odours and others, and between male and female odours. 81 per cent of the males and 69 per cent of the females identified their own shirts correctly. When asked to characterize the odours of the shirts, the subjects generally said the males' shirts smelled musky and the females' shirts smelled sweet. [22] Women say they feel more relaxed in the presence of male axillary extracts. [23] Several studies in babies of only a few weeks old, have demonstrated that they can identify, and are attracted to both the axillary and the breast odours of their own mother, but not of other women. [24] [25] Other studies have shown that humans rate the axillary odour of *dissimilar* people as more pleasant than those who share similar genetic material such as close relatives.[26] [27] Women with irregular menstrual cycles became regular when exposed to male underarm extract. [28] Other studies have demonstrated that the smell of androstadienone, a chemical component of male sweat, influence the endocrine (hormonal) balance of the opposite sex, causing higher levels of cortisol in females. They argue that it is a human pheromonal chemosignal. [29]

Human beings use the sense of smell to select their mates

Both homosexual males and heterosexual females react in a common manner when they are sexually aroused by male odours. Using a brain imaging technique in 2005 and 2006, Swedish researchers have shown that homosexual and heterosexual males' brains respond differently to two odours that may be involved in sexual arousal, and that the homosexual men respond in the same way as heterosexual women; though it could not be determined whether this was cause or effect. The study was expanded to include homosexual women. The results were consistent with previous findings, meaning that homosexual women were not as responsive to male identified odours, while their response to female cues were similar to that of heterosexual males. This research suggests a possible role for human pheromones in the biological basis of sexual orientation. [31] [32]

Female body odour is a potential cue to ovulation

In a further study conducted in 2001 by researchers at the University of Texas, Department of Psychology, men described the smell of a woman's t-shirt as more sexy or pleasant during the fertile stage of her menstrual cycle, than the shirt of the same woman during her infertile stage. This is a fascinating finding since men now have a cue when it is most appropriate to do the deed. So the next time you are swept away by the subtle odour of your lover, you are just a victim of this age old excitement carrier. [33] [34]

Do women have a hidden heat period?

Juan J. Tarín, et al in a paper published in 2002, reported that studies focused on cycling changes in women's olfactory and visual perception, show that, in comparison with women at other phases of the menstrual cycle, women at mid-cycle exhibit increased sexual motivation that bias recognition performance towards objects with a sexual meaning, evaluate the unattractive sweat substance androstenone as more pleasant, and display enhanced preference for the odour and face shape of masculinised, physically attractive and symmetric men. On the other hand, men find the scent of women at mid-cycle more pleasant and sexually attractive than during the luteal phase. As discussed in the previous study.[35]

In summary, the role of the human nose in detecting odour as a sexual stimulant has not been given the recognition it deserves. However, increasing evidence from the research just described, indicates irrefutably, that pheromones play a critical role in mate selection and sexual behaviour.

Aromas are sexually enticing

It is accepted as a truism that various aromas are sexually enticing and some common aromas believed to enhance desire are: banana nut bread, cola, cucumber, doughnut, cinnamon, frankincense, jasmine, lavender, licorice, musk, peppermint, pumpkin pie, vanilla, strawberry, cherry, orange, cranberry, popcorn, male cologne and perfume.

However, there has not been a scientific study to prove their effectiveness until in 1996, when Dr. Alan Hirsch, the founder and neurological director of the Smell & Taste Treatment and research foundation in Chicago, and colleague Dr. Jason Gruss, conducted a study called '*Olfactory Stimuli and Sexual Response in the Human Male*'. The purpose of the study was to investigate the relationship between sexual arousal and smell by exposing 31 male research subjects aged 18 to 64 years to a variety of different scents, and the average increase in penile blood flow was noted. In 1998, they also studied the effect of aromas on vaginal blood flow in nineteen non-menstruating, non-anorgasmic women. The study, known as the '*Effects of Odours on Female Sexual Arousal*', revealed that in men the combined odour of lavender and pumpkin pie had the greatest effect, increasing median penile blood flow by 40 per cent.

Next in effectiveness, was the combination of black liquorice and doughnut, which increased arousal by 31.5 per cent, pumpkin pie and doughnut by 20.0 per cent, orange by 19.5 per cent, lavender & doughnut by 18 per cent, black liquorice and cola by 13 per cent, doughnut and cola by 12.5 per cent, lily of the valley by 11 per cent and buttered popcorn 9 per cent. There was a notable difference in the response between young men and older men who responded strongly to vanilla. Baked cinnamon buns had more effect than all the perfumes together. Men also responded strongly to the smell of cheese pizza.

Men who had frequent sexual intercourse were quite responsive to the scent of strawberries.

The authors concluded that since pleasant odours tend to positively increase other behaviours, they would be likely to increase penile blood flow. They also argued that the odours could induce a 'pavlovian conditioned response' reminding partners of sexual partners or their favourite foods, or that the odours could have evoked nostalgic recall. The results in women revealed that Good & Plenty (black liquorice candy combined with cucumber) increased vaginal blood flow by 14 per cent, baby powder by 13 per cent, pumpkin pie combined with lavender 11 per cent, baby powder combined with chocolate 4 per cent and perfume 1 per cent. What turned the women off, were things usually associated with masculinity such as men's colognes and the scent of barbecued meat and cherries. [36] [37] [38] [39] [40] [41] [42]

Based on the above study, aromatic scents can be titillating and seductive so here are my suggestions to spice up your love life:

The love recipe:

- Bake a cinnamon cake or a pumpkin pie for your lover, the rich aroma could be a potent aphrodisiac

- Light lavender or jasmine candles to aromatize the air

- Dab on a vanilla scent or perfume

- Smear aromatic oils like jasmine or lavender on a low wattage bulb to diffuse the scent into the air

- Offer your partner a cup of peppermint, vanilla, liquorice, or jasmine tea as a prelude to intimacy

- Perfume the air with jasmine or peppermint air freshener

- Eat doughnuts, liquorice, candy, chocolate, strawberries or popcorns as a snack to energize you during foreplay

- Bathe with a cucumber scented soap or use lotions, oils or shampoos containing aromatic oils

References

1. Jäger, G.(1880). Die Entdeckung der Seele (2nd ed). *"The Discovery of The Soul".* Leipzig: Gunther.

2. Stowers, L. & Marton, T. F. (2005). *What is a Pheromone? Mammalian Pheromones Reconsidered. Neuron,* 46(5), 699-702.

3. Wysocki, C. J. & Preti, G. (2004). *Facts, Fallacies, Fears, and Frustrations with Human Pheromones. The Anatomical Record Part A: Discoveries in Molecular, Cellular, and Evolutionary Biology,* 281(1), 1201-1211.

4. Bhutta, M. F. (2007). *Sex and the Nose: Human Pheromonal Responses. JRSM,* 100(6), 268-274.

5. Kalogerakis, M. G. (1963). *The Role of Olfaction in Sexual Development. Psychosomatic Medicine,* 25(5), 420-432.

6. Russell, M. J. (1976). *Human Olfactory Communication. Nature.* 260, 520-522.

7. Comfort, A. (1971). *Likelihood of Human Pheromones. Nature.* 230: 432-479.

8. Le Magnen, M.J. (1952). *Les Phénomènes Olfacto-sexuel Chez L'homme.* Arch Scient Physiol 6:125-1.

9. Le Magnen, M. J. (1948). *Nouvelles Donnees Sur Le Phénome-ne De L'exaltolide Comptes Rendus de L'Academie Des Sciences.* Paris, 1948, 226, 694.

10. Doty, R. L. (1976). *Mammalian Olfaction, Reproductive Processes, and Behavior.* New York: Academic Press.

11. Udry, J. R., & Morris, N. M. (1968). *Distribution of Coitus in the Menstrual Cycle. Nature,* 220 (5167), 593-596.

12. Doty, R. L., Snyder, P. J., Huggins, G. R., & Lowry, L. D. (1981). *Endocrine, Cardiovascular, and Psychological Correlates of Olfactory Sensitivity Changes During the Human Menstrual Cycle. Journal of Comparative and Physiological Psychology,* 95(1), 45 -60.

13. Good, P. R, Geary, N. & Engen, T. (1976). *The Effect of Estrogen on Odor Detection. Chemical Senses,* 2(1), 45-50.

14. Vierling, J. S. & Rock, J. O. H. N. (1967). *Variations in Olfactory Sensitivity to Exaltolide During the Menstrual Cycle. Journal of Applied Physiology,* 22(2), 311-315.

15. Doty, R. L., Ford, M., Preti, G. & Huggins, G. R. (1975). *Changes in the Intensity and Pleasantness of Human Vaginal Odors During the Menstrual Cycle. Science*

190(4221), 1316-8.

16. Michael, R. P., Bonsall, R. W., & Warner, P. (1974). *Human Vaginal Secretions: Volatile Fatty Acid Content. Science, 186,* 1217-1219.

17. McClintock, M.K. (1971). "Menstrual Synchrony and Suppression". *Nature* 229 (5282): 244-5.

18. Stern, K., & McClintock, M. K. (1998). *Regulation of Ovulation by Human Pheromones. Nature,* 392(6672), 177-178.

19. Yang, Z. & Schank, J. C. (2006). *Women Do Not Synchronize Their Menstrual Cycles. Human Nature,* 17(4), 434-447.

20. Russell, M. J., Switz, G. M. & Thompson, K. (1980). *Olfactory Influences on the Human Menstrual Cycle. Pharmacology Biochemistry and Behavior,* 13(5), 737-738.

21. Cutler, W. B., Preti, G., Krieger, A., Huggins, G. R., Garcia, C. R. & Lawley, H. J. (1986). *Human Axillary Secretions Influence Women's Menstrual Cycles: The Role of Donor Extract from Men. Hormones and Behavior,* 20(4), 463-473.

22. Russell, M. J. (1976). *Human Olfactory Communication. Nature.* 260 (5551), 520-522.

23. Preti, G., Wysocki, C. J., Barnhart, K. T., Sondheimer, S. J. & Leyden, J. J. (2003). *Male Axillary Extracts Contain Pheromones That Affect Pulsatile Secretion of Luteinizing Hormone and Mood in Women Recipients. Biology of Reproduction,* 68(6), 2107-2113.

24. Cernoch, J. M. & Porter, R. H. (1985). *Recognition of Maternal Axillary Odors By Infants. Child Development,* 1593-1598.

25. Varendi, H., & Porter, R. H. (2001). *Breast Odour As the Only Maternal Stimulus Elicits Crawling Towards the Odour Source. Acta Paediatrica,* 90(4), 372-375.

26. Wedekind, C., Seebeck, T., Bettens, F., & Paepke, A. J. (1995). MHC-dependent Mate Preferences in Humans. *Proceedings of the Royal Society of London. Series B: Biological Sciences,* 260(1359), 245-249.

27. Wedekind, C., & Füri, S. (1997). *Body Odour Preferences in Men and Women: Do They Aim For Specific MHC Combinations or Simply Heterozygosity? Proceedings of the Royal Society of London. Series B: Biological Sciences,* 264(1387), 1471-1479.

28. Preti, G., Wysocki, C. J., Barnhart, K. T., Sondheimer, S. J., & Leyden, J. J.

(2003). *Male Axillary Extracts Contain Pheromones That Affect Pulsatile Secretion of Luteinizing Hormone and Mood in Women Recipients. Biology of Reproduction*, 68(6), 2107-2113.

29. Wyart, C., Webster, W. W., Chen, J. H., Wilson, S. R., McClary, A., Khan, R. M., & Sobel, N. (2007). *Smelling a Single Component of Male Sweat Alters Levels of Cortisol in Women. The Journal of Neuroscience*, 27(6), 1261-1265.

30. Savic, I., Hedén‐Blomqvist, E., & Berglund, H. (2009). *Pheromone Signal Transduction in Humans: What Can Be Learned from Olfactory Loss. Human Brain Mapping*, 30(9), 3057-3065.

31. Savic, I., Berglund, H., & Lindström, P. (2005). *Brain Response to Putative Pheromones in Homosexual Men. Proceedings of the National Academy of Sciences of the United States of America*, 102(20), 7356-7361.

32. Berglund, H., Lindström, P., & Savic, I. (2006). *Brain Response to Putative Pheromones in Lesbian Women. Proceedings of the National Academy of Sciences*, 103(21), 8269-8274.

33. Singh, D., & Bronstad, P. M. (2001). *Female Body Odour is A Potential Cue to Ovulation. Proceedings of the Royal Society of London. Series B: Biological Sciences*, 268(1469), 797-801.

34. Poran, N.S. (1994). *Cyclic Attractivity of Human Female Odours. Adv Biosci* 93:555-60.

35. Tarín, J. J., & Gómez-Piquer, V. (2002). *Do Women Have a Hidden Heat Period?. Human Reproduction*, *17*(9), 2243-2248.

36. Hirsch, A.R. and Gruss, J.J. (1996) *Olfactory Stimuli and Sexual Response in the Human Male*. The Proceedings of the World of Aromatherapy, edited by Jeanne Rose, San Francisco, CA, 1996, p. 26-76.

37. Hirsch, A.R., Gruss J., Bermele C, Zagorski D & Schroder, M.A (1998): "The Effects of Odors on Female Sexual Arousal." *Psychosomatic Medicine, 60*, 95.

38. Herz, R. (2007). *The Scent of Desire: Discovering our Enigmatic Sense of Smell*. New York NY: William Morrow.

39. Hirsch, A.R. (1998) "Scent and Sexual Arousal," *Medical Aspects of Human Sexuality*, 1 (3), 9-12.

40. Hirsch, A.R., Schroder, M., Gruss, J., Bermele, C.& Zagorski, D. (1999). *Scentsational Sex. Olfactory Stimuli and Sexual Response in the Human Female. The International Journal of Aromatherapy*, 9(2), 75-81.

41. Hirsch, A.R., and Gruss, J.J.: (1999). *Human Male Sexual Response to Olfactory Stimuli, J. Neurol. Orthop. Med. Surg.*, 19, 14-19.

42. Hirsch, A. R. (1998). *Scentsational Sex: The Secret to Using Aroma for Arousal.* Boston, Massachusetts: Element.

Erogenous Zones
Male and Female Hot Spots

"For women the best aphrodisiacs are words. The G-spot is in the ears.
He who looks for it below there is wasting his time".
~Isabel Aliened

Do you agree with Isabel, or would you like to find out if there are any hidden erogenous zones in men and women? This section will unveil for you those hidden hot spots.

Female hot spots

A guided tour through her hot spots.

The skin is the largest sensory organ of the human body and is for many an unexplored territory which can unleash a well of pent up passions. Let me therefore guide you along these sensual tactile pathways called erogenous zones. Precisely which body parts are sources of sexual arousal is a very individual experience. Let us now explore her hot spots.

The C spot - the clitoris

The clitoris is a very sensitive sexual organ which contains over eight thousand nerve endings. It is the prime hot spot for woman because up to 75 per cent of women need direct clitoral stimulation to have an orgasm. This structure is very sensitive to touch, pressure and temperature. Stimulation of the clitoris can cause an intense clitoral orgasm.

The G spot

The Grafenburg or G spot is a cluster of erectile tissue surrounding the urethra which becomes engorged with blood during sexual excitement. In some women, if this area is stimulated, they will experience an intense and fulfilling vaginal orgasm. [1]

The A spot

The anterior fornix erogenous zone or A spot is the area on the front wall of the vagina mid way between the cervix and the G spot. It plays a role in vaginal lubrication and if stimulated can alleviate vaginal dryness.

The U spot

The U spot refers to the urethral opening which in some women is very sensitive and can be a source of pleasure.

The P spot

The perineum or P spot is the soft tissue between the vaginal opening and the anus and is composed of spongy erectile tissue. It is referred to as Hui - Yin in acupressure (gate of life and death). When stimulated, it increases female sexual desire.

The X spot

The X spot refers to the cervix; it is very sensitive to pressure and when stimulated can induce a cervical orgasm.

The M spot

The M spot lies just below the mouth of the uterus and when stimulated can be quite gratifying.

Other female hot spots

Many parts of the female body not involved in reproduction are sensitive to sexual touch. Caressing and massaging of these areas can enhance sensual pleasure or they can be invitations to further sexual activity. These hot spots can significantly enhance your sexual experience, but you must take time to explore them and only through active communication can you determine if your partner finds them stimulating.

These spots are:

- **The mouth** — including the lips and tongue. For most people, this is an area of high erotic potential. Kissing is one act that uses the sensitivity of this region in a sexually stimulating way.

- **The breasts** — these are called the 'bells of love' by Chinese sexologists. They have many pleasure receptive nerve endings that send sensations to the brain in the same way as the genitals do.

- **The nipples** — have love points called centres of the breasts which arouse sexual energy when stimulated. Another sex point is called the heavenly pond; this is a thumb width away from each nipple. They increase sexual intimacy and help to express love and affection when touched, caressed and kissed. Some women can reach orgasm through breast stimulation alone.

- **The neck** — sensual neck play has been shown to facilitate arousal in women.

- **The scalp** — massaging the scalp help women to relax due to the release of oxytocin which produces a feeling of well being and enhances intimacy.

- **The ears** — many women enjoy having their ears tickled or kissed.

- **Other erogenous zones** — to explore are: the eyelids, shoulders, nose, abdomen, shin and calves, hands and feet. The buttocks (which is sometimes a target for spanking and stroking; an activity which is erotically appealing to some women) is also known as an erogenous zone.[2]

Male hot spots

A guided tour through his hot spots

Men also have many unique hot spots which, when discovered, will transform your relationship. So, let us continue to explore:

The penis

The penis is the seat of a man's virility; it ranges in size and shape. The average flaccid penis is two to four inches in length. The average erect penis ranges in length from 4 5/8 to 6 ¼ inches, 12 per cent of males are above average and 12 per cent is below average.

The penis is not one big erogenous zone, but has several specialized erotic areas such as the glans, the corona, the frenulum and the foreskin.

The frenulum or F spot

This is a tiny loose band of skin located near the indentation on the underside of the penis where the glans meet the shaft. Its function is thought to be that of providing pleasure by stretching during sexual intercourse.

The U spot

The male urethral and opening or U spot is the orifice through which urine and semen are released and is an erogenous zone for some men. For most men orgasm is attained through penile stimulation; the penis induced orgasm.

The perineum or P spot

The perineum or P spot is the patch of skin that lies between a man's testes and the anus. It is an acupressure point known as the Gate of Life and Death or Hui - Yin. When stimulated it results in prostate and penile stimulation.

The scrotum or R spot

The R spot is found on the scrotum. It is a visible line along the centre and underside of the scrotum called the scrotal raphe it can be stimulated by gently running your finger tips along it.

The thigh or T spot

There are three sensitive acupressure spots inside the upper thigh which are located close to the crease that join the thigh to the trunk. During sex play, try to hold them and press them for greater sexual fulfilment.

Other male hot spots

Many parts of the male body not involved in reproduction are sensitive to sexual touch. Caressing and massaging of these erogenous zones can be titillating forms of sensual pleasure in and of themselves, or they can be invitations to further sexual activity. These hot spots can significantly enhance your sexual experience but you must take time out to explore them and only through active communication can you determine if your partner find them stimulating.

These spots are:

- **The mouth** — including the lips and tongue; for most people, this is an area of high erotic potential. Kissing is one act that uses the sensitivity of this region in a sexually stimulating way.

- **The breasts** — these are called the bells of love by Chinese sexologists. They are packed with pleasure receptive nerve endings that send sensations to the brain in the same way as the genitals do.

- **The nipples** — the nipples have love points called centres of the breasts which arouse sexual energy when stimulated. The heavenly pond points are one thumb width away from each nipple and when stimulated increase sexual intimacy and help to express love and affection.

- **The neck** — sensual neck play has been shown to facilitate arousal in men.

- **The scalp** — massaging the scalp help men to relax and produces a feeling of well being and enhances intimacy.

- **The ears** — most men enjoy having their ears tickled or kissed.

- **Other erogenous zones** — include the eyelids, shoulders, nose, abdomen, shin and calves, and the hands and feet. The buttocks which are sometimes a target for spanking and stroking is also erotically appealing to some men. [3]

Deliberately exploring yourself and your partner are the first steps in discovering which body parts are sexually responsive and the types of stimulations that feel best. Varying the pressure of touching and stroking the body from head to toe with different materials such as a silk scarf, a soft brush, or a feather, may help to identify previously undiscovered erogenous zones. So go for it.

References

1. Gräfenberg, E. (1950). *The Role of the Urethra in Female Orgasm. Int. J. Sexol,* 3, 145-148.

2. Morris, D. (2007). *The Naked Woman: A Study of the Female Body.* NY: St. Martin's Griffin.

3. Morris, D. (2009). *The Naked Man: A Study of the Male Body.* NY: Thomas Dunne Books.

Bibliography

4. Ladas, A. K., Whipple, B., & Perry, J. D. (1982). *The G spot and Other Recent Discoveries About Human Sexuality* (pp. 144-145). Austin TX:Holt, Rinehart, and Winston.

5. Morris, D. (1968). *The Naked Ape: A Zoologist's Study of the Human Animal.* Cape May, NJ: Cape Publishing, Inc.

Aphrodisiacs
Give Your Sex Life A Boost

I trust as you launch forth on this journey of discovery, it will be for you and your partner, a most stimulating experience. The following section will up the tempo a bit as I walk you through the exotic herbs, spices and foods called aphrodisiacs.

Exotic foods and spices

Caribbean people usually place great emphasis on their sexuality, and for generations have sought out many local and foreign exotic foods and spices to boost their libido and enhance their fertility. The debate rages about whether the effect on the libido and virility is real. In the next few pages I will try to shed some light on this fascinating conundrum.

An aphrodisiac is a food, drink, drug, scent, or device that can arouse or increase sexual desire, or libido. It is named after Aphrodite, the Greek goddess of sexual love and beauty.

Many ancient peoples believed in the so-called law of similarity, which means that an object resembling the genitalia may possess sexual powers. Ginseng, rhinoceros horn, and oysters are three typical examples. Aside from resemblance to sex organs, people throughout history have made aphrodisiac associations with animals that are known to be virile and prolific reproducers such as rabbits, tigers, goats and bulls, which have reputations for prolific reproduction, strength or virility. The sex organs of these animals have been eaten to achieve an aphrodisiac effect or to enhance sexual performance. The Roman physician Galen, wrote that foods worked as aphrodisiacs if they were warm and moist and also windy, meaning they produced flatulence. He thought that a wind, or as one sixteenth century writer put it, an insensible pollution, inflated the penis to cause an erection, so anything that made you gassy would also make you erect!

According to the Food and Drug Administration, the alleged sexual effects of so-called aphrodisiacs are based in folklore, not fact. In 1989, the agency declared that there is no scientific proof that any over-the-counter aphrodisiacs work to treat sexual dysfunction and that they were ineffective and sometimes even dangerous, but many people still use them to give their sex lives a boost. [19] Aphrodisiacs work in many ways. They may directly increase the physical desire to have sex, stimulate the strength and endurance of an erection in men, and increase lubrication and genital sensitivity in women. However, there are very few substances that are scientifically proven to do this on a consistent basis. Most alleged aphrodisiacs act as tonics, increasing virility over time. Aphrodisiacs are classified in two principal groups:

Psycho-physiological - visual, tactile, olfactory, aural.

Internal - stemming from food, alcoholic drinks, drugs, love potions and medical preparations.

Aphrodisiac herbs and spices

I will now describe for you the most common herbs, spices and supplements which are used for their aphrodisiac effect.

Arginine

Arginine is an amino acid found in meat, nuts, eggs, coconut milk and cheese. It has many important functions in the body, including the formation of nitric oxide, which increases blood flow to the genitals. Arginine is touted as an anti-aging factor due to its ability to increase strength and lean muscle mass. It has been shown to increase sperm motility and male fertility, and may be useful for erectile dysfunction. In women, Arginine combined with other supplements, has been found to enhance sexual desire, reduce vaginal dryness, increase the frequency of intercourse and orgasm and improve clitoral sensation and sexual arousal.

Damiana (Turnera aphrodisiaca)

Damaina is a shrub native to Central America, Mexico, South America, and the Caribbean. It is known as the woman's sexuality herb. It contains alkaloids and various aromatic oils that have a stimulant effect on the reproductive organs. These nutrients work to restore and enhance sexual functions by increasing blood flow to these organs. It has a long history of use as an herbal medicine in Mexico, dating back to the ancient Aztec and Mayan civilizations. In Jamaica it is called 'ram goat dash along'.

Deer antler velvet

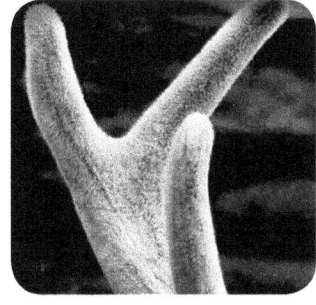

Antlers are the usually large and complex bony appendages on the heads of most deer species. While an antler is growing, it is covered with highly vascular skin called velvet, which supplies oxygen and nutrients to the growing bone. Collected while in the velvet stage, antlers of elk and deer are commonly used as a dietary supplement. Deer antler velvet is prized in Chinese medicine for its use as a sexual stimulant as well as a tonic.

Epimedium

Epimedium, also known as 'horny goat weed', has been used in traditional Chinese medicine for hundreds of years as an aphrodisiac. Its active ingredient, icariin, is also an active ingredient in Viagra and other sexual enhancement medications. Icariin works by increasing blood flow to the penis. According to folklore, horny goat weed's reputed aphrodisiac qualities were discovered when a Chinese goat herder noticed increased sexual activity in his flock after they ingested the weed.[1]

Fennel (Foeniculum vulgare)

Fennel is a hardy, perennial herb, with yellow flowers and feathery leaves. It is highly aromatic and flavourful with culinary and medicinal uses. Fennel has compounds that mimic the female hormone oestrogen.

Fenugreek (Trigonella foenum-graceum

Fenugreek is used as a herb (the leaves) and as a spice (the seed). It is frequently used in curry and has been recognized as a medicinal plant for centuries. The Egyptians, Greeks and Romans used the aromatic seeds extensively. It was a staple in the diet of Harem woman to increase the size and roundness of their breasts.

Fo-ti (Polygonum multiflorum)

Fo-ti is a plant native to China that is also found in Japan and Taiwan. The medicinal part of the plant is the root. It is also called 'He Shou Wu', which means black-haired Mr. He, in Chinese. This name refers to a legend of an older villager named Mr. He who took Fo-ti and restored his black hair, youthful appearance and sexual vitality.

Ginseng (Panax ginseng)

Korean ginseng is another well known aphrodisiac. It grows primarily in China and has been used there for over 5 thousand years and is considered the strongest form of ginseng. The word ginseng means man root and the plant's reputation as an aphrodisiac probably arises from its similarity to the human body. It contains thirteen different ginsenosides and is said to boost the immune system thus helping to combat infections and improve health.

Recently, the *Journal of Urology* reported that 'the mean International Index of Erectile Function scores were significantly higher in patients treated with Korean red ginseng than in those who received placebo.' [2]

Ginko (Ginkgo biloba)

Ginkgo biloba is an ancient tree found in China and Japan, and this species has been around for over 200 million years. Its leaves are used medicinally as an ancient Chinese remedy for coughs, asthma and allergies. It increases the blood flow and oxygen to the brain and the sexual organs and has been found to be useful for treating dementia and erectile dysfunction. [3]

Kelp (Ascophyllum nodosum)

Kelps are large seaweeds (algae) belonging to the brown algae. It grows in underwater forests (kelp forests) in shallow ocean and is a good source of iodine and other important minerals that support thyroid function. Iodine deficiency can impair sexual functioning.

Lychii fruit (Lycium barbarum)

Lychii fruit, also called 'wolfberry' and 'go-qi-zi', has traditionally been used in China for thousands of years for its rejuvenating effects on sexuality and fertility. Lychii

90

is a small red berry which is dried and prepared as a tea. Scientific studies have found that polysaccharides found in lychii fruit protect both male and female sex organs from free radical damage.

Maca (lepidium meyenii)

Maca is a cruciferous vegetable like kale and broccoli that grows in the Andes Mountains in Peru. Native people dig up the root-like tuber and brew it into a strong drink. Both men and women partake of this brew shortly before going off in couples for erotic enjoyment. Incan warriors used maca before battle to increase strength and endurance. [4]

Muira puama (ptychopetalum olacoides)

Muira puama is a native shrub with white flowers found in Brazil and the Amazon forest area. It is known as potency wood since it is thought to improve sexual function. It is used as a traditional aphrodisiac in Brazil. Muira puama has been used successfully in France to treat erectile dysfunction and to improve libido.

Reishi mushroom (ganoderma lucidum)

Reishi mushroom grows in the coastal areas of China and is found on decaying logs and tree stumps. In Asian medicine, the reishi mushroom is prized for its health-promoting effects. The Chinese call it 'herb of spiritual potency' and uses it to treat fatigue, asthma, insomnia, coughs and erectile dysfunction.

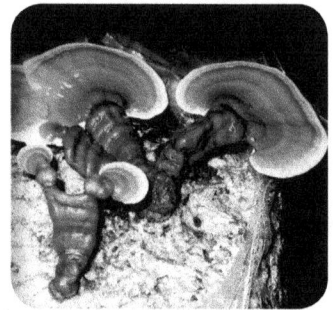

Rhino horn

The rhino horn is primarily fibrous tissue with fairly large amounts of calcium and phosphorus.
Since low levels of these minerals can lead to weakness and general fatigue, taking large doses of these elements could increase stamina if the levels are low. This might explain why it has been historically considered to be an aphrodisiac

in addition to its resemblance to an erect penis.

Saw palmetto (serenoa repens)

Saw palmetto is a small palm tree that grows wild from Texas to South Carolina, and is a native plant to North America. Saw palmetto bears blue-black berries that are used medicinally. They have long been used in Europe and the United States by herbalists to treat problems of the genitourinary tract in both sexes and for its reputed aphrodisiac effects.

Spanish fly (lytta vesicatoria)

Spanish fly is one of the most famous aphrodisiacs. It is made from a beetle that secretes an acid-like juice, called cantharidin, from its leg joints when threatened. Because it would be more difficult to remove just the juice, the entire beetle is dried and crushed to produce the powder. When spanish fly powder is ingested, the body excretes the cantharidin in the urine. This causes intense irritation and burning in the urogenital tract, which then leads to itching and swelling of the genitals. This swelling and burning was once assumed to be sexual arousal and led to the belief that spanish fly had aphrodisiac qualities, but cantharidin is highly toxic. The kidneys are affected also and can be permanently damaged. Spanish fly can also cause severe gastrointestinal disturbances, convulsions (fits) and even death. [5]

Sarsaparilla (smilax regelii)

Jamaican sarsaparilla is a perennial trailing vine with prickly stems that is native to Central America. Its name, which is 'zarzaparrilla' in Spanish comes from the Spanish words zarza for shrub and parrilla for little grape vine. Sarsaparilla is used as the basis for a soft drink sold for its taste, it is said to contain a testosterone-like substance which boost men's libido.

Tribulus (Tribulus terrestri)

Tribulus terrestris is a flowering plant, native to warm temperate and tropical regions of the old world. It has long been a constituent in tonics in Indian ayurveda practice, where it is known by its Sanskrit name, 'gokshura'. It is also used as an aphrodisiac in ayurveda. Tribulus is also called the natural Viagra and is said to increase testosterone levels. It is smoked or drunk as a tea. [6]

Wild yam (Dioscorea villosa)

Wild yam is a species of a twining tuberous vine that is native to and found growing wild in North America. Its fame is based on its steroid-like saponins which can be chemically converted to progesterone contraceptives, and cortisone. Extracts of the plant have been used to treat painful menstruation, hot flashes and other symptoms associated with menopause. Wild yam has a traditional use as an aphrodisiac and chemical analysis shows that it contains chemicals that can increase sensitivity in the genitals. It also has a reputation for inducing erotic dreams, when drunk at bedtime.

Yohimbine (Pausinvstalia yohimbe)

Yohimbine is an alkaloid extracted from the bark, stripped from a West African evergreen tree, pausinystalia yohimbe. It is also found naturally in rauwolfia serpentina (Indian Snakeroot). Yohimbine is used as a herbal aphrodisiac and in a prescription drug for erectile dysfunction in men. It has also been used for the treatment of sexual side effects caused by some antidepressants (SSRIs), and in female hyposexual disorders (low sex drive). The active ingredient of yohimbine causes vasodilatation (increased blood flow) and therefore is useful in erectile dysfunction. [7]

Aphrodisiac foods

The following is a list of foods that reportedly act as aphrodisiacs. Some are said to be aphrodisiacs simply because of their shape and some because of their aromas, while others claim a chemical basis for their love powers. However, there is no readily available research to substantiate these claims.

Aniseed (Pimpinella anisum)

Aniseed is a flowering plant, native to the eastern Mediterranean region and southwest Asia. Anise leaves are used to treat digestive problems, relieve toothache, and its essential oil is used to treat lice and scabies. The ancient Greeks and Romans believed that you could increase desire by sucking on anise seeds.

Ambergris

Ambergris comes from the guts of whales and is used in perfumes. Some consider ambergris an aphrodisiac and there is evidence to support this notion. In animal studies, it increased levels of testosterone in the blood, which is essential to the male sex drive, and is thought to play a part in women's libido as well.

Alcohol

Alcohol has traditionally been used to enhance desire and sexual functioning but overindulgence also has some profound negative consequences. Both are outlined below:

Short term sexual effects of alcohol:

- Alcohol has a dis-inhibiting effect, which can make people loosen up and feel more comfortable initiating or engaging in sex

- Alcohol might make you feel more socially confident and in small quantities facilitate more socializing and sexual communication

- In small amounts, alcohol has been reported to have a positive impact on sexual desire and arousal

- As drinking increases, both men and women will experience a reduction in sexual arousal, men may have difficulty getting erections, and both men and women may have difficulty experiencing orgasms

Long term sexual effects of alcohol:

- Erectile disorders and dysfunction in men
- Loss of sexual desire; significant decrease in sexual arousal for men and women
- Difficulty experiencing orgasm for men

Almonds (Prunus dulcis)

The almond is a specie of trees native to the Middle East. Almond is also the name of the edible and widely cultivated seed of this tree. Almonds were regarded as fertility symbols throughout antiquity. Its aroma supposedly arouses passion in females. Alexandre Dumas dined on almond soup every night before meeting his mistress, and Samson is said to have wooed Delilah with these tasty nuts. Almonds provide high doses of vitamin E, magnesium and even fibre to improve your general well-being.

Asparagus (Asparagus officinalis)

Asparagus is a flowering plant species native to most of Europe, Northern Africa and Western Asia, and is now widely cultivated as a vegetable crop. Man's affection for this member of the lily family dates back hundreds of years. Asparagus 'stirs up lust in man and woman,' wrote English herbalist Nicholas Culpepper in the seventeenth century. [20] In nineteenth century France, bridegrooms were served three courses of the sexy shoots at their prenuptial dinner.

Avocado (Persea americana)

The avocado, native to Central America is cultivated mainly for its fruit in tropical and subtropical regions, which include Israel, Spain, and South Africa. It is an evergreen tree that grows up to seventy feet, with dark green, leathery leaves and white flowers. The fruit is picked when fully grown, and the leaves are harvested as needed. The avocado tree was called a 'testicle tree' by the

Aztecs because its fruit hangs in pairs on the tree, resembling the male testicles, they also have a voluptuous and feminine shape. Its aphrodisiac value is based on this resemblance. The Spanish is said to have found avocados so obscenely sexy, that Catholic priests forbade them to their parishioners. The creamy fruit is quite good for pregnant women due to its high content of folic acid, as well as vitamin B6 and potassium.

Bananas (Musa paradisiacal)

Bananas come in a variety of sizes and colours when ripe, including yellow, purple, and red. In addition to the phallic shape of the banana itself, the banana flower also has a phallic shape. Bananas are rich in potassium and B vitamins, which are said to be necessary for sex-hormone production. The rationale for ascribing aphrodisiacs properties to bananas is that it contains the enzyme bromelain and other chelating minerals which are suspected to improve the libido of men This may explain why central Americans drink the sap of the red banana as an aphrodisiac, while Hindus regard it as a symbol of fertility. The fruit has a high concentration of potassium, magnesium and B vitamins. A banana left on a doorstep indicates that a marriage is about to take place. Bananas made an early appearance in the Garden of Eden; according to Islamic myth, Adam and Eve covered themselves not with fig but banana leaves.

Basil (Ocimum basilicum)

Basil is a culinary herb prominently featured in Italian cuisine, and also plays a major role in the Southeast Asian cuisines of Thailand, Vietnam, Cambodia, and Laos.

The leaves of basil and its many close relatives are used as medicine. The seeds are also used medicinally in India and Southeast Asia. Though it originated on the shores of the Mediterranean Sea and the Middle East, common basil now grows in gardens all over the world. For centuries, people said that basil stimulated the sex drive and boosted fertility, it is also said to produce a general sense of well being. The scent of basil was said to drive men wild; so much so, that women would dust their breasts with dried and powdered basil.

Bois bandé (Roupala montana)

Bois bande is the name commonly used in a large part of the Caribbean for the tree 'roupala montana'. The plant is not only found in Grenada and Trinidad, but also in Dominica, where it is known as 'gimauve' or 'gommier tree' and is known in Costa Rica as 'danto amarillo' or 'zorillo'. The bark of this tree is famous for its aphrodisiac properties. Locals soak a strip of the bark for a week in rum, then filter the rum and take a small glass of the extract. The extract is also known as macoucherie rum. No studies are available in the Western literature to give us any clues on this herb's aphrodisiac benefits or mechanism of action. Bois bande is also available in a liquid and capsule form.

Cardamom (Elettaria subulatum)

The name cardamom is used for herbs within two genera of the ginger family. Both forms of cardamom are used as flavourings in both food and drink, as cooking spices and as a medicine. Cardamom has a strong, unique taste with an intensely aromatic fragrance. Certain cultures deem it a powerful aphrodisiac and also claim it is beneficial in treating impotence. It is high in cineole, which can increase blood flow in areas where it is applied.

Carrots (Daucus carota)

The carrot is a root vegetable, usually orange in colour, though purple, red, white, or yellow varieties exist and have a crisp texture when fresh. The edible part of a carrot is a taproot.

The carrot gets its characteristic and bright orange colour from β-carotene, which is metabolised into vitamin A in humans when bile salts are present in the intestines.

The phallus-shaped carrot has been associated with sexual stimulation since ancient times and was used by early Middle Eastern royalty to aid seduction. The vitamins and beta-carotene found in carrots is said to enhance the male libido.

Chilli peppers (Capsicum annuum, c. frutescen)

Chilli pepper is the fruit of the plants from the genus capsicum; members of the nightshade family. Red chilli's contain high amounts of vitamin C and carotene (provitamin A). Yellow and especially green chilli's (which are essentially unripe fruit) contain a considerably lower amount of both substances. In addition, peppers are a good source of most B vitamins, and vitamin B6 in particular. They are very high in potassium and high in magnesium and iron. Eating chilli peppers generates physiological responses in our bodies (such as: sweating, increased heart rate and warmth) that are similar to those experienced when having sex. The capsaicin they contain is responsible for the effects and is also a good pain reliever. Another reported effect of eating large quantities of chilli peppers is an irritation of the genitals and urinary tract that could simulate sexual excitement.

Chocolate (Theobroma)

Chocolate comprises a number of raw and processed foods produced from the seed of the tropical theobroma cacao tree. Cacao has been cultivated for at least three millennia in Mexico, Central and South America, with its earliest documented use around 1100 BC.

The Aztecs referred to chocolate as nourishment of the gods. Chocolate has always been associated with love and romance. It was originally found in the South American rainforests. The Mayan civilizations worshipped the cacao tree and called it food of the gods. Rumour has it that the Aztec ruler Montezuma drank 50 goblets of chocolate each day to enhance his sexual abilities. Researchers have studied chocolate and found it to contain phenylethylamine and serotonin, which are both feel good chemicals. They occur naturally in our bodies and are released by our brains when we are happy or feeling loving or passionate. It produces a euphoric feeling, like when you're in love. In addition to those two chemicals, researchers at the Neuroscience Institute in San Diego, California, say that chocolate may also contain substances that have the same effect on the brain as marijuana. [21] The substance is a neurotransmitter called anandamide. The amount of anandamide in chocolate is not enough to get a person high like marijuana, but it could be enough to contribute to the good feelings that serotonin and phenylethylamine induce.

Coffee (Coffea canephora and coffea arabica)

Coffee is a brewed drink prepared from roasted seeds, commonly called coffee beans, of the coffee plant. Coffee is sometimes considered an aphrodisiac because it stimulates the central nervous system, but it has no specific effect on sexual desire.

Cucumbers (Cucumis sativus)

The cucumber has a phallic shape and therefore is deemed to be erotically arousing; it is even used by some women for solo sex. The scent of cucumbers is believed to stimulate women by increasing blood flow to the vagina. (See Scentsational Sex)

Caviar

Caviar is a luxury food consisting of processed, salted, non-fertilized sturgeon roe. It is high in zinc, which stimulates the formation of testosterone, and improves male libido.

Cilantro seed (Coriandrum sativum)

Coriander is also known as 'Chinese parsley' or particularly in the Americas it is called 'cilantro'. All parts of the plant are edible, but the fresh leaves and the dried seeds are commonly used in cooking. Cilantro seeds have been an aphrodisiac for centuries. It has a stimulant effect on the body and the seed is also used as an appetite stimulant.

Celery (Apium graveolens var dulce)

Celery is used around the world as a vegetable, either for the crisp petiole (leaf stalk) or the fleshy taproot. In temperate countries, celery is also grown for its seeds which are very small fruits. These seeds yield a valuable volatile oil used in the perfume and pharmaceutical industries. Celery is said to be an aphrodisiac by some people because it is thought to contain androsterone, a metabolic product of testosterone.

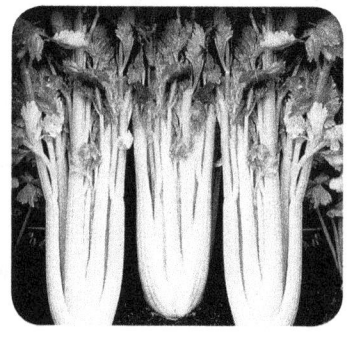

Cowcod soup

Cow cod soup is a traditional dish in Jamaican cuisine that is considered to be an aphrodisiac. It is made with bull's penis (or cod) cooked with bananas and scotch bonnet pepper in a white rum-based broth.

Conch (Strombus gigas)

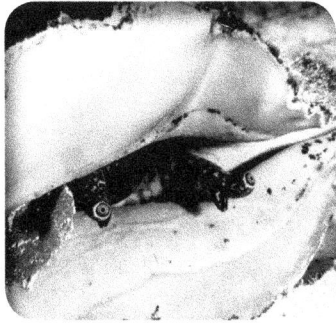

Conchs produce a large amount of meat, and are especially treasured in the Caribbean region, where the giant pink (or queen) conch is farmed extensively. Cooked conch, pickled conch and raw conch meat are considered to be an aphrodisiac. In the West Indies, a rod shaped portion of the conch's stomach called the crystalline style is swallowed by males to enhance their potency.

Egg

The egg is one of the most ancient fertility symbols. Eggs are high in vitamin B5 (Pantothenic acid) and vitamin B6 (Pyridoxine). Raw chicken eggs eaten before sex are considered to enhance the libido.

Energy drinks

Energy drinks are widely used in Jamaica as sexual boosters and are often mixed with alcohol to increase desire and enhance performance (Energy drinks are soft drinks advertised to boost energy). These drinks usually do not emphasize energy derived from the sugars they contain, but rather through a variety of stimulants, vitamins, and herbal supplements the manufacturer has added to the drink. Typical examples are: Red Bull, Monster, Rockstar, Spunk, Nitro, Superman, Cocaine, Full Throttle, Arizona, Hype, Spike Shooter and Cocaine.

Energy drinks generally contain methylxanthines (including caffeine), vitamin B, and herbs. Other commonly used ingredients are carbonated water, guarana, yerba mate, acai and taurine, plus various forms of ginseng, maltodextrin, inositol, carnitine, creatine, glucuronolactone, and ginkgo biloba. Some contain high levels of sugar, and many brands offer artificially sweetened diet versions.
[22]

The main ingredient in most energy drinks is caffeine (often in the form of guarana or yerba mate). The caffeine content of energy drinks range from 70-300 mg per 8-oz serving, whereas an eight ounce cup of generic brewed coffee can contain 102-200 milligrams of caffeine.[8] In November of 2010, the University of Texas Medical School at Houston, reported that energy drinks contain more caffeine than a strong cup of coffee, and that the caffeine combined with other ingredients such as guarana, amino acid taurine, other herbs, vitamins and minerals may have adverse interactions.

A variety of physiological and psychological effects have been attributed to energy drinks and their ingredients.

Two studies reported significant improvement in mental and cognitive performances as well as increased subjective alertness but excess consumption of energy drinks may induce mild to moderate euphoria primarily caused by the stimulant properties of caffeine and may also induce agitation, anxiety, irritability and insomnia. [9] [10] In the US, energy drinks have been linked with reports of nausea, abnormal heart rhythms and emergency room visits. The drinks may also cause seizures due to the crash following the energy high that occurs after consumption.[11] Norway and France have banned Red Bull.

Caffeinated alcoholic energy drinks

Energy drinks such as Red Bull are often used as mixers with alcoholic beverages producing mixed drinks such as Vodka Red Bull, which are similar to, but stronger than, Rum and Coke with respect to the amount of caffeine they contain. They are also sold in a wide variety of formulations such as Four Loko and Joose which combine caffeine and alcohol. Energy drinks consumed with alcohol may cause palpitations, increase blood pressure and panic attacks. There appears to be little or no protective benefit from the addition of caffeine to alcohol.

A study, headed by Jonathan Howland of the Boston University School of Public Health and the Center for Alcohol and Addiction Studies, indicated that caffeine does not mitigate the impairment effects of alcohol. On the driving test, the effect of alcohol on performance was significant, but the addition of caffeine did not make a noticeable difference. On the test for sustained attention and reaction times, the addition of caffeine made only a slight difference that the study deemed 'borderline significant.' The study was published in the *Journal Addiction*. [12]

Figs (Ficus carica)

The common fig is a fruit that claims aphrodisiac qualities based on its appearance. An open fig is thought to look similar to the female sex organ. To the ancient Greeks, they were 'more precious than gold' and many cultures associated figs with fertility.

Foie gras

Foie gras (pronounced fwa gra) in English; (French for fat liver) is a food product made of the liver of a duck or goose that has been specially fattened. This fattening is achieved through gavage (force-feeding) corn. Foie gras is a popular and well-known delicacy in French cuisine. Its flavour is described as rich and buttery. Like diamonds, furs, champagne and caviar, it is associated with fine living; its buttery texture and mythical status are guaranteed to put you in a sexy mood.

Garlic (Allium sativum)

Allium sativum, commonly known as 'garlic', is a specie in the onion family.

Garlic has been used as both food and medicine in many cultures for thousands of years. Garlic is also alleged to help regulate blood sugar levels. Regular and prolonged use of therapeutic amounts of aged garlic extract lowers blood homocysteine levels and has been shown to prevent some complications of diabetes mellitus and in doing so prevent erectile dysfunction. Tibetan monks were not allowed to enter the monastery if they had been eating garlic because of its reputation for stirring up passions.

Ginger (Zingiber officinale)

Ginger is a tuber that is consumed whole as a delicacy, medicine, or spice. The characteristic odour and flavour of ginger is caused by a mixture of zingerone, shogaols and gingerols, volatile oils that compose one to three percent of the weight of fresh ginger.

The medical form of ginger historically was called 'Jamaica ginger'; it was classified as a stimulant and carminative, and used frequently for dyspepsia and colic.

People have deemed ginger root an aphrodisiac for centuries because of its scent and because it stimulates the circulatory system.

Honey

Honey is a sweet food made by certain insects using nectar from flowers. The variety produced by honey bees (the genus apis) is the one most commonly referred to and is the type of honey collected by beekeepers. In medieval times, people drank mead, a fermented drink made from honey, to promote sexual desire. In ancient Persia, couples drank mead every day for a month (known as the honey month a.k.a. honeymoon) after they married in order to get in the right frame of mind for a successful marriage. Honey is rich in B vitamins (needed for testosterone production) as well as boron (which helps the body to metabolize and use oestrogen). Some studies have suggested that it may also enhance the blood levels of testosterone.

Irish moss (Chondrus crispus)

Irish moss is a very common and commercially important seaweed in the Atlantic, the Caribbean and Canada. Irish moss are sources of natural thickeners and stabilizers called carrageenans, which are widely used in processed foods such as lunch meat and ice cream. It is also quite popular in the Caribbean where it is used as a health drink as well as an aphrodisiac.

Liquorice (Glycyrrhiza glabra)

The liquorice plant is a legume (related to beans and peas), native to southern Europe and parts of Asia. The flavour of liquorice comes mainly from a sweet-tasting compound called anethole.

Liquorice is popular in Italy (particularly in the South) and Spain in its natural form. The root of the plant is simply dug up, washed and chewed as a mouth freshener. In ancient China, people used liquorice to enhance love and passion. The smell appears to be particu-

larly stimulating. Alan R. Hirsch, neurological director of the Smell and Taste Treatment and Research Foundation in Chicago, conducted a study that looked at how different smells stimulated sexual arousal. He found that the smell of black liquorice increased the blood flow to the penis by 13 per cent. When combined with the smell of doughnuts, that percentage jumped to 32 percent. [15]

Meat

Meat is animal flesh that is used as food. Most often, this means the skeletal muscle and associated fat, but it may also describe other edible tissues such as organs, livers, skin, brains, bone marrow, kidneys, or lungs. St. Thomas Aquinas, a thirteenth century friar, wrote a thesis on aphrodisiacs. [23] Like Galen, he thought aphrodisiac foods had to produce vital spirit and provide good nutrition. So meat, considered the heartiest food, was for him an aphrodisiac.

Mustard seed (Brassica nigra)

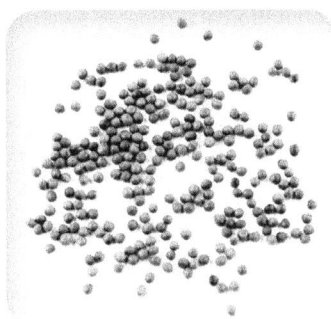

Mustard seeds of the various mustard plants are among the smallest of seeds. The seeds are about 3mm in diameter, and may be colored from yellowish white to black. They are important spices in many regional cuisines. Indians have used mustard seeds and almonds in their food for over two thousand years. Mustard seeds are said to act as a stimulant to the sexual glands and increase libido.

Mannish water

Mannish water also called 'power water' in Jamaica, is a spicy soup made with goat head (some cooks include tripe, brains and feet as well), garlic, escallion, cho-cho, green bananas, yam, dumpling and scotch bonnet peppers, White rum is an optional ingredient. It is highly regarded by Jamaican men as a potent aphrodisiac.

Oats (Avena sativa)

The common oat (Avena sativa) is a specie of cereal grain grown for its seed, which is known by the same name. It is rich in body-building nutrients including silicon, manganese, zinc, calcium, phosphorus and vitamins A, B1, B2 and E. This particular grain encourages the release of testosterone in men thus improving their libido.

Oysters

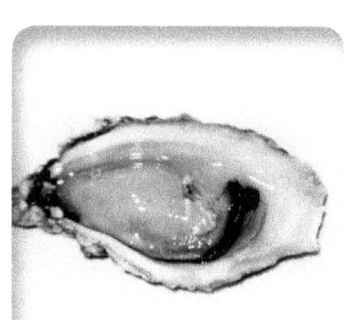

The word oyster is used as a common name for a number of distinct groups of bivalve molluscs which live in marine or brackish habitats. Some kinds of oyster are commonly consumed by humans, cooked or raw. Other kinds, such as pearl oysters, are not.

Oysters, especially wild, are excellent sources of several minerals, including iron, zinc and selenium. They are also an excellent source of vitamin B12, omega-3 fatty acids and dopamine. Oysters are considered the healthiest when eaten raw on the half shell. Because Aphrodite was said to be born from the sea, many types of seafood have the reputation of being aphrodisiacs. Oysters are particularly esteemed as sex aids, possibly gaining their reputation at a time when their contribution of zinc to the nutritionally deficient diets of the day could improve overall health and so lead to an increased sex drive. Oysters, also look like the female's anatomy. The zinc in oysters facilitate sperm production, and raw oysters also contain D-aspartic acid and N-methyl-D-aspartate, which may boost testosterone production.

Pomegranate (Punica granatum)

A pomegranate is a fruit-bearing deciduous shrub or small tree. Pomegranate aril juice provides about 16 per cent of an adult's daily vitamin C requirement per 100 ml serving, and is a good source of vitamin B5, potassium and the antioxidant polyphenols. In Chinese folklore, this fruit, due to its abundance of seeds, is a symbol of prosperity and is widely believed to enhance fertility.

Potatoes (Solanum tuberosum)

The potato is a starchy, tuberous crop. Potatoes, both sweet and white, were once known as aphrodisiacs in Europe, probably because they were a rare delicacy when they were first transplanted from the Americas.

Papaya (Carica papaya)

The papaya is the fruit of the plant carica papaya and is native to the tropics of the Americas. Papaya (like aniseed) is oestrogenic, meaning it has compounds that act as the female hormone oestrogen. It has been used as a folk remedy in promoting menstruation and milk production, facilitating childbirth and increasing the female libido.

Pine nuts (Pinus)

Pine nuts are the edible seeds of pines. People have been using pine nuts to make up love potions and stimulate the libido since medieval times. Like oysters, they are high in zinc. The Arabian medical scholar Galen recommended eating one hundred pine nuts before going to bed.

Perfumes

Perfumes: made of natural foodstuffs such as almond, vanilla, and other herbs and spices act as a pheromone to communicate emotions by smell. The sexual impact of odours and aromas are discussed extensively in part 2.

Puffer fish (Tetraodontidae)

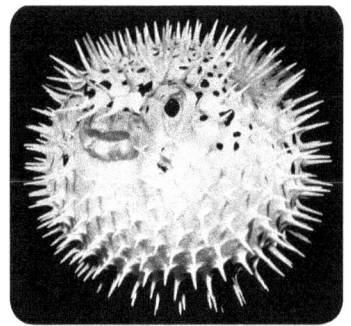

The puffer fish is the second most poisonous vertebrate in the world, after the golden poison frog. The puffer's skin and certain internal organs are highly toxic to humans, but nevertheless the meat of some species is considered a delicacy and an aphrodisiac in both Japan (as fugu) and Korea (as bok) when prepared by cooks who know what is safe to eat. Thick gloves should be worn to avoid poisoning and bites when removing the hook from a caught animal. The flirt with death is said to give a sexual thrill.

Radish (Raphanus sativus)

The radish is an edible root vegetable. It was considered to be a divine aphrodisiac by Egyptian pharaohs, most likely because its spicy taste stimulated the palate.

| APHRODISIACS

Strawberries (Fragaria)

The garden strawberry is a common plant which is cultivated worldwide for its fruit, the (common) strawberry. The fruit is greatly favoured, mainly for its characteristic aroma but also for its bright red colour. It is consumed in large quantities; either fresh, or in prepared foods such as preserves, fruit juice, pies, ice creams and shakes. Strawberries are rich in vitamin C, which improves your sexual stamina. It is also used during foreplay to enhance arousal.

Skink (Eumeces laticeps)

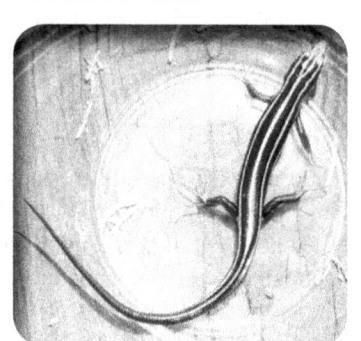

Skinks are the most diverse group of lizards. They make up the family scincidae. For centuries parts of the skink were thought to be an aphrodisiac.

Sparrows (Passer domesticus)

A sparrow is a small passerine bird, also known as 'old-world sparrows'. Some sparrows make their nests near houses or buildings. Aphrodite, the Greek goddess of love (from whose name, of course, aphrodisiac is derived) was said to have held sparrows sacred. Europeans were inclined to eat sparrows, particularly their brains, as aphrodisiacs.

Truffles (Tuber aestivum)

The Greeks and the Romans considered the rare truffle to be an aphrodisiac. Truffles are fungi that grow underground near the roots of oak, elm, aspen, and willow trees. Specially trained dogs and pigs detect the scent of truffles and dig them up. The musky scent is said to stimulate and sensitize the skin to touch. Truffles, because of its rarity and musky aroma, have long been considered to be an appetite stimulant and a tonic. To sustain his masculinity, an ancient lover in folklore was said to have gorged himself to death on Alba truffles during the wedding feast.

Vanilla (Vanilla planifolia)

Vanilla is a flavouring derived from orchids of the genus vanilla, native to Mexico.

The scent and flavour of vanilla is believed to increase lust. In old medicinal literature, vanilla is described as an aphrodisiac and a remedy for fevers. These alleged usages have never been scientifically proven, but it has been shown that vanilla does increase the levels of catecholamines (epinephrine) and may be considered mildly addictive.

The potpourri of plant and animal products that have just been described should have provided for you an in depth overview of the myriad of aphrodisiacs used by many people to augment their sexuality. I hope if you do use these boosters, that you will exercise caution to minimize adverse effects.

References

1. *Epimedium Grandiflorum* (Large Flowered Barrenwort, Bishop's Hat). Retrieved April 2012, from http://www.memidex.com/epimedium-grandiflorum

2. Murphy, L. L., & Lee, T. J. F. (2002). *Ginseng, Sex Behavior, and Nitric Oxide.* Annals of the New York Academy of Sciences, 962(1), 372-377.

3. Cohen, A. J., & Bartlik, B. (1998). *Ginkgo Biloba For Antidepressant-induced Sexual Dysfunction.* Journal of Sex & Marital Therapy, 24(2), 139-143.

4. Gonzales, G. F., Cordova, A., Vega, K., Chung, A., Villena, A., & Góñez, C. (2003). *Effect of Lepidium meyenii (Maca), A Root with Aphrodisiac and Fertility-enhancing Properties, On Serum Reproductive Hormone Levels in Adult Healthy Men.* Journal of Endocrinology, 176(1), 163-168.

5. Karras, D. J., Farrell, S. E., Harrigan, R. A., Henretig, F. M. & Gealt, L. (1996). *Poisoning from "Spanish fly"(cantharidin).* The American Journal of Emergency Medicine, 14(5), 478-483.

6. Neychev, V. K., & Mitev, V. I. (2005). *The Aphrodisiac Herb - Tribulus terrestris - Does Not Influence the Androgen Production in Young Men.* Journal of Ethnopharmacology, 101(1), 319-323.

7. Adeniyi, A. A., Brindley, G. S., Pryor, J. P., & Ralph, D. J. (2007). *Yohimbine in the Treatment of Orgasmic Dysfunction.* Asian Journal of Andrology, 9(3), 403-407.

8. Juliano, L.M. & Griffiths, R.R. (2005). "Caffeine." In Lowinson, J.H., Ruiz, P., Millman, R.B., Langrod, J.G. (Eds.). *Substance Abuse: A Comprehensive Textbook, Fourth Edition. (pp 403-421).* Baltimore: Lippincott, Williams, & Wilkins.

9. Alford, C., Cox, H., & Wescott, R. (2001). *The Effects of Red Bull Energy Drink on Human Performance and Mood.* Amino acids, 21(2), 139-150.

10. Van den Eynde, F., Van Baelen, P. C., Portzky, M., & Audenaert, K. (2008). *The Effects of Energy Drinks on Cognitive Performance.* Tijdschrift voor psychiatrie, 50(5), 273

11. Iyadurai, S. J. P., & Chung, S. S. (2007). *New-onset Seizures in Adults: Possible Association With Consumption of Popular Energy Drinks.* Epilepsy and Behavior, 10(3), 504-508.

12. Howland, J., Rohsenow, D. J., Arnedt, J. T., Bliss, C. A., Hunt, S. K., Calise, T. V. & Gottlieb, D. J. (2011). *The Acute Effects of Caffeinated Versus Non - caffeinated Alcoholic Beverage on Driving Performance and Attention/Reaction Time.* Addiction, 106(2), 335-341.

Bibliography

13. Henderson, M. (2007). *Cannabis Puts Females in the Mood for Love.* The Times. 2001-01-29. Retrieved April 2012, from http://www.cannabisnews.com/news/8/thread8414.shtml.

14. Hopkins, M. Lockridge, R. (2007). *The New InterCourses: An Aphrodisiac Cookbook.* Waco, TX: Terrace Publishing.

15. Hirsch, A.R(1999). *Smell and Sexual Arousal - in Francis, F. J. (1999).* Wiley Encyclopedia of Food Science and Technology (2nd Edition) Volumes 1-4. New York: John Wiley & Sons. pp. 81-87.

16. Hirsch, A.R. (2000). "Aphrodisiacs and Stimulants," *Food Science and Technology, 1,* 81-87.

17. Kilham, C. (2004). *Hot Plants: Nature's Proven Sex Boosters for Men and Women.* New York: St. Martin's Griffin.

18. MacKay, D.(2004). *Nutrients and Botanicals for Erectile Dysfunction: Examining the Evidence. Altern Med Rev,* 9, 4–16.

19. *Health: FDA Bans Purported Aphrodisiacs,* July 10, 1989, from Times Wire Services. Retrieved February 4, 2013, from http://www.articles.latimes.com/1989-07-10/news/mn-2720_1_fda-ban

20. Culpeper, N.(1995). *Culpeper's Complete Herbal: A Book of Natural Remedies of Ancient Ills The Wordsworth Collection Reference Library.* Chicago IL:NTC/Contemporary Publishing Company

21. Tomaso, E di, Beltramo,M. & Piomelli,*D. (22 august 1996). *Nature* **382,** 677 – 678.

22. Higgins, J.P., Tuttle T.D. & Higgins C.L. *Energy Beverages: Content and Safety. Mayo Clinic Proceedings* 2010, 85(11), 1033–41.

23. Kiple, K. F., & Ornelas, K. C. (2001). *The Cambridge World History of Food. Food Service Technology,* 1(1), 61-62.

The Art of Kissing

Enjoy One of Life's Sweetest Pleasures

How important is kissing in your love life? Believe me it is one of life's sweetest pleasures. So get ready to discover the joys of kissing.

An integral part of human nature

Many lovers revel in the joys of a deep sensual kiss, but did you know that kissing is an integral part of human nature and over 90 per cent of humans kiss? We kiss each other to reveal affection, to portray deep love, to comfort, to greet, to bid farewell, to show homage and as part of religious rituals. Evolutionary psychologists have posited the view that kissing is a learned phenomenon and have cited the behaviour of chimpanzees who feed their young with premasticated food with puckered lips as evidence. Others have proposed that kissing is a innate instinct and cite bonobo apes who use the kiss to comfort and bond with each other.

The historical origin of kissing remains obscure. It is described in Indian Sanskrit texts around 1500 BC and in the *Kama Sutra* in the sixth century AD. The Romans were known to use the kiss in many of their social, religious and political rituals.

Kissing styles

The type and intensity of the kiss is determined by the nature of the relationship between the giver and the recipient

A peck or a smooch on the cheek or fore head is used to greet or comfort someone or to bid good bye. Friends or casual acquaintances sometimes blow each other a kiss while touching cheeks

An Eskimo kiss is the term which describes nose touching

A butterfly kiss is one in which you flutter your eyelids against your partners face

A dry kiss is one in which the couple press their lips firmly together as an expression of deep affection

A deep, wet or French kiss characterized by the sensual interplay of the tongue and lips is often shared by intimate partners as a sign of strong passion and a prelude to sexual intercourse

Sensual kissing involves the use of the lips to titillate one's partner on various parts of the body to enhance arousal during foreplay

The kissing study

Personally, I really thought that kissing was just a brief prelude to the main event until I read this seminal study done in 2007, by psychologists Susan M. Hughes et al, published in the *Journal Evolutionary Psychology*. The study was entitled '*Sex Differences in Romantic Kissing Among College Students: An Evolutionary Perspective*,' which surveyed 1,041 college students, most of them aged 18 to 25.

The study concluded that 'romantic kissing may have evolved as a courtship strategy that functions as a mate-assessment technique, a means of initiating sexual arousal and receptivity, and a way of maintaining a bonded relationship,' and that 'the information conveyed by a kiss can have profound consequences for romantic relationships, and can even be a major factor in ending one.' [1]

Their findings are summarized below, for men and women:

Women:

- Were less than half as likely to have sex with a man without first enjoying a kiss

- Placed a greater emphasis on kissing for making mate assessments

- Treat kissing as a means to induce bonding and to help them assess whether their partners have remained faithful and interested

- Were less likely to encourage deep French kissing on a first date

- Are more likely to base evaluations of their partner's kissing ability on chemical clues, i.e., the breath and taste

- Were less likely to want sex with a bad kisser

- Were much more likely to kiss a partner after sex than men were

- Continued to give kisses a high priority once a relationship was established

Men:

- Over 50 per cent of the men said they would have sex with someone without kissing

- Found kissing more erotic than women

- Regarded kissing as a prelude to sex

- Regarded a good kiss as one in which deep French kissing was allowed

- Were more likely to continue to want sex even with a bad kisser

- Were less interested in kissing once a relationship was established.

From this study, it is obvious that kissing is regarded by women as a major part of their courtship experience, whereas men really just regard it almost as a courtesy. So now that the scales have been removed from your eyes, I can now invite you to enjoy a good kiss.

Kiss - the stress reducer

Have you ever experienced a sense of deep contentment after a soulful kiss? Well, the experts now tell us that kissing is a great stress reliever. To prove this thesis, in 2007 a study was designed by psychologist Wendy L. Hill and her student Carey A. Wilson of Lafayette College, Easton, Pennsylvania. They compared the levels of two important hormones in 15 college male-female couples before and after they kissed, and before and after they talked to each other while holding hands. One hormone, oxytocin, is involved in social bonding - the cuddling hormone - and cortisol, a stress hormone released when we are under duress. Wilson predicted that kissing would boost the levels of oxytocin, which also influences social recognition, male and female orgasm, and childbirth. They expected this effect to be most pronounced in the females in the study population, who reported higher levels of intimacy in their relationships. They also predicted a fall in the cortisol levels, because kissing is deemed to be a stress reliever.

However, the researchers were surprised to find that oxytocin levels rose only in the males, whereas it decreased in the females, after either kissing or talking while holding hands. They concluded that females must require more than a kiss to feel emotionally connected or sexually excited during physical contact. The cortisol levels dropped for both sexes after kissing or holding hands. This proved their theory that kissing does relieve stress. The study was reported in November, 2007, at the annual meeting of the Society for Neuroscience. [2]

The joys of kissing

These studies and our own experiences have therefore revealed that kissing, whether it is just a friendly peck on the cheek, a symbol of worship, an indicator of deep affection or an expression of intense passion, evokes a myriad of reactions psychologically, biologically and socially. It promotes feelings of bonding and closeness between humans.

The act itself also releases a variety of pleasure hormones such as oxytocin, the cuddling hormone; dopamine, the pleasure hormone and serotonin, which elevates the mood. Also released is adrenaline, which causes the dry mouth, sweaty palms, palpitations and the sexual flush and endorphin which produces a feeling of euphoria. So, go for it and enjoy one of life sweetest pleasures.

A word of caution

Despite the obvious pleasure that one can experience with kissing, deep kissing does result in exchange of saliva and therefore exposes you to the risk of contracting a number of diseases, such as Herpes simplex virus (cold sores), Infectious Mononucleosis (the kissing disease), the common cold and others. HIV transmission from kissing is unlikely unless one or both partners have an oral ulcer or bleeding gums. Let me encourage you therefore to chose your partners carefully and practice safe sex so that you can truly experience the joys of kissing.

References

1. Hughes, S. M., Harrison, M. A. & Gallup Jr, G. G. (2007). *Sex Differences in Romantic Kissing Among College Students: An Evolutionary Perspective. Evolutionary Psychology. 5*(3), 612-63.

2. Walter, C. (2008). *Affairs of the Lips. Scientific American Mind, 19*(1), 24-29.

Bibliography

3. BBC News *"How Animals Kiss and Make Up"* October 13, 2003. Retrieved April 2012, from http://www.news.bbc.co.uk/2/hi/uk_news/scotland/3183516.stm

4. Cane, W. (1998). *The Art of Kissing. Book of Questions and Answers: Everything You Ever Wanted to Know About Perfecting Your Kissing Technique.* New York: St. Martin's Griffin.

5. Demirjian, A. (2006). *Kissing: Everything You Ever Wanted to Know about One of Life's Sweetest Pleasures.* New York NY: Perigee Trade.

6. Dyer, T. T. F. "The History of Kissing". *The American Magazine, 14* (1882), 611–614.

Sex Toys
An Insider's Guide to Experiencing "Toygasms"

The time has now come for us to explore what for many is a taboo subject - marital aids.

Marital aids

Many of my female patients have confided in me that they are regular users of sex toys for a variety of reasons, but the most common one is to relieve sexual frustration. On the other hand, even though men rarely admit to using toys, there are many closet users out there and this chapter will hopefully de-mystify this taboo subject.

A sex toy is any object or device that is primarily used to facilitate human sexual pleasure. The most popular sex toys are designed to resemble human genitals and can be classified as vibrating or non-vibrating. Another term used to describe them are adult toys or marital aids. Sex aids or sex toys are used primarily on the genitals or around the genitals, but some can be used on other parts of the body. People use them personally or with partners, but there are many persons who object strongly to the use of sex toys and many myths abound pertaining to their usage.

Some of the more common myths are:

- The use of sexual aids suggests that you are a pervert

- Using sexual devices in a relationship is a sign that the relationship is dysfunctional

- People who use sexual aids become addicted to them

- Homosexuals use sex aids more than heterosexuals do

Many people therefore feel ambivalent about using sex aids. Some persons feel that using mechanical devices during intimate moments is unnatural, de-personalizing or replacing their partner. An insecure individual may wonder if his or her partner is using a sex aid because of dissatisfaction with him or her. While these concerns are understandable, it is not really the use of sex aids that contributes to ill feelings, but how they are used and what their use means to an individual or to a couple.

If the use of sexual aids objectifies or de-personalizes sexual experiences, there may be a problem in the relationship that requires attention. If people are using sexual devices as a crutch because they feel inadequate or inferior, then their negative feelings may need to be explored. Under these circumstances, the use of sexual aids is an unhealthy substitute for addressing interpersonal conflicts. However, some couples find that a healthy relationship can comfortably accommodate the addition of sex toys, while others may find that after some experimentation, they prefer not to use them. As a rule, people who use sex aids tend not use them every time they engage in sex and do not always use the same aid on each occasion. These issues and any others that may be raised as a result of introducing sexual aids should be seen as an opportunity for individuals and couples to explore their feelings and discover the problems in their relationships.

It is important to consider that using sex aids is normal, but if you opt not to use them, there is no cause for concern. It is simply a matter of individual choice. Although the majority of sex aids and toys are sold to people who use them just to enhance their pleasure, some can be used in the treatment of sexual problems such as anorgasmia (difficulty reaching an orgasm).

I will now introduce you to the myriad of sex toys that are available.

Female sex toys

Vibrators

Vibrators are electrical machines powered by batteries or plugged into electrical outlets. They come in different sizes and shapes; some have variable speed controls to allow the user to personalize the intensity of the stimulation. The more popular kinds of personal vibrators are battery powered, cylindrical or penis shaped in different diameters and lengths, and sometimes come with attachments for different parts of the body. The sexual sensations produced by a vibrator can be intense and overpowering. They must be used gently on sensitive body tissues. Some people use a towel between the skin and the vibrator to cut down on the intensity of the sensation. Using a water-based lubricant can also make a vibrator more comfortable and stimulating.

Types of erotic vibrators

There is an enormous range of vibrators but most of them fall into several broad categories described below:

Penetrative vibrators — usually measure twelve to eighteen centimetres (five to seven inches) in length, and two to five centimetres (one to two inches) wide to mimic the size of an actual penis.

Dual area vibrators — these vibrators are designed to stimulate two erogenous zones simultaneously or independently. They are usually found in the form of a clitoral stimulator and vaginal stimulator. An example is the Sybian.

Triple area vibrators — these vibrators are designed to stimulate three erogenous zones simultaneously or independently. These provide stimulation to the vagina, clitoris and anal regions.

Multispeed vibrators — multispeed vibrators allow users to customize how fast the vibrator's pulsing or massaging movement occurs. Depending on the specific type of vibrator, the speed change is made by simply pushing a button a certain number of times, allowing users to change speed several times throughout the usage.

Anal vibrators

Vibrators designed for anal use have either a flared base or a long handle to grip, to prevent them from slipping inside and becoming lodged in the rectum. Anal vibrators come in different shapes but they are commonly anal plugs or phallus-like vibrators. They are recommended to be used with a significant amount of lubrication and to be inserted gently and carefully to prevent any potential damage to the rectal lining.

The average size of an anal vibrator is smaller than vibrators intended for vaginal penetration and may vary from four to six inches long and about one inch wide. As with other vibrators designed for external and internal stimulation, anal vibrators are usually battery operated. The batteries may be inside the unit or connected by wire to a power pack.

Types of anal vibrators

Vibrating anal probes — anal probes, with vibrating effect are smaller than usual butt plugs–about the size of a finger.

Vibrating anal plugs — vibrating anal plugs are made to stay inside the anus to create fullness and vibrating stimulation at the same time.

Vibrating anal beads and balls — vibrating beads and balls are a number of small beads or balls joined together through a long retrievable cord to a power control. They may not only be inserted and pulled out, but also vibrate at different speeds.

Clitoral vibrators

Clitoral vibrators are sex toys designed for stimulating the clitoris, to achieve sexual pleasure and orgasm. Normally clitoral vibrators are created for massaging the clitoris, and are not penetrating sex toys, although the shape of some vibrators allows for penetration and the stimulation of inner erogenous zones.

Types of clitoral vibrators

While most vibrators are suitable for clitoral stimulation, there are a few distinct types of vibrators designed exclusively for this purpose: the hands-free and the manual.

Hands-free clitoral vibrators — hands-free vibrators can be used to stimulate the clitoris and labia. They are held in place by straps or a harness, freeing the wearer's hands during use. Butterfly strap-ons, vibrating panties, and penis rings are all examples of hands- free clitoral vibrators.

Butterfly strap-ons — small sex toys, usually made in the shape of a butterfly, flower or animal. Their adjustable straps are worn on the woman's waist and hips. They comes in three variations: traditional, remote control and with anal and/or vaginal stimulators. They are made of silicone, plastic, latex or jelly.

Vibrating panties — are lingerie with a vibrating element attached for intense, localized vibration. They are usually remote controlled, and can be worn discreetly under normal clothing. The vibrating bullet or some other shaped elements are located against the female genitalia (clitoris and labia), but there are also some penetrative sex toys attached from the inner side of the panties for stimulating the vagina.

Penis rings — feature a vibrating bullet, to stimulate the clitoris during intercourse. This clitoral vibrator and erection enhancer in one single device is intended for couples' pleasure.

Manual clitoral vibrators — manual vibrators come in a wide variety of designs. Some are powered from wall sockets, such as the Hitachi Magic Wand. This makes them somewhat less convenient, but generally allows the vibrator to offer more intense stimulation and better durability. At the other end of the spectrum are small battery operated vibrators that can be worn on a finger; a design particularly suited for couples' play.

The EROS Clitoral Therapy Device — the EROS Clitoral Therapy Device is a small, handheld female sexual health medical device that improves sexual responses by increasing blood flow to the clitoris and external genitalia. A small, soft plastic cup is placed over the clitoris. When this device is turned on, a gentle vacuum is created, increasing blood flow to the genitalia causing the clitoris to become engorged. Increased blood flow to the genitalia results in increased vaginal lubrication and enhanced ability to achieve orgasm. The Eros Therapy Clitoral Device for Female Sexual Dysfunction received FDA clearance-to-market in April 2000. [1]

Other vibrators

Egg-shaped vibrators — can be used for stimulation of the clitoris or insertion into the vagina. They are considered discrete sex toys as they do not measure more than three inches in length and ¾ inches in width.

G-spot vibrators — are similar to the traditional vibrator but with a curve and often a soft jelly-like coating. The curve makes it easier for them to stimulate the G-spot or prostate. They are made of materials such as silicone or acrylic. They also come in different colours, shapes and sizes and can be used with or without the vibrations. Many users state that vibration enhances the sensations during G-spot or prostate stimulation. They are recommended to be used with a significant amount of lubricant, especially when used to provoke sexual pleasure in men.

Luxury vibrators — were introduced into the market around the year 2000, with an increased focus on design and the use of precious materials that appeal to the more upscale market.

Rabbit vibrators — are popular female sex toys popularized by the television series 'Sex and the City'. They comprise an insertable shaft which often has additional functionality, such as rotation and internal beads or a thrusting action. Attached to the shaft is a vibrating clitoral stimulator; for most rabbit vibrators, this comes in the form of bunny ears, which sit on either side of the clitoris. They are normally made of rubber, jelly, silicone and latex and they come in a wide variety of colours, sizes and designs.

Undercover vibrators — are discreetly shaped as everyday objects, such as lipstick tubes, cell phones, or art pieces. Occasionally, some women use actual mobile phones in this function. This type of vibrator is made from a wide range of materials and is available in different shapes and colours. Undercover vibrators are usually relatively small, have only one speed and are powered by a single battery. They tend to copy an exact shape and design of the object they are intended to be mistaken for.

The pocket rocket — is shaped like a cylinder and one of its ends has some vibrating bulges. It is meant to stimulate the clitoris or nipples, not for vaginal insertion. A pocket rocket is a mini-vibrator that is typically about five inches long and which resembles a small, travel-sized flashlight. This vibrator is a discreet sex toy that may be carried around in one's purse or briefcase. It is specially designed to provide clitoral stimulation and although it is said to be discreet, many users claim that it is quite noisy. Due to its small dimension, it is powered by a single battery and usually has only one speed.

Bullet vibrators — are small, bullet-shaped vibrators that can be used for direct stimulation or inserted into other sex toys to increase stimulation.

Dildos

A dildo is a non-vibrating device which is used for sexual stimulation of the vagina or anus. Dildos are generally made of silicone, rubber, metal or glass and often made to resemble a penis.

If a dildo is inserted in the anus and remains in place for a period of time it is called an anal plug. There are also double-ended dildos, with different-sized shafts pointing in the same direction, used by women to accomplish both anal and vaginal penetration at once, or for two partners to share a single dildo. In this case, the dildo acts as a sort of see-saw; each partner takes an end and receives stimulation.

There are dildos designed to be worn in a harness, sometimes called a strap-on harness or strap-on dildo, or to be worn inside, sometimes with vibrating devices attached externally.

Strap-on dildos may be double-ended, in which case they are meant to be worn by users who want to experience vaginal or anal penetration while also penetrating a partner.

Other types of dildos include those designed to be fitted to the face of one party, inflatable dildos, and dildos with suction cups attached to the base (sometimes referred to as a wall mount). Other types of harness mounts for dildos (besides strapping to the groin) include thigh mount, face mount, or furniture mounting straps.

Ben wa balls

This device, which originated in the Orient, consists of a set of two metal balls. One is solid and is placed in the vagina near the cervix; the other one is partially filled with mercury and is also placed in the vagina, near the first one. They are also known as Burmese bells, benoît balls, orgasm balls, venus balls or geisha balls. They are small, marble-sized balls, usually hollow and containing a small weight that rolls around. Any movement causes the mercury filled ball to hit the deeper one, spreading vibrations through the vaginal area. Women primarily use them on their own, but they can also be incorporated into sexual activity with a partner.

Nipple toys

Nipple clamps — used to stimulate the nipples by applying varying degrees of pressure.

Suction devices — are usually made of rubber or glass which fit around the nipple, causing them to become more sensitive due to engorgement. Glass suction devices may use either heat or a pump to create suction.

Kegel exercisers

Kegel exercisers, also known as vaginal barbells or vagina jugglers, are designed to improve muscle tone in the PC muscle (the pelvic floor) and can be used for sexual pleasure as well as enhancing vaginal response.

Male sex toys

Masturbators — are devices with soft, usually latex sleeves, often designed to resemble the female vagina, into which a man can place his erect penis. If this sexual aid is an electrically or battery powered model, it can be controlled by the user to operate at varying desired speeds to create a rhythmic motion, stimulating the man to reach orgasm and ejaculate.

Penile rings — are ring-shaped devices made of metal, leather, silicone or rubber, usually from and a half to two inches in diameter. Penis rings can be worn around just the penis or penis and scrotum, or just the scrotum alone, though this is usually designated as a testicle cuff. The testicles and the erect penis are slipped through the ring, which fits tightly, putting pressure on the dorsal vein of the penis. The idea is that the ring will keep the blood that has engorged the penis from flowing out. The man will therefore retain his erection longer and be able to prolong his sexual activity.

A man may wear this ring because he has erectile dysfunction (ED) or wants to prolong his erection, or as a sex toy because he likes the particular sensation of tightness and extreme engorgement that wearing one provides. When used for ED, a vacuum pump is used to produce an erection in spite of vascular or nerve damage, and the ring slides off the pump's cylinder onto the base of the penis to maintain the erection.

Some men also wear rings when they want their genitals to look larger under their pants. Some models include a protruding clitoral stimulator, designed to stimulate the clitoris during sex. Others vibrate, either vibrating the ring itself, or in a popular dolphin variant using two removable bullet vibrators to provide stimulation to the testicles and clitoris. Proper fit is important so that the penis and testicles do not get bruised. Men using this device should be cautioned not to wear the rings too tightly or for an extended period of time, since they act as a tourniquet limiting blood flow and can cause severe damage to the genitals. Some common examples of penile rings are: single-strap penis ring (adjustable), single penis ring (solid), testicle-spreader (double crown), ball-stretcher (triple crown).

A triple penis ring or triple crown is a ring that has additional rings for restraining the testicles. In orgasm, the testicles usually retract towards the body before ejaculation. A triple crown changes and intensifies the sensation of orgasm by forcing the testicles to stay away from the body.

A **balls lock** — is an ordinary padlock fastened around the male scrotum, separating the testicles away from the penis and not removable except by key or combination.

A **penile harness** — is a contraption designed to be worn around the penis and scrotum. It is used to enhance the man's erectile capacity. Multi strap penis harness fits around the base and testicles and then five straps with small buckles go up the shaft.

Warning:

Do not use penis rings if you bleed easily or have a blood clotting disorder, if you are diabetic, or if you suffer from any peripheral vascular or nerve disease. Do not use these toys if you are taking anti-coagulants, aspirin, or any other blood-thinning medication. In the event of discomfort or any unusual body changes including bruising, pain, bleeding or loss of sensation, discontinue use immediately and check with a physician. Do not place over sore, swollen, or infected areas or areas without sensation.

A **penis sleeve** — is a cylindrical device that is placed on the shaft of the penis, with the aim of increasing stimulation for the person being penetrated. They often have soft bumps intended to provide further stimulation.

A **penis extender** — is a partially hollow device like a very short dildo, with the hollow end placed on the end of the penis, intended to increase the effective length of the penis, again for the benefit of the person being penetrated. These are generally worn with condoms to prevent them from falling off during use.

French ticklers — are devices that fit over the penis and are designed to tickle and increase sensation in the vagina during intercourse. These devices are pre-shaped (unlike condoms, which come rolled up) and their surfaces are equipped with ridges and small probes or hair-like protrusions. French ticklers can be reused after thorough washing. It is important to note that while they fit over the penis in a fashion similar to condoms, they are not birth control devices.

Anal plugs — are often shorter dildos intended for anal insertion. They tend to have a flared base to prevent the device from becoming lodged in the rectum.

Anal plugs are usually used covered by condoms for hygiene, and to allow for the easy disposal of any faeces that they may come in contact with. They should not be shared with other people, due to the risk of blood-borne diseases, including HIV that can arise from the transfer of body fluids from one person to another. These should also never be used to stimulate any area other than the rectum.

Anal beads — are balls or bumps on a string or a semi-rigid wand. They are inserted into the rectum and then removed with varying speeds. The beads can be uniform or vary in size, and number from three to as many as eight. They are commonly made of silicone, plastic, rubber, latex, glass or metal and end with a ring or similar handle designed for pulling.

Prostate massage toys — are specially curved toys that are designed to stimulate the prostate, such as the Aneros.

Wireless sex toys

Wireless sex toys have been designed to provide as much sexual pleasure as the regular sex toys do but with more comfort. These types of sex toys come in a variety of shapes, sizes, colours and forms and are usually powered by batteries. They are suitable to be used both individually and with a partner for clitoral, vaginal or anal stimulation. They can be anything from vibrating panties, clitoral stimulators, regular vibrators, or butt plugs.

The care and maintenance of sex toys

Now that you have chosen your favourite sex toy, you must treat it gently and maintain it for it to provide you with years of satisfaction. Sex toys are made of silicone, cyberskin or latex and should be maintained as outlined below.

Silicone — is soft and lifelike. It is hypoallergenic, warms up quickly to body temperature, non-porous and so is easy to clean (with mild soap and water, or boiled for sterilization). Unlike jelly rubber and other porous materials, silicone can be sterilized in temperatures up to 300 ° C (572 ° F). In addition, it can be bleached in a ten per cent bleach solution. When using lubricants with silicone sex toys, it is important that silicone or silicone-based lubricants are not used, to avoid damage to the toys.

Cyberskin — is a thermal plastic elastomer and feels like real skin. It is made from ingredients on the FDA approved lists and does not contain phthalates, polyvinyl chloride (PVC), heavy metals or latex. It is easy to clean and maintain by washing with soap and water. It should be used with water based lubricants and stored in a dry place.

Latex rubber, also called jelly rubber — is commonly used for sex toys and are less expensive than silicone, glass and cyberskin. However, they can be allergenic to some people. It is also porous and should be cleaned thoroughly with an antibacterial soap and water and not shared with others. Some latex toys contain phthalates which are used to soften rubber, but they carry serious health risks. Water and silicone-based lubricants can be used with these toys, but oil-based lubricants and petroleum jelly should not be used as these cause deterioration of the latex.

As you can see, the options you have are many. Don't feel obliged to use them if they make you feel uncomfortable or guilty. But remember, in this era of HIV and widespread STDs, sex toys can offer individuals a safe alternative to penetrative intercourse.

Shared toys can transmit STDs

Shared toys can transmit STDs and over enthusiastic usage can irritate and bruise delicate membranes. It is also important to note that those devices which use household electricity can electrocute you if not properly grounded. Videos, audiotapes and written material can be helpful in assisting an individual or a couple to overcome anxiety or lack of information if one partner expresses an interest in using sex toys. Sexual devices can be particularly helpful for some disabled people whose disability inhibits their sexual expression.

In order to improve communication and intimacy, marital and sex therapists suggest that couples who have concerns or fears about the use of sex aids or toys should be encouraged to talk openly with their partner about their feelings and choose a toy which is non threatening and mutually acceptable.

References

1. Schroder, M., Mell, L. K., Hurteau, J. A., Collins, Y. C., Rotmensch, J., Waggoner, S. E. & Mundt, A. J. (2005). Clitoral Therapy Device For Treatment of Sexual Dysfunction in Irradiated Cervical Cancer Patients. *International Journal of Radiation Oncology* Biology* Physics, 61*(4), 1078-1086.

Bibliography

2. Allison, S. (2003). *Toygasms!: The Insider's Guide to Sex Toys & Techniques.* San Francisco: Tickle Kitty Press.

3. Venning, R. & Cavanah, C. (2003). *Sex toys 101: A Playfully Uninhibited Guide.* Kochi, India: Touchstone.

4. Maines, R. P. (2001). *The Technology of Orgasm: "Hysteria", the Vibrator, and Women's Sexual Satisfaction.* Baltimore: Johns Hopkins University Press.

The Top 20 Sexual Positions
Which Ones Are Best For You?

Are you ready to now launch forth into the world of deep intimacy? Are you intimidated by the perceived demand to rise to the occasion and prove your worth? The next chapter contains some good news for you, because; despite all the hype, everyone can have fulfilling sex if they only know which positions are best for them.

The mystery of sexual positions

I am sure that many readers will turn to this chapter initially because sexual positions have such an erotic appeal. Most people can only fantasize about many of the positions they have heard about, because they lack the fitness or the dexterity to try many of the myriad of positions adequately discussed in many sex manuals. The primary aim of this chapter is to debunk the myth that all lovers can and should try all the known sexual positions but rather, to encourage you to try the ones which are right for you.

For millennia, questions have been raised about sexual positions. Which positions provide maximal gratification for both partners? Are some positions immoral? Which positions are best in: pregnancy, persons with disabilities, debilitating medical conditions (such as heart disease, lung disease, spinal cord injuries, severe arthritis and low back pain), women who experience deep dyspareunia (painful sex on deep thrusting), men who are not well endowed, or too well endowed or people who are obese. Let us unravel the mystery of sexual positions and provide you with a variety of options which should enhance your sex life.

Sexual positions and religion

I am usually astounded when female patients ask me if I think certain positions are immoral; interestingly men never ask that question. I find it difficult to make the link between morality and positions between two consenting adults and so I searched the literature and discovered that; although *The Bible* does not mention sexual positions, from the sixth to sixteenth centuries, church authorities taught that intercourse should be face-to-face, man-on-top, primarily because they believed that semen would flow with gravity, leading to conception. Exceptions were made for couples challenged by illnesses, obesity or pregnancy.

The medieval Catholic Church observed that animals copulated in the vendor-dorsal (doggy style) position, and concluded that it was unnatural to humans. According to John Bancroft author of *Human Sexuality and Its Problems*, Thomas Aquinas believed that crimes against nature included intercourse in unnatural positions, with the missionary position being considered the only natural one. It is commonly believed that the term missionary position arose in response to Christian missionaries, who taught that the position was the only proper way to engage in sexual intercourse. However, the missionary position has been used for millennia.

Robert Francoeur, a futurist, evolutionary biologist, and Catholic priest married with Vatican approval, has dedicated many years studying human sexuality. He notes in his paper '*Dominant Theory*' that evidence of the missionary position's use appears in ancient pottery and art in the fertile crescent as well as in the art of early Greeks, Romans, Peruvians, Indian, Chinese and Japanese cultures. He also points out that the majority of the positions described in the *Kama Sutra*, written years before Christianity, involved the woman lying on her back with her legs in a variety of positions. [1] [2]

Now readers, I am really sorry to disappoint you, but there are only five or six sexual positions with many variations on each theme. I will now describe my top twenty as described in *'The Perfumed Garden', Kama Sutra, The Ananga Ranga* and *Tao* sexual practices. They are broadly classified as: penetrating partner on top with front entry, penetrating from behind, receiving partner on top, sitting and kneeling, standing and exotic positions.

The Perfumed Garden by Muhammad ibn Muhammad al-Nafzawi is a fifteenth-century and work of erotic literature. The full title of the book is *The Perfumed Garden of Sensual Delight.* The book presents opinions on what qualities men and women should have to be attractive, gives advice on sexual technique, warnings about and recipes to remedy sexual maladies. It lists names for the penis and vagina; has a section on the interpretation of dreams, and briefly describes sex among animals. Interspersed with these are a number of amusing stories. The book first became widely known in the English speaking world through a translation from the French in 1886, by Sir Richard Francis Burton. [3]

The Ananga Ranga (Stage of Love) or *'Kamaledhiplava'* *(Boat in the Sea of Love)* is an Indian sex manual written by Kalyana Malla in the fifteenth or sixteenth century. The poet wrote the work in honour of Lad Khan, son of Ahmed Khan Lodi. He was related to the Lodi dynasty, which from 1451 to 1526, ruled from Delhi. Later, commentators have said it is aimed specifically at preventing the separation of a husband and wife. This work is often compared to the *Kama Sutra*. It was translated into English in the year 1885, under the editorship of Sir Burton. The work was intended to show that a single woman is enough for a man. The book provides instructions in how a husband can enhance the love for his wife through sexual pleasure in addition to an extensive catalogue of sexual positions for both partners. [4]

Taoist sexual practices literally means the bedroom arts, the *Tao* is a collection of ancient Chinese wisdom. It predates the *Kama Sutra, The Perfumed Garden,* and *The Ananga Ranga.* These practices were also known as joining energy or the joining of the essences. Practitioners believed that by performing these sexual arts, one could stay in good health, and eventually with some other spiritual or alchemical practices, attain immortality. The retention of the semen is one of the fundamental tenets of Taoist sexual practice. Many Taoist practitioners link the loss of ejaculatory fluids to the loss of vital life force. The visual names given to *Tao* positions indicate that the Chinese viewed sex as an art form. The terminology of the *Tao* is very colourful. Here are some examples: the penis is called jade stem; the vagina is called coral gate; the clitoris is called pearl on the jade step; orgasm is called the great typhoon and intercourse is called the mists and the rain. [5]

The *Kama Sutra* is an ancient Indian Hindu text widely considered to be the standard work on human sexual behaviour in Sanskrit literature written by Mallanāga Vātsyāyana. A portion of the work consists of practical advice on sexual intercourse. It is largely in prose, with many inserted poetry verses. Kāma means sensual or sexual pleasure, and sūtra literally means a thread or line that holds things together, and more metaphorically refers to an aphorism (or line, rule, formula), or a collection of such aphorisms in the form of a manual.

The *Kama Sutra* is the oldest and most notable of a group of texts known generically as *Kama Shastra* (Sanskrit: Kāma Shāstra) In the *Kama Sutra*, eighty-four sex positions are explained as arts. These may be considered yoga positions for a couple. [6]

The Missionary

The missionary position is probably the most common, first position people try, which is most likely related to its simplicity and the high level of intimacy experienced. In this position the receiving partner lies on her back and the penetrating partner lies on top of the receiving partner facing her.

Among humans, the missionary position is the most commonly-used sex position. Prior to the release of Alfred Kinsey's work, the missionary position was known by several names, including the matrimonial, the mama-papa position, the English-American position, and the male superior position. In his seminal study *Sexual Behaviour in the Human Female* (1953), which focused on American women, researcher Alfred Kinsey stated that 91 per cent of married women surveyed, reported using this position most often, whereas nine percent reported using it exclusively.[7] There are many variations to this position namely the stopperage, the anvil, the viennese oyster, the coital alignment technique, the galloping triangle the scissors and a few others. A brief description of these positions is given below.

The Stopperage

The receiving partner lies on her back with a cushion beneath her buttocks, legs pulled up straight and knees near to the head. The penetrating partner holds the receiving partner's legs and penetrates from above. This position is called 'the stopperage' (*The Perfumed Garden*), the Dragon Turn (*Tao*), the raised feet posture (*The Ananga Ranga*) and the crab posture (*Kama Sutra*). Men with very long penises should exercise restraint in this position to avoid discomfort to the receiving partner.

The Anvil

In this position commonly called the anvil the receiving partner lies on her back while she raises her feet and places them onto the penetrating partner's shoulders, who then enters her from a kneeling position while supporting some of his weight on the receiver's legs. This allows a deeper penetration for stimulation of her vagina and clitoris. This is also called the fourth posture (*The Perfumed Garden*), rising position and variant yawing (*Kama Sutra*) level feet posture (*The Ananga Ranga*) and the ape or pine tree (*Tao*).

The Viennese Oyster position

The Viennese oyster position was first described in '*The Joy of Sex*' by Alex Comfort, in 1972. In this position, the receiver lays on their back with their lower back and legs raised all the way up so that the ankles are crossed behind their own head. The exact end position will depend on the flexibility of the receiver. This position totally exposes the groin area to the giving partner who lays atop the receiver. The penetrating partner moves up and down on the receiver to create friction. The giver needs to use their hands to support their own body weight to avoid crushing the receiver. This position requires considerable flexibility on the part of the receiver and it cannot be (fully) achieved by most, but is quite erotic due to the feeling of being totally exposed. Those less flexible might try getting into the position, but stop at the point where the position starts to become uncomfortable. The giver can also help those less flexible by using their hands to support the receiver's thighs at the mid-point. This is also described as the second posture of '*The Perfumed*

Garden' and Sheikh Nefzawi recommends it for a man whose member is a short one to minimise discomfort to his partner.[8]

The Coital Alignment Technique (CAT)

The coital alignment technique is a variant of the missionary position designed to maximize clitoral stimulation during coitus. The penetrating partner lies above the receiving partner as in the missionary position, but moves upward along the woman's body, until the erection, which would otherwise point up, is pointing down. The dorsal (upper) side of the penis now presses against the clitoris; and as opposed to the missionary position, the male's body moves downward (relative to the female's) during the inward stroke, and upward for the outward stroke. She may also wrap her legs around his.

Sexual movement is focused in the pelvises, without leverage from the arms or legs. The rocking upward stroke (female leads) and downward stroke (male leads) of sexual movement stimulates the clitoris and is an effective way to give a woman a clitoral orgasm. The technique for coital alignment was formulated by American psychotherapist Edward Eichel and the original study was published by Eichel, De Simone Eichel, and Kule in 1988, in the *Journal of Sex & Marital Therapy*. [9] [10] [11] [12] [13] [14]

The Galloping Horse

In this position, the receiving partner lies beneath while the penetrating partner enters her from above as she thrusts her pelvis forward to meet him. The penetrating partner should support his weight on his hands and knees to control his thrusting. This position is also called the First Posture of *The Perfumed Garden*. The *Kama Sutra* describes this as the pressing position and *The Ananga Ranga* as the gaping posture while the *Tao* is far more descriptive and calls it the galloping horse or silk worm spinning a cocoon. This position is primarily recommended for men with a long member.

The Scissors Position

In this position the receiving partner lies on her side so that her bottom leg is between her partners legs and her top leg is draped over his side. The penetrating partner lies facing her so that his bottom leg is under her bottom leg and his upper between her legs. This affords very deep penetration and intimate interaction. It is also called, the crab embrace (*The Ananga Ranga*), the fifth sexual posture (*The Perfumed Garden*) and side by side clasping (*Kama Sutra*).

Receiving Partner on Top - The Female Dominant Position

In this position the receiving partner assumes the dominant role and again there are many variations such as: the lateral coital, the reverse cow girl and cow girl.

The Lateral Coital Position

The lateral coital position recommended by Masters and Johnson is one in which the penetrative partner lies on his back, with the receiving is rolled slightly to the side so that her pelvis is atop his, also called the inverted embrace (*The Ananga Ranga*).

The Reverse Cowgirl

The reverse cowgirl position is one in which the penetrating partner lies on his back and the receiving partner kneels on top of the penetrator with her back towards him. This is called reciprocal sights of the posterior or the mares position (*The Perfumed Garden*), the swing (*Kama Sutra*) and birds fly on back and rabbit grooming (*Tao*).

The Cowgirl

The cowgirl position is one in which the penetrating partner lies on his back and the receiving partner kneels on top of the penetrator with her abdomen facing him she usually leans forward on her arms. This position allows the receiver to have more control over depth and angle of penetration. This is called 'interchange of coition' or 'the race of the member' (*The Perfumed Garden*), the pair of tongs or the top (*Kama Sutra*), the butterfly (*Tao)* and the ascending position (*The Ananga Ranga).*

Penetrating from behind

The Spoons Position

In the spoons position, the penetrative partner lies on his side, with his knees bent and the receptive partner lies on her side, with her back pressed against the penetrative partner. The penetration angle is ideal for G-spot stimulation. Nefzawi called this 'coitus from the back' and the Taoists 'mandarin ducks'.

The Rear Entry Positions

The rear entry position is also known as kitty style, retrocopulation, doggy style, or by its Latin name, coitus more ferarum (sex after the custom of beasts).

There are many direct variations of doggy style, some of the more common ones are:

- The receiving partner is on all fours with their torso horizontal. The penetrating partner inserts from behind called the sixth posture (*Perfumed Garden)*, the deer (*Kama Sutra)*, tiger step and cicada on a bough (*Tao*).

- The penetrating partner lies flat on the receivers back who has a pillow placed underneath her pelvis. It is also called coitus from behind (*The Perfumed Garden*), and the elephant posture (*Kama Sutra*).
- The receiving partner kneels at the edge of the bed and rests her torso on the bed and the penetrating partner enters her gently from behind. It is also called the quickie and the ninth posture (*The Perfumed Garden*).

Standing positions

One partner stands while holding up the other without a support or with the support of furniture. Ordinary furniture can be used for this purpose, but you can try other forms of erotic furniture and other apparatus such as fisting slings and trapezes to enhance the experience.

Here are some techniques you can try:

Late Spring Donkey

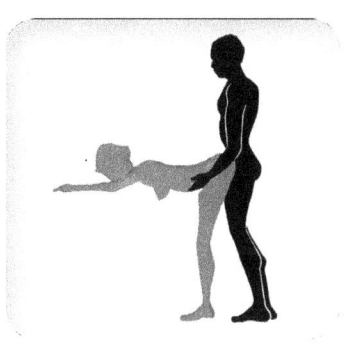

This position is normally used in a venue where lying down is undesirable. The receiving partner lies face down across a bed with her knees on the floor or stand and lean forward over the bed. The penetrating partner enters her from behind. This is the simplest standing position often called standing doggy-style. It allows for deep penetration and is called the ninth posture (*The Perfumed Garden*), congress of a cow (*Kama Sutra*) and late spring donkey (*Tao*).

The Supported Congress

In this position, both partners stand facing each other, the receiver raises one of their legs to give easier access while their partner helps support it. If the receiver is very flexible, you may want to try putting the raised leg onto the shoulder of the giver for an even more erotic experience. This position is called belly to belly (*The Perfumed Garden*) or the supported congress (*Kama Sutra*).

Suspended Congress

The receiver wraps her leg around the penetrating partner who leans against a wall and locks his hands underneath her buttocks or thighs. This position allows for more contact of the man's body against the woman's clitoris, giving her greater pleasure. It also enables the man to thrust more effectively. This is called the suspended congress (*Kama Sutra*).

The Butterfly

The receiving partner lies on a flat surface. The penetrating partner stands in front of the receiver and lifts her hips until her vagina is lined up with his penis. The receiver places her legs either on the man's shoulders or on his waist to help support her weight. The penetrator then inserts his penis. This is known as the butterfly position. The angle of the penetration makes it excellent for G-spot stimulation.

Sitting and kneeling

The Lotus

In the lotus position (*The Ananga Ranga*), the penetrating partner sits crossed legs (lotus style). The receiving partner sits on top and wraps their legs around the penetrating partner. Both wrap their arms around each other for support. This forms a wheel-like figure for which this position is named. The giver and receiver together can set up a rocking motion to facilitate movement during penetration. This is also called pounding on the spot (*The Perfumed Garden*) and singing monkey (*Tao*). It is said that this position combines sex and meditation to bring lovers to a higher level of awareness and in fact is a popular position while enjoying Tantric sex.

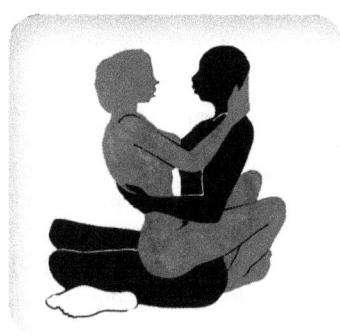

The Lap Dance

In the lap dance the penetrating partner sits in a chair or the edge of a bathtub. The receiving partner then straddles the penetrating partner and sits, facing the penetrating partner or with her back towards him, she can place her feet on the floor or around his neck.

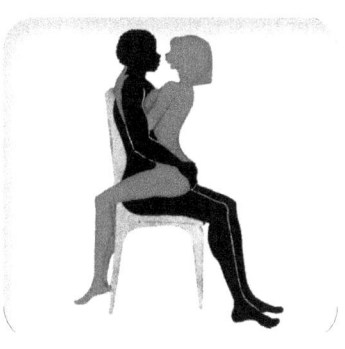

Exotic positions

These positions are quite innovative, and not as widely known or practiced as the ones listed above. Typical examples are: the t square, the modified t square, the seventh position of Burton and the pile driver.

The T-Square Position

The receiving partner is on the bottom and raises the knees up and spread the legs apart. A pillow under the small of the back often helps maintain this position. The penetrating partner lies perpendicularly to her with his hips under the arch formed by her raised legs forming a tee. This position is described in *The Perfumed Garden* as the rainbow arch or drawing the bow.

The Modified T-square or X Position

The X position is another form of acrobatic copulation. The receiving partner lies on her back with her legs bent at the hips and her thighs spread as wide as possible. The penetrating partner enters her frontally at a 45 degree angle forming a large X.

The Seventh Posture of Burton

The seventh posture of Burton's translation of *The Perfumed Garden* is an unusual position not described in many sex manuals. The receiving partner lies on her back, the penetrating partner sits back on his heels with one of her legs over his shoulder and the other between his thighs.

The Piledriver

The receiver lies on her back, then raises her hips as high as possible, the penetrative partner while standing holds her legs against his chest as he enters her. The position places considerable strain on the woman's neck, so firm cushions should be used to support her. This is called the tail of The ostrich (*The Perfumed Garden*) and the rising position *(Kama Sutra)*.

Which positions are best for you?

Now that you are acquainted with my top twenty positions, you are now equipped with the knowledge to make an informed decision and choose the ones best for you.

The missionary position — both receptive and penetrative is comfortable, allows deep penetration, whole body contact, eye contact, kissing and closeness. It also can be sustained for reasonable periods. However, if your partner is heavy or suffers from arthritis (hip, knee, leg or arm) or you are pregnant, this position is not recommended.

In many women the missionary position places the penis at an incorrect angle with minimum stimulation of the G-spot or clitoris and some women feel pinned underneath the partner and have difficulty responding with appropriate pelvic movements. On the other hand the penetrative partner has good control of the depth of penetration as well as the speed of his thrusts. The coital alignment technique (CAT) takes pride of place among all the missionary positions since it puts rhythmic pressure on the clitoris during penetration. Many women who have difficulty experiencing vaginal orgasm find this technique quite stimulating.

The female dominant position (receptive on top) — is ideal where the person lying down is heavier, less athletic or has back problems. It is also a useful approach for men who suffer from premature ejaculation as well as during early pregnancy, since it offers the benefit of the woman being in control of the depth and angle of penetration. Women who experience deep dyspareunia might find this position more comfortable. It is important for me to remind you that in the reverse cow girl position the penis might be bent forcefully forward and cause a penile fracture.

Retro copulation (receptive from behind) — is excellent for overweight couples as it imposes less strain on their muscles. It is also good for men who are not well endowed as this position shortens the vaginal barrel and makes penetration feel deeper. It is also excellent for G-spot stimulation and during pregnancy, but it can be painful for some women during deep thrusting. It is also important to note that this position does not stimulate the clitoris directly so the penetrative partner should incorporate some manual stimulation of the clitoris into foreplay.

Spooning (penetrative from behind) — is recommended for couples of different weights, pregnant women, women who do not enjoy deep thrusting, and the elderly with arthritis, or those who are less mobile. It is deemed to be the most intimate and relaxed position for intercourse.

Standing — is a useful approach for quickies in confined spaces. This position is ideal for couples who are equally matched in heights. If one or both partners suffer from arthritis this is a useful position to try.

Sitting positions — are ideal for couples of different sizes if the lighter one is on top, it is also an excellent position during pregnancy. The lotus position is a favourite for those who practice Tantric sex.

Exotic positions — are reserved for agile and fit lovers who want to experiment with new and exciting variations of posture during sex. Of course, you must always ensure that discomfort is minimized by using appropriate cushions and changing a posture if fatigue is experienced.

The T- square position — is a good position to try during pregnancy since it minimizes pressure on the abdomen. However, it may provide too much deep penetration for use during the last trimester. It is also a winner for those with arthritis since it allows penetration with minimal pressure on the joints and the hands are free for some sensual massage. Obese patients might also find this position quite an ideal option.

So whether you are young or old, pregnant or non pregnant, arthritic, obese or totally disease free, there are sexual positions which can add sparkle to your love life.

References

1. Bancroft, J. (1989). *Human Sexuality and its Problems.* London, United Kingdom: Churchill Livingstone.

2. Francoeur, R. (2002). *Nerve.* Retrieved April 2012, from http://www.nerve.com/dispatches/francoeur/hwjdi/.

3. Netzawi. S. (Author), Sir Richard Francis Burton (Translator) (May 1, 1999). *The Perfumed Garden of Cheikh Nefzawi: A Manual of Arabian Erotology.* New York NY: Signet Classics.

4. Kalyanamalla, F. M.(Author), Karene H. ed (2010). *Ananga Ranga: Erotic Art of Love & Sex: An Illustrated Ancient Indian Guide for Couples: Sacred Erotic Texts:*

5. Lai, H. (2001). *The Sexual Teachings of the White Tigress: Secrets of the Female Taoist Masters.* Rochester, VT:Destiny Books.

6. Burton, S. R. & Arbuthnot, F. F. (1966). trans. *The Kama Sutra of Vatsayana.* New York: Putnam's

7. Kinsey, A. C., Wardell B. P., Martin, C. E., & Gebhard,P.H. (1953). *Sexual Behavior in the Human Female.* Philadelphia: W.B. Saunders Company.

8. Comfort, A. (1975). *The Joy of Sex: A Gourmet Guide to Lovemaking.* London: Quartet pb.

9. Eichel, E. W., Eichel, J. D. S. & Kule, S. (1988). *The Technique of Coital Alignment and its Relation to Female Orgasmic Response and Simultaneous Orgasm.* Journal of Sex & Marital Therapy, *14*(2), 129-141.

10. Eichel, E. W. & Nobile, P. (1992). *The Perfect Fit: How to Achieve Mutual Fulfillment and Monogamous Passion Through the New Intercourse.* New York: Dutton Adult.

11. Kaplan, H. S. (1992). *Does the CAT Technique Enhance Female Orgasm?.* Journal of Sex & Marital Therapy, *18*(4), 285-291.

12. Hurlbert, D. F., & Apt, C. (1995). *The Coital Alignment Technique and Directed Masturbation: A Comparative Study on Female Orgasm.* Journal of Sex & Marital Therapy, *21*(1), 21-29.

13. Pierce, A. P. (2000). *The Coital Alignment Technique (CAT): An Overview Of Studies.* Journal of Sex &Marital Therapy, *26*(3), 257-268.

14. Eichel, E.W.(1999). *Orgasm Defined by the C.A.T. Research. Sexuality in the New Millennium: Proceedings of the 14th World Congress of Sexology,* Hong

Kong.

Bibliography

15. Sweet, L. (2009). *365 Sex Positions: A New Way Every Day For a Steamy, Erotic Year.* Churchville, PA: Amorata Press.

16. Hooper, A. (2008). *Kama Sutra - Sexual Positions For Him and For Her.* London, United Kingdom: Dorling Kindersley

17. Bodansky, S. & Bodansky, V. (2002). *The Illustrated Guide to Extended Massive Orgasm.* Alameda: Hunter House.

18. *Top 20 Sex Positions.* Retrieved January 23, 2013, from http://www.goodtoknow.co.uk/relationships/galleries/9278/top-20-sex-positions

19. *Sexual Positions* – Retrieved April 2012, from http://www.cosmopolitan.com/sex-love/positions/the-spider-web-sex-position

20. Kaplan, H. S. (1992). *Does the CAT Technique Enhance Female Orgasm?. Journal of Sex & Marital Therapy, 18*(4), 285-291.

Tantric Sex
The Science of Ecstasy

Having mastered your sexual positions you can now graduate to the next level where you will learn how to extend the peak of your sexual ecstasy, so that you and your partner can experience several orgasms in a single sexual encounter, let me therefore introduce you to Tantric sex.

The science of ecstasy

We all day dream of a sexual encounter that lasts forever and leaves us in a state of eternal bliss. In the real world the closest thing that can get you there is Tantric sex.

Tantra embraces the natural energies of the bodies and connects you with cosmic, universal energy. It is becoming one with the other, and the very cosmos itself (Swami Nostradamus Virato; Guru and Enlightened Spiritual Teacher of Human Potential and Holistic Health).

Tantric sex originated in India some three thousand years ago, and is called by practitioners 'The Science of Ecstasy'. The word Tantric is derived from the Sanskrit word Tantra, which means to manifest, to expand, to show and to weave. Tantric sex is said to expand consciousness and to weave together the polarities of male (represented by the Hindu god, Shiva), and female (embodied by the Hindu goddess, Shakti), into a harmonious whole. Tantra emerged as a rebellion against organized religion, which held that sexuality should be rejected in order to reach enlightenment. Tantra challenged the ascetic beliefs (to abstain from worldly pleasures and comfort) of that time, and proposed that sexuality was a doorway to the divine, and that earthly pleasures, such as eating, dancing and creative expressions were sacred acts. Making love was seen as a gift to God. So there was no repression or guilt attached to sex. It taught that when a man approaches his beloved he should have a sacred feeling as if he were going into a temple. Tantra teaches lovers how to extend the peak of their sexual ecstasy so that women and men can experience several orgasms in a single sexual encounter.

Tantric intimacy exercises

The Tantric tradition emphasizes preparation for lovemaking. Erotic rituals focus on exchanging pleasures, awakening the senses and allowing couples to communicate deeply, physically and emotionally.

The following exercises will help you reconnect with your body and with your partner in a special way. As you move through these steps, do not focus on intercourse as the ultimate goal. But simply enjoy giving and receiving pleasure using sensual touch and words of love:

Plan a sexual rendezvous — at least once per week set aside an hour or more of uninterrupted time to be together.

Create a temple of love — whether you meet in your bedroom, living room or another space in your house, creating a sacred space for each other will help relax you and set the mood. You can transform any room into a temple of love using candles, fresh flowers, erotic art, finger foods and tantalizing aromas.

Dress provocatively — experiment with clothing or accessories that make you feel sexy and excite your partner.

Use ritual to develop intimacy — begin your journey with a ritual. Feed each other aphrodisiac foods or share a glass of wine in the nude. Some couples enjoy bathing together in order to connect with each other. Sensual massage is also an excellent way to fuse your energies. I also recommend that you read poetry to each other, dance, play, listen to music etc. Use this time to communicate, sharing what you admire most about each other.

Harmonize your breathing — breathing is an important concept for Tantric practitioners. Partners should learn to concentrate and synchronize their breathing, with the male and female taking alternate breaths.

Try this exercise: sit quietly, cross-legged, facing each other. Rest your hands on your knees with your palms facing up. As you gaze into your partner's eyes, take soft but deep breaths. Keep your eyes open, gazing beyond the eyes into your partner's soul. Sustained eye contact is essential for building intimacy. Practice this exercise until you can sustain eye contact and harmonize breathing for about ten minutes.

Try to spend several weeks practicing the Tantric intimacy exercises without necessarily engaging in intercourse, Then you may move into the next exercise.

Erotic touch — pleasurable practice will help you become better lovers, guide your partner as you take turns stimulating each other. Describe exactly how you would like to be touched. Share your desires in an encouraging way, making requests in a clear and loving manner. Once you become comfortable with this process, you may wish to create a pleasure chest. Include whatever excites you and your partner; a feather, marital aids, massage oil, blindfold, soft fabric, erotica and love notes to each other. Explore new and creative ways to awaken each other's minds and bodies. Then, you will be ready for Tantric lovemaking.

Tantric love making

As you make the transition into sex, the idea is to maintain a state of sexual ecstasy for as long as possible. Tantric lovemaking is not result-oriented, but rather, timeless and unstructured.

Maintain a deep level of intimacy — continue to gaze into each other's eyes as much as possible. It has been said that a woman's most powerful sex organ lies between her ears. Since desire can be inhibited by fear, guilt and stress. Women often need to concentrate on feelings rather than thinking when making love.

Keep it slow — a long, slow build up helps men control orgasm and enhance women's arousal. Gently stimulate the clitoris and the G-spot. Commence slow unhurried intercourse. According to Tantric teacher, Robert Frey, "the longer you linger in this process of building energy, the longer men can resist ejaculation and the woman's response will be more intense."

Bring your attention back to your breath — resist the urge to breathe quickly. Instead, take long, slow, deep breaths from the belly and exhale gradually. You may match your breathing to that of your partner, or try breathing alternately— as you inhale, your partner exhales. This moves energy back and forth and connects you to your lover.

Vary your positions — different sex positions add to sexual pleasure and balance male and female energies.

Mini orgasms in men — male initiates are taught the four phases of sexual activity. Phase one is arousal; phase two is realized when the male approaches orgasm, phase three is orgasm itself and phase four is ejaculation. By learning to distinguish between the four states, Tantric practitioners are able to maintain and repeat phase three indefinitely. By holding back, men can experience a series of mini-orgasms as follows: when you feel the undulations of ejaculation, relax and tighten your PC muscles. Take a slow, deep breath and stop making love long enough for your arousal to subside. Resume your lovemaking, continuing to generate excitement, then relax again, contract your PC's and breathe slowly. Repeat this as often as you can to experience the joy of sex without ejaculating.

Multiple orgasms in women

For women to enhance their own ecstasy they must use the PC muscles and breathing exercises also. They can do this at peaks of energy to spread the orgasmic energy throughout the body and so may be able to achieve one, two, three or even more orgasms.

A lifetime of bliss

The practice of Tantra shows us how to reclaim the sexual intimacy that is often lost in most relationships and allows us to discover new joys and transform mere moments of sexual ecstasy into a lifetime of sexual bliss.

Bibliography

1. Bhattacharyya, N. N. (1982). *History of the Tantric Religion: A Historical, Ritualistic, and Philosophical Study.* New Delhi, India: Manohar Publishers & Distributors,

2. Feuerstein, G. (1998). *Tantra: Path of Ecstasy.* Boston: Shambhala Publications

3. Richardson, D. (2010). *Heart of Tantric Sex.* Amsterdam: O-Books.

Part 3 - AFTER PLAY

Part three of this book is dedicated to all the readers who are experiencing a sexual slump.

Overcoming Emotional Barriers to Sex

Sex is a major cause for marital conflict

A few years ago, a patient came to see me and bemoaned the fact that after a mere six months he had lost desire for his wife. To his dismay, she just did not meet his sexual expectations and he was at a loss on how to tell her that sex for him had become tiresome. This young man was having one of the seven quarrels of marriage – Sex. Dr Robie McCauley, in his book, *The Seven Basic Quarrels of Marriage: Recognize, Defuse, Negotiate, and Resolve Your Conflicts*, reminds us that sex is a major cause for marital conflict, primarily due to: lack of confidence, communication difficulties, inexperience, lack of skill, unrealistic expectations, and refusal to take responsibility for our own sexual pleasure. [1]

So what are the emotional barriers to sex?

Bernard Zilbergeld addressed this issue elegantly in his book, *Men and Sex*. He posited the argument that the emotional barriers are: your belief systems, your sexual conditions, your affect (mood) and your degree of empathy (the power of entering into your partner's personality and imaginatively experiencing his feelings). [2]

Belief systems

Our belief systems are taboos and phobias about sex that we all have and take with us into each sexual encounter. Most of us are not aware of these biases and expectations, but these un-examined, yet rigid convictions have the potential to impact negatively on our sexual experiences.

Sexual conditions

Are you unhappy with your sex life? Has sex for you become a chore? Perhaps your sexual conditions are not being met. In many sexual encounters each partner is primarily concerned with the others satisfaction. The woman is trying to figure out what the man wants and expects, while he is trying to determine how to satisfy her. Each is looking out for each other and neither is addressing his or her own needs.

To truly enjoy good sex you must determine the ideal conditions which would facilitate maximum gratification; that is:

- Becoming aroused

- Achieving erection or vaginal lubrication

- Having an orgasm if desired

A condition is anything that affects your sexuality such as your emotional state, your physical state, how you feel about your partner, what you expect from him/her, the type of stimulation you desire, the setting you are in as well as other factors. Ideal conditions should make you more relaxed, confident and sensuous. As human beings we have unique preferences, styles and needs.

Your conditions reflect your uniqueness and you should not be embarrassed for having special needs. In order to truly achieve these conditions you must communicate your feelings to your partner.

Your mood

Are you in the mood for sex? If not, why not? Share your feelings and your fantasies with your partner. Explore your fears, taboos and sexual preferences.

Is there a novel experience that you crave but are unwilling to verbalize?

Are you experiencing a physical challenge such as erectile dysfunction, PMS, hot flashes, tiredness, etc?

Are you on any drug that has suppressed your desire?

What is your mood like?

Are you feeling depressed, anxious or angry?

Do you have performance anxiety?

How much do you empathize with your partner?

How do you feel about your partner? Do you really find him/ her attractive?

Do you think he/ she really cares for you?

Are you aware of his/ her specific desires?

Are you willing to meet these needs?

Are they contrary to your mores, value systems, etc?

Let us review some guidelines for improving your communication skills.

Improving your communication skills

- The male partner should reflect on the needs of his penis. What are the conditions which would facilitate its optimum functioning? And what would retard its performance? Share these with your partner.

- The female partner should reflect on her emotional, physical and situational needs. Does her partner know these needs?

- Because of the pressure to satisfy their partner's needs, both men and women often sacrifice their own enjoyment, and make love when they don't want to, when they are too tense to respond appropriately, in ways they don't like and even with partners they find unattractive.

- To meet your conditions you must be assertive, while showing appropriate concerns for your partners needs.

- Let your partner know that you are not in the mood for sex even though he/she is interested.

- Tell your partner that you don't want intercourse but would like some other form of sex. Indicate in a clear way that you want to stop in the middle of a sexual experience if it is uncomfortable.

- Let your partner know that certain feelings such as anger, anxiety or boredom are interfering with your sexual feelings and functioning.

- Give your partner directions on how to stimulate you in a way you find most pleasurable.

- Be frank and express your wishes clearly but don't criticise, just say what you want or do not want.

- It is essential that you give a rationale for your request or rejection but be firm and persistent.

- If you are unwilling to grant a request as it is made, but want to do something else, discuss this option with your spouse.

- At the end of this period of intimacy, express your appreciation when your requests are granted.

Please remember that assertiveness should not be regarded as rudeness, bullying or aggression; it affords you the opportunity to pay serious attention to your own needs. Your partner may not always be responsive and you will have to negotiate compromises to overcome emotional barriers to sex.

References

1. Betcher, W., & Macauley, R. (1990). *The Seven Basic Quarrels of Marriage: Recognize, Defuse, Negotiate, and Resolve your Conflicts.* New York: Villard Books.

2. Zilbergeld, B. & Ullman, J. (1979). Men and Sex: A Guide to Sexual Fulfilment. London WC1B 3PA: Souvenir Press.

Bibliography

3. Goldsmith, B. (2009). *Emotional Fitness for Intimacy: Sweeten & Deepen Your Love in Only 10 Minutes a Day.* Oakland: New Harbinger Publications.

4. Notarius, C. & Markman, H. (1994). *We Can Work It Out: How to Solve Conflicts, Save Your Marriage, and Strengthen Your Love For Each Other.* New York:Perigee.

5. Penner, C. J. & Penner, J. (1993). *Restoring the Pleasure: Complete Step-by-Step Programs to Help Couples Overcome the Most Common Sexual Barriers.* Dallas: Word.

Sexual Healing

An Intimacy Inoculation

Having resolved your communication issues, I want to share with you in the next chapter, some real benefits that sex brings; not only to your relationship, but to your overall health.

An intimacy inoculation

I have always felt that sexually active people look happier, walk with a kind of bounce and live longer than their celibate counterparts, but was there any evidence to support my thesis? Well, scientific evidence now shows what many of us have suspected for some time; that good sex not only adds great enjoyment to our lives, but it also improves our health and may even contribute to our longevity.

In his book called *Sexual Healing,* Dr. Paul Pearsall, Director of Behavioural Medicine at Detroit's Beaumont Hospital, writes that the joys and pleasures of living life and loving may provide us with something called an intimacy inoculation that actually protects us from diseases.

Sexual healing is achieved primarily by maintaining a close, intimate relationship which, when accomplished, leads to better health. Can lack of sexual intimacy create a risk factor for certain diseases? Dr. Pearsall cites research and his own clinical experience which indicate that sexual dissatisfaction seems to be prevalent prior to a heart attack in a high percentage of persons. [1]

Here are some of the benefits of sex:

Longevity (long life)

In French, an orgasm means 'the little death' (la petite mort). This was so described because after an orgasm, an intense wave of calm and relaxation overcomes humans (that's why men usually fall asleep) and it's a time when people can truly liberate themselves and let go. They experience a spiritual release called transcendence. Sexual experts now say that having sex at least two times a week can increase your life span! Just before orgasm and ejaculation, the hormone DHEA (Dehydroepiandrosterone) spikes to levels three to five times higher than usual. DHEA can boost your immune system, repair tissues, improve cognition, keep the skin healthy, and act as an antidepressant. Lets us review the evidence:

David Weeks, a clinical neuropsychologist, head of Old Age Psychology at the Royal Edinburgh Hospital in Scotland, did an elegant long term study on sex and longevity and published his findings in his book *Secrets of the Superyoung,* in 1999. He concluded that, 'The key ingredients for looking younger are staying active and maintaining a good sex life.' In a study of 3,500 people, ages 30 to 101, Weeks found that 'sex helps you look between four and seven years younger,' according to impartial ratings of the subjects' photos. [2]

In another study at the Royal Edinburgh Hospital in Scotland, a panel of judges viewed participants through a one-way mirror and guessed their ages. Those who looked seven to 12 years younger than their age (labelled super young) were also enjoying more sex—four times a week, on average.

George Davey Smith, et al, of Queen's University of Belfast conducted a study called *Sex and Death: Are They Related?* Findings from the Caerphilly cohort study tracked the mortality of about 1,000 middle-aged men over the course of a decade. The study was designed to compare persons of comparable circumstances, age and health. Its findings, published in 1997 in the *British Medical Journal*, revealed that the mortality risk was 50 per cent lower in the group with high orgasmic frequency than in the group with low orgasmic frequency. [3]

Improved sense of smell

After sex there is an increased production of oxytocin; this in turn causes stem cells in the brain to develop new neurons in the brain's olfactory bulb, its smell centre. Regular sex therefore improves your sense of smell. [4]

Reduced risk of heart disease

When we are aroused, our pulse quickens and the blood flow to our brain increases, and so do our cognitive function and oxygenation of our tissues. In 2001, a follow-up to the Queens University study mentioned above, researchers focused on cardiovascular health. They found that by having sex three or more times a week, men reduced their risk of heart attack or stroke by half. In reporting these results, the co-author of the study, Shah Ebrahim stated that, 'the relationship found between frequency of sexual intercourse and mortality is of considerable public interest.' Making love regularly can also lower levels of the body's total cholesterol while positively changing the ratio of good-to-bad cholesterol. [5] [6] [7]

Can semen combat breast cancer?

It has been shown that semen contain two cancer fighting agents namely, Glycoproteins and Selenium. In 1978, Gjorgov published a study in Oncology titled *Barrier Contraceptive Practice and Male Infertility as Related Factors To Breast Cancer in Married Women*. He concluded that the reduction of the incidence of breast cancer by eliminating the barrier contraceptive techniques would be less than 50 per cent in married women in the population studied. [8]

Improved fitness and well being

A vigorous episode of sex, work the pelvis, thighs, buttocks, arms, neck and thorax and can burn about 200 calories (about the same as running 15 minutes on a treadmill or playing a hectic game of squash). The pulse rate, in a sexually aroused person, rises from about 70 beats per minute to 150, the same as that of an athlete expending maximum effort.

Sex also boosts production of testosterone, which leads to stronger bones and muscles.

Men's Health magazine has called the bed, the single greatest piece of exercise equipment ever invented. Regular lovemaking can also increase a woman's oestrogen level, protect her heart and keep her vaginal tissues more supple. Dr. Claire Bailey of the University of Bristol says "there is little or no risk of a woman overdosing on sex". In fact, she says, "regular sex can firm a woman's tummy and buttocks and improve her posture." [9]

Reduction of blood pressure

Can sex stabilize your blood pressure? Have you ever been freaked out by a challenging assignment and longed to reach for a valium? Well; I have an alternative option for you – sex.

Stuart Brody, from the University of Paisley, Scotland, UK in 2000 and 2006, determined that penile–vaginal intercourse (PVI), but not other sexual behaviour, is associated with better psychological and physiological function. He examined the relationship of sexual behaviour patterns to blood pressure (BP) and its reactivity to stress (public speaking and verbal arithmetic). For a fortnight, 24 women and 22 men used daily diaries to record PVI, masturbation, and partnered sexual behaviour in the absence of PVI. Persons who reported PVI (but no other sexual activities) had better stress response (a lower rise in blood pressure) when asked to speak in public or solve a mathematics problem than persons reporting other or no sexual behaviours. The conclusion is clear. Sex; prior to a stressful engagement is a potent anxiloytic. [10] [11] Light also showed in 2005, that more frequent partners hugs and higher oxytocin levels are linked to lower blood pressure and heart rate in pre-menopausal women. [12]

Improved mental health

We all know that sex makes us feel good, but is there any proof that sex is a mood enhancer? In 2007, the Arizona State University conducted a study on 58 middle-aged women, to determine if sex was a mood enhancer. They concluded that physical affection or sexual behaviour with a partner significantly predicted lower negative mood and stress, and higher positive mood the following day. In other words, sex can lead you to feel less stressed, and being less stressed can lead to more sex. [13] [14]

If you are still not convinced check this one out. In a 2002 study of 293 women, American psychologist Gordon Gallup reported that sexually active participants whose male partners did not use condoms were less subject to depression than those whose partners did. One theory is that prostaglandin, a hormone found in semen, may be absorbed in the female genital tract, thus modulating female hormones. [15]

Wound healing

Some evidence suggests sex may actually help wounds to heal faster due to the release of oxytocin. This might prove quite useful in those suffering from chronic ulcers due to peripheral vascular disease such as diabetics. [16]

Pain-relief

Immediately before orgasm, the level of the hormone oxytocin increases to five times its normal level. This in turn releases endorphins (a hormone-like chemical that is chemically related to morphine), which is a potent analgesic (pain reliever). Sex, therefore, can alleviate a myriad of painful conditions such as arthritis, migraine, pelvic congestion syndrome, lumbago, prostatitis and sinusitis. In women, sex also elevates the levels of oestrogen, which can reduce the pain of premenstrual syndrome (PMS). [17][18]

A study done by Beverly Whipple, professor emeritus at Rutgers University in 1985 revealed that, when women masturbated to orgasm, the pain tolerance threshold and pain detection threshold increased significantly by 74.6 per cent and 106.7 per cent respectively. [19] She repeated the study in 1988, and revealed that two types of self-stimulation, pressure and pleasurable, applied by ten women to the anterior vaginal wall, the posterior vaginal wall, and the clitoris resulted in significant increase in pain thresholds. [20]

Less-frequent colds and flu

Individuals who have sex once or twice a week show 30 per cent higher levels of an antibody called immunoglobulin A. This is known to boost the immune system and reduce the frequency of common respiratory infections (coughs and colds). [21]

Sex exercises the pelvic floor muscles

Regular sex exercises the PC muscles which not only enhance the quality of sex, but can strengthen the bladder sphincter and prevent incontinence and utero-vaginal prolapse.

Prostate protection

A team in Australia, led by Graham Giles of the Cancer Council Victoria in Melbourne in 2003, asked 1079 men with prostate cancer to fill in a questionnaire detailing their sexual habits, and compared their responses with those of 1259 healthy men of the same age. The team concluded that the more men ejaculate between the ages of 20 and 50, the less likely they are to develop prostate cancer. The protective effect is greatest while men are in their twenties. Those who had ejaculated more than five times per week in their twenties, for instance, were one-third less likely to develop aggressive prostate cancer later in life. Giles described it as a 'prostatic stagnation hypothesis,' he opined that 'the more you flush the ducts out, the less there is to hang around and damage the cells that line them.'

Leitzmann, et al in 2004, concluded in their study that ejaculation frequency is not related to increased risk of prostate cancer. The above results contradict those of previous studies, which had suggested that having had many sexual partners, or a high frequency of sexual activity, increased the risk of prostate cancer by up to 40 per cent. The key difference is that these earlier studies defined sexual activity as sexual intercourse, whereas the latest studies focused on the number of ejaculations, whether or not intercourse was involved.
[22] [23] [24] [25]

Regular menstrual cycles

A series of studies by Behavioural Endocrinologist, Winnifred Cutler and her colleagues at both Columbia and Stanford University found that women who have intercourse at least once per week have more regular cycles than abstainers or the sporadically active. Cutler argues that regular exposure to a loving partner has extraordinary effects on health and well-being. [26]

Practice safe sex

As I have shown you, there are many health benefits of sex. In today's stressful society, it has become more difficult to have la petit mort as often as one would like, but if you make a conscious effort to change, you'll realize that it's really worth it. The health benefits of sex will induce in you a sense of well being within and without, and you will gradually notice that the more sex you have the more bounce you will have in each step.

Happiness isn't just a function of sex itself, but sex does play a role in human happiness. But remember, sexually transmitted infections (STIs) know no age boundary; so if you are sexually active, always practice safe sex.

References

1. Pearsall, P. (1994). *Sexual Healing: Using the Power of an Intimate, Loving Relationship to Heal Your Body and Soul.* New York: Crown Publishers.

2. Weeks, D. J., James, J., James, J., & Weeks, D. (1998). *Secrets of the Superyoung: The Scientific Reasons Some People Look Ten Years Younger Than They Really Are--and how You Can, Too.* New York: Villard.

3. Smith, G. D., Frankel, S. & Yarnell, J. (1997). *Sex and Death: Are They Related? Findings from the Caerphilly Cohort Study. BMJ, 315*(7123), 1641-1644.

4. Wood, H. (2003). Sex Cells. *Nature Reviews Neuroscience, 4*(2), 88-88.

5. Ebrahim, S., May, M., Shlomo, Y. B., McCarron, P., Frankel, S., Yarnell, J. & Smith, G. D. (2002). *Sexual Intercourse and Risk of Ischaemic Stroke and Coronary Heart Disease: The Caerphilly Study. Journal of Epidemiology and Community Health, 56*(2), 99-102.

6. Rerkpattanapipat, P., Stanek, M. S., & Kotler, M. N. (2001). *Sex and the Heart: What is the Role of the Cardiologist?. European Heart Journal, 22*(3), 201-208.

7. Larson, J. L., McNaughton, M. W., Kennedy, J. W. & Mansfield, L. W. (1980). *Heart Rate and Blood Pressure Responses to Sexual Activity and a Stair-climbing Test. Heart & Lung: The Journal of Critical Care, 9*(6), 1025.

8. Gorgov, A. N. (1978). *Barrier Contraceptive Practice and Male Infertility as Related Factors to Breast Cancer in Married Women. Medical Hypotheses, 4*(2), 79-88.

9 *Sex-as-exercise the-hard-facts.* Retrieved April 2012, from http://www.healthnews.ediets.com/fitness-exercise/sex-as-exercise-the-hard-facts.html

10. Brody, S. (2006). *Blood Pressure Reactivity to Stress is Better for People Who Recently Had Penile–Vaginal Intercourse Than for People Who Had Other or No Sexual Activity. Biological Psychology, 71*(2), 214-222.

11. Brody, S., Veit, R., & Rau, H. (2000). *A Preliminary Report Relating Frequency of Vaginal Intercourse to Heart Rate Variability, Valsalva Ratio, Blood Pressure, and Cohabitation Status. Biological Psychology, 52*(3), 251-257.

12. Light, K. C., Grewen, K. M., & Amico, J. A. (2005). *More Frequent Partner Hugs and Higher Oxytocin Levels are Linked to Lower Blood Pressure and Heart Rate in Premenopausal Women. Biological Psychology, 69*(1), 5-21.

13. Burleson, M. H., Trevathan, W. R., & Todd, M. (2007). *In the Mood for Love or Vice Versa? Exploring the Relations Among Sexual Activity, Physical Affection,*

Affect, and Stress in the Daily Lives of Mid-aged Women. Archives of Sexual Behavior, 36(3), 357-368.

14. Montorsi, F., Padma-Nathan, H. & Glina, S. (2006). *Erectile Function and Assessments of Erection Hardness Correlate Positively with Measures of Emotional Well-being, Sexual Satisfaction, and Treatment Satisfaction in Men with Erectile Dysfunction Treated with Sildenafil Citrate (Viagra). Urology, 68*(3 Suppl), 26.

15. Gallup, G. G. J., Burch, R. L. & Platek, S. M. (2002). *Does Semen Have Antidepressant Properties?. Archives of Sexual Behavior, 31*(3), 289-293.

16. Gouin, J. P., Carter, C. S., Pournajafi-Nazarloo, H., Glaser, R., Malarkey, W. B., Loving, T. J., & Kiecolt-Glaser, J. K. (2010). *Marital Behavior, Oxytocin, Vasopressin, and Wound Healing. Psychoneuroendocrinology, 35*(7), 1082-1090.

17. Phillips, W. J., Ostrovsky, O., Galli, R. L. & Dickey, S. (2006). *Relief of Acute Migraine Headache with Intravenous Oxytocin. Journal of Pain and Palliative Care Pharmacotherapy, 20*(3), 25-28.

18. Uryvaev, Y. V., & Petrov, G. A. (1996). *Extremely Low Doses of Oxytocin Reduce Pain Sensitivity in Men. Bulletin of Experimental Biology and Medicine, 122*(5), 1071-1073.

19. Whipple, B. & Komisaruk, B. R. (1985). *Elevation of Pain Threshold By Vaginal Stimulation in Women. Pain, 21*(4), 357-367.

20. Whipple, B., & Komisaruk, B. R. (1988). *Analgesia Produced in Women By Genital Self-stimulation. Journal of Sex Research, 24*(1), 130-140.

21. Charnetski, C. J. & Brennan, F.X. (2004). *Sexual Frequency and Salivary Immunoglobulin a (IgA). Psychological Reports, 94*(3), 839-844.

22. Giles, G. G., Severi, G., English, D. R., McCredie, M. R. E., Borland, R., Boyle, P. & Hopper, J. L. (2003). *Sexual Factors and Prostate Cancer. BJU International, 92*(3), 211-216.

23. Leitzmann, M. F., Platz, E. A., Stampfer, M. J., Willett, W. C., & Giovannucci, E. (2004). *Ejaculation Frequency and Subsequent Risk of Prostate Cancer. JAMA: The Journal of the American Medical Association, 291*(13), 1578-1586.

24. Fox, D. (2003). *Masturbating May Protect Against Prostate Cancer. New Scientist.* Retrieved January 23, 2013 from http://www.newscientist.com/article/dn3942-.html

25. Eeles, R. & Dearnaley, D. (2009). *Sexual Activity and Prostate Cancer Risk in Men Diagnosed at a Younger Age. BJU International, 103*(2), 178-185.

26. Cutler, W. B., Garcia, C. R., & Krieger, A. M. (1979). *Sexual Behavior Frequency and Menstrual Cycle Length in Mature Premenopausal Women. Psychoneuroendocrinology,* 4(4), 297-309.

Bibliography

27. Foster, D. K. (2005). *Sexual Healing.* Ventura CA. Regal Books.

28. Keesling, B. (2006). *Sexual Healing: The Completest Guide to Overcoming Common Sexual Problems.* Alameda: Hunter House.

29. Levine, P. A. (2003). Audio CD. *Sexual Healing.* Louisville, CO: Sounds True, Incorporated.

30. Maltz, W. (2002). *Treating the Sexual Intimacy Concerns of Sexual Abuse Survivors. Sexual and Relationship Therapy,* 17(4), 321-327.

31. Nelson, J. (2005). *Sexual Healing: A Novel.* Rockefeller Center, New York: Pocket Books.

Sexercise
Get Fit For Sex

Your sexual performance is enhanced and the quality of the pleasure experienced is improved if you are fit. So, let us show you how to get fit for sex in this chapter.

Exercise boosts sexual performance!

We all know that being physically fit confers all kinds of benefits, but did you know that regular exercise can boost sexual desire and enhance sexual pleasure? Regretfully, it is one of the most important and often overlooked components of a good sex life. Good sex is as an act of intimacy that promotes health and well-being, providing us with significant physical and physiological benefits especially if enjoyed in the context of a happy relationship, says Paul Pearsall, author of the book, *Super Immunity: Master Your Emotions and Improve Your Health*. He also reminds us that "sex boosts chemicals in the body that protect us against diseases." [1]

Is there any proof that exercise can enhance your sexuality? A study done in 1982, found that increased time spent in physical activity was associated with a higher reported frequency of sexual behaviour and frequency of desired sexual activity among a population of college undergraduate students. [2] In 2000, a further study concluded that physical endurance, muscle tone, and body composition all improved sexual functioning.[3] The most common question that my male patients ask is, 'Can exercise prevent erectile dysfunction (ED) and lead to an increase in staying power?' Well, I have some good news. Researchers have shown that, exercise activates the sympathetic nervous system, encouraging blood-flow to the genital region. Here is also a wake up call for all you couch potatoes; according to the literature, sedentary men could significantly lower their risk of erectile dysfunction by burning at least 200 calories per day (equal to fast-walking for about 2 miles). It has also been reported that women were more sexually responsive following 20 minutes of vigorous exercise. [4] So a pre-sex work out should definitely be part of your fore play.

Among males, short intense exercise is linked with increased testosterone levels, which may stimulate sexual interest and behaviour. Conversely, too much exercise is associated with a decrease in testosterone and other male hormones, which may decrease sexual desire.[3]

So if your partner is experiencing a sexual slump send him to the gym, if you are not yet convinced, here is the most compelling evidence I have seen so far. An extensive long term study was reported in 2003, by Bacon, et al. The researchers examined data from 31,742 men, ages 53-90 in the health professionals follow-up study of dentists, optometrists, podiatrists, pharmacists, and veterinarians to determine which lifestyle factors affected the risk of erectile dysfunction. Results of this study found that men over 50 who were physically active had a 30 per cent lower risk of impotence compared with inactive men. [5] Finally, a Harvard University study of 160 male and female swimmers in their 40s and 60s showed a positive relationship between regular physical activity and the frequency and enjoyment of sexual intercourse. [3] The conclusions drawn from the above studies are that physical exercise will boost your sexual appetite and improve your sexual performance.

A good work out will elevate your endorphin levels, relieve stress, promote weight loss and rejuvenate the body. An active exercise program will therefore fill you with renewed vigour, boost your confidence and slow the aging process. Regular exercise also increases blood flow to the genitals, in men and women- a natural Viagra. Remember that good sex can be physically demanding, so improving cardiovascular fitness with aerobic activities such as walking, running, cycling or swimming for at least 30 minutes, three times per week, will help you and your partner to perform longer and more frequently. To strengthen the shoulders, chest and abdominal, all of which are utilized during sexual intercourse I would also like to recommend that you add push-ups and sit-ups or crunches.

Novel sexercises

Let me now introduce you to some novel 'sexercises' recommended by Amy Painter a writer for *Discovery Health*. [6]

Kegel's exercises

The muscles of locomotion in your arms or legs are quite active during the day but the secret sex muscles are rarely active when you do your routine chores. However, by strengthening these muscles, you and your partner can enjoy more intense and fulfilling sex. This secret muscle is called *'The PC'* muscle, which stands for pubococcygeus muscles. It is actually a sling of muscles that support the pelvic floor and surround the internal genitalia. These muscles are involved in urination (when you stop yourself from urinating in mid-stream, you're using your PC muscles). Both men and women have PC muscles. Like any muscles in the body, the PC muscles can become weak for many reasons such as: childbirth, old age, severe weight loss, radiation treatments for cancer etc.

Here are four tips to find your PC muscle:

- Try to stop the flow of urine when you are sitting on the toilet. If you can do it, you are using the right muscles

- Imagine that you are trying to stop passing gas. Squeeze the muscles you would use. If you sense a pulling feeling, those are the right muscles for pelvic exercises

- For women, lie down and put your finger inside your vagina. Squeeze as if you were trying to stop urine from coming out. If you feel tightness on your finger, you are squeezing the right pelvic muscle.

- For men you can also determine that you've got the right muscle by inserting a lubricated finger covered by a finger cot in the anus and squeezing your PC muscle. If you feel pressure around your finger, you're using the right muscles.

'Kegel's exercises restore muscle tone and strength to the pubococcygeus muscles. They are named after Los Angeles physician Arnold Kegel. These exercises are recommended for both men and women:

- To prevent or reduce pelvic floor problems and to increase sexual gratification
- To treat vaginal prolapse and prevent uterine prolapse in women
- For treating prostate pain and swelling resulting from benign prostatic hyperplasia (BPH) and prostatitis in men
- For treating urinary incontinence in both men and women
- To enhance sexual enjoyment and change the way orgasms feel
- To help men learn greater ejaculatory control

You can make these pelvic floor muscles stronger with a few minutes of exercise every day. The basic exercise can be done anytime and anywhere. Just squeeze your PC muscles as hard as you can, and hold them. Start by squeezing and holding for a count of 3-5 seconds, then release and relax for 5 seconds. As a guideline, try to work up to a point where you can hold the squeeze for ten seconds. And try to work up to doing ten repetitions of Kegel exercises per set. So you squeeze, hold for ten second, release, relax for ten seconds, and repeat ten times. Do the exercise 3-4 times per day. Do them during foreplay, before you have an orgasm, and even while having an orgasm. You may notice that Kegel's enhances sexual excitement and increases the intensity of your orgasms.

Pelvic Lifts

The following pelvic exercises will help keep the muscles used during sex strong and flexible and help facilitate orgasm. Each activity can be done in the bedroom on a firm mattress or on the floor. Wear either loose clothing or nothing at all, and consider playing your favourite mood music. Lie on your back with knees bent and slightly apart. Feet should be flat on the floor and arms at your side.

Inhale, clenching your abdominal and buttocks and lifting the pelvis until your back is straight. Take care not to arch your back. Breathe as you hold the position for at least ten seconds. Exhale as you lower your body and repeat the exercise.

The pelvic bounce

After you complete your lifts, try a few pelvic bounces, an exercise that can evoke strong sexual feelings. As with the pelvic lift, knees are bent and slightly apart. Your palms should face up. Inhale and lift your pelvis just slightly off the ground. Then, exhale and let it down so your lower back bounces gently against the floor.

The butterfly

Lie on your back with knees bent, feet should be together and flat on the bed. Next, pull your feet in until they touch your buttocks. Turn your ankles so the soles of your feet are facing each other and touching. Your knees will point out to the sides of the bed.

Lower your knees toward the bed taking care not to force them down. You or your partner may gently press downward on your inner thighs. When your knees are as far apart as is comfortable, hold for 60 seconds. Gently bring the knees back together with your hands and relax.

This exercise can also be done sitting up, back-to-back with your partner. Sit up as straight as possible with your spines pressed gently together. Relax your shoulders and keep your head in line with your spine. Bring your feet in as close to your body as possible, and turn them so your soles touch and knees point out. Clasp your feet. Breathe deeply and watch as your knees begin to lower, taking care not to force the knees down.

The butterfly is also beneficial for menstrual irregularities, urinary problems and is thought to help ease the pain of childbirth.

Aerobics

There are many other exercises and stretches that can enhance not only your sex lives but your mental and physical health. Yoga and dance classes offer good workouts and help stretch the pelvic region. Swimming and other sports that involve kicking motions are also beneficial.

| SEXERCISE

Regular exercise of almost any kind releases the pleasure hormone endorphin and improves cardiovascular fitness, strength and endurance. So, commit yourself to start a sexercise program today, it might be that added boost you need to add sparkle to your relationship.

References

1. Pearsall, P. (1987). *Superimmunity: Master Your Emotions & Improve Your Health.* New York:McGraw-Hill Book Company.

2. Frauman, D. C. (1982). *The Relationship Between Physical Exercise, Sexual Activity, and Desire For Sexually Activity.* The Journal of Sex Research, 18(1), 41-46.

3. Krucoff, C., & Krucoff, M. (2000). *Peak Performance. How A Regular Exercise Program Can Enhance Sexuality and Help Prevent Prostate Cancer.* American Fitness, 18(6), 32-37.

4. Stanten, M. (2003). *4 Workouts to Improve Your Love Life.* Prevention, 55(5), 76.

5. Bacon, C. G., Mittleman, M. A., Kawachi, I., Giovannucci, E., Glasser, D. B., & Rimm, E. B. (2003). *Sexual Function in Men Older Than 50 Years of Age: Results from the Health Professionals Follow-up Study.* Ann Intern Med, 139(3), 161-168.

6. *Exercises for Sex.* Retrieved January 23,2013,from http://www.sexual-health/sexuality/exercises-for-sex-dictionary.html

Bibliography

7. Bordo, S. (2004). *Unbearable Weight: Feminism, Western Culture, and the Body.* Berkeley, California: University of California Press.

8. Bortz, W. M. (1999). *Physical Fitness, Aging, and Sexuality.* Western Journal of Medicine, 170(3), 167.

9. Haavio-Mannila, E., & Purhonen, S. (2001). *Slimness and Self-rated Sexual Attractiveness: Comparisons of Men and Women in Two Cultures.* Journal of Sex Research, 38(2), 102-110.

10. O'Relly, E. (1967). *Sexercises, Isometric and Isotonic.* Gravesend, Kent: Bell Publishing Company.

11. Russell, W. D., & Cox, R. H. (2003). *Social Physique Anxiety, Body Dissatisfaction, and Self-esteem in College Females of Differing Exercise Frequency, Perceived Weight Discrepancy, and Race.* Journal of Sport Behavior, Vol 26(3), 297-318.

12. Summers, A. (2006). *Sexercise: Spice Up Your Sex Life and Get Fit in the Process.* London: Ebury Press (A Division of the Random House Group Ltd).

13. Sussman,L.(2002). *Sexercise*. London: Carlton books Ltd.

14. Falk, P. (1994). *The Consuming Body* (Vol. 30). London, United Kingdom: Sage Publications Limited.

15. Turner, B. S. (2008). *The Body and Society: Explorations in Social Theory.* London, United Kingdom: Sage Publications Limited.

16. Weiss, J. (1997). *Not Tonight Honey, I've Got a Body Ache: Physique Honed But Sex Life Sagging? Maybe You Should Change the Focus of Your Workouts. Womens Sports and Fitness, 19,* 66-68.

17. Wiederman, M. W., & Hurst, S. R. (1998). *Body Size, Physical Attractiveness, and Body Image Among Young Adult Women: Relationships to Sexual Experience and Sexual Esteem. Journal of Sex Research, 35*(3), 272-281.

18. Wilmore, J. H. (2003). *Aerobic Exercise and Endurance: Improving Fitness for Health Benefits. The Physician and Sports Medicine, 31*(5), 45.

Rekindling Desire
How To Do It

You are now fit for sex, but to quote Mignon McLaughlin, "Desire is in men a hunger, in women only an appetite". Your desire is waxing and waning. The fire that once burnt bright is going dim. You need to rekindle the fire. This chapter will show you how.

Sex can be a terrible wedge

As we discussed in chapter one, passion fades with time and has to be replaced by intimacy and commitment. So, many couples have been to see me quite perturbed that their love has grown cold and their sex life has lost its appeal. Let me therefore remind you of the admonition given by Mark Schoen, Director of Sex Education for the Sinclair Intimacy Institute. He states that 'a good sex **life** is an important part of an individual's overall health' and that 'people who have a good sex life feel better mentally and physically'. Dr. Linda Banner, a licensed sex therapist specializing in marriage and relationship counselling and a researcher associated with Stanford University Medical School, also advises us that 'sex can be a wonderful cementer or a terrible wedge' for relationships.

In the beginning of a new relationship most couples experience very passionate sex. Just the thought of your lover evokes paroxysms of desire. This is the result of chemistry and novelty. It's always exciting to explore unknown territory but over time the chemistry and novelty wear off and passion diminishes. I must emphasize to all couples that passion inevitably decreases over time. When lovers settle into the comfort and stability of a long term relationship, it is natural and normal for it to change and become less intense and sometimes boredom sets in. In other words, love may remain constant, but passion comes and goes in waves. It needs fuel in order to stay alive. To sustain passion over time takes work, creativity and commitment. It requires a conscious decision from each partner to make it a priority. Remember, losing that 'in love feeling' is a normal developmental stage of love relationships. In order to bring romance back into your relationship, you first need to understand why it left. [1]

What has happened neuro-chemically?

When you and your partner were in the early stages of courtship, the euphoria of infatuation had help from your brain. There is strong evidence that the altered state, or high of infatuation and attraction is accompanied by neurochemical changes. In this stage, your brain was flooded with a powerful chemical cocktail (including phenyl ethylamine (PEA), an amphetamine-like neurotransmitter - dopamine, a neurotransmitter associated with pleasure, and nor epinephrine, a neurotransmitter associated with exhilaration, excessive energy, and feelings of excitement) that let you feel boundless energy, optimistic, hyper-aroused, etc. The effects of this cocktail is short-lived, however, and when the high is gone, you and your partner might experience a condition called dysphoria. This is not the end of love, but the beginning. Now you can see your partner how he or she really is, instead of a love-blind, idealized version of him/her, and enter the next phases of your relationship, intimacy and commitment.

What has happened behaviourally?

The first noticeable change often coincides with living together. When you know that you'll see each other tomorrow and the next day and the next day sex becomes less urgent. You're also likely to be seeing a lot more of each other's daily living habits. You may also have children around which can make it harder to find the time and the privacy that you used to enjoy. You must now nurture and maintain the relationship. Nurturance includes the meaningful and rewarding activities couples engage in to strengthen the relationship, such as give massages, send flowers, take baths, go for long walks, dine out, send a card, dance, laugh, exercise, play cards or board games, express love, gratitude, appreciation, attraction, dreams and hopes.

Maintenance includes the day-to-day responsibilities we all have to attend to in order to get by, such as earn a living, clean the house, pay the bills, shop for groceries, do the laundry and run errands. Early in your relationship you probably spent 90 per cent of your time on nurturance, and only ten per cent on maintenance. As time passed, the percentages naturally evened out to a more realistic and sustainable 50/50. However, as more time passed, the scales may have tipped far in the other direction perhaps your nurturance activities are only ten per cent while the maintenance activities are 90 per cent. If you feel distressed, disconnected or disappointed, it means that it's time to shift the balance and engage in more nurturance behaviours. It's time to work hard at love, just like you did when you were dating.

What has happened sexually?

Your sexual relationship has probably stagnated. You can usually predict with close to 100 per cent accuracy what will happen the next time you and your partner will have sex. Sex has become routine, predictable and boring. You can generate more sexual passion by ending the conspiracy of silence and bringing your full sexual and erotic self to the bedroom. [2]

How to rekindle the spark

Now that we understand why the glow of love fades, let us put in place the formula for resuscitating your flagging desire. Here are just a few ideas to get you started:

Communication — talking and touching bring you and your partner closer together. Opening up the lines of communication, when both partners are willing to try something different, can be arousing in itself. Try it and see what happens. Discuss the changes you are going through and how you can accommodate each other during sex.

Try different positions — a little bit of lubrication, massage and cuddling. Ask your partner about his or her needs. Instead of saying what you don't like or criticizing, try being positive and offering an alternative. 'Instead of...' is a good starter, instead of starting by lying down on the bed, let's start by standing up in the hallway.

Share fantasies - caution here! — some fantasies are best kept to yourself.

Introduce new behaviour — instead of beginning by kissing, then breast play, genital play and ending in intercourse, begin with genital play; move to breast stimulation, then kissing then ear stimulation and back to intercourse. In other words change your routine, incorporate erotica, or sex toys in foreplay. Initiate sex in an unexpected place, or at an unexpected time.

Allow for and create different types of sexual experiences: playful, tender, explicit, fast, light-hearted, emotional, brief, prolonged, etc. Devote time to visualizing and anticipating a sexual encounter with your partner. Make an effort to always look your best for your partner and keep yourself in good health.

Create romance — while it may take a little longer to get aroused, take that time to explore each other's bodies and put a little bit of romance back into your lives together.

- Light a candle
- Give each other a sensual massage
- Dress up (or down!)
- Take a shower or a bath together
- Buy something sexy for your partner or yourself and stimulate your partner visually
- Change the scenery - bathroom, living room, dining room
- Watch an erotic movie together to get you in the mood or share an erotic story
- Experiment with new sexual positions
- Change the way you initiate sex - maybe something more daring or more romantic

- Play sex games

- Learn a new stimulation technique

- Go to your local bookstore and read sex books with your partner and then talk about what you just read. What did you like, dislike, want to try etc.

- Be bold, daring and adventurous.

Keeping the sexual spark alive in a marriage or in a long-term relationship can be challenging. However, if couples take time to cultivate and maintain healthy and satisfying sexual relations they will keep the flames of love burning for many years to come.

I hope you will soon bask in the glow of re-united love.

References

1. Banner, L. (2004). *Advanced Sexual Techniques* (Vol. 2). Philadelphia PA: Running Press.

2. Banner, L., et al (2005). Sexplorations.Widescreen Studio: Sinclair Institute.

Coping Skills For The Frustrated Woman
Circumventing Sexual Obstacles

Sometimes, despite the intensity of the passion and the depth of the arousal, many women find sex quite challenging due to either emotional or physical obstacles. We will review in the chapter some techniques for circumventing them.

COPING SKILLS FOR THE FRUSTRATED WOMAN

Many sexually active women become quite frustrated when the anticipated pleasure is not realized, or is replaced by pain or disappointment. This chapter will walk you through the sexual challenges some women face and propose the appropriate skills to circumvent these.

Coping with a large member

Most women are quite unperturbed about penis size but there is a small subgroup that is challenged by a really large penis or an abnormally small one. The average penis is five to seven inches long in its erect state and about 10 per cent of men fall below or above this range. If your partner is larger than average, sex can be uncomfortable or painful, but you can still enjoy it if you follow these guidelines:

- Extend your foreplay to enhance your arousal
- Use adequate lubrication such as Astroglide or KY jelly
- Approach insertion gently, preferably using the male dominant position (man on top)
- Avoid retro-copulation (doggy style) sex since this shortens the vagina and could cause discomfort
- Try the female dominant position (woman on top) since this allows the woman to exercise better control over the depth of penetration. The sitting position is also a reasonable option
- Please encourage your partner to have slow gentle sex and a potentially painful experience could become a very pleasurable one

Coping with a small member

If you partner's penis is below average, sex can also be gratifying. Try these techniques:

The best position for a small penis is rear entry since this allows your partner maximal penetration. A reasonable alternative is the sitting position. Let your partner have a warm shower before sex it will enhance his turgidity.

Coping with a bent member

Men who have bent penises (Peyronie's disease) might find penetration a bit problematic. In this case the spoon position or rear entry is recommended; of course this condition might have to be surgically corrected to enable them to return to normal functioning.

Coping with an impotent man

If your man is impotent this could be quite challenging to a relationship; but do not despair. Nowadays, there are many treatment options for men with erectile dysfunction (ED).

Don't be overly critical of him but gently encourage him to seek help so that the cause of his ED can be identified and appropriate treatment given. Your man might be unwilling to admit that he has ED, but of course you know.

Please remind him that these treatment options are available:

Phosphodiesterase inhibitors — Sildenafil, Tadalafil, and Vardenafil which increase blood flow to the penis after adequate stimulation.

The vacuum pump — which creates suction and promotes engorgement of his member.

Intra cavernosal injection — which is a technique in which a special medicine is injected into the shaft of the penis causing it to become erect.

MUSE — 'medicated urethral suppository for erection', another approach in which a medical pellet is squeezed into the urethra causing an erection.

Penile implants — is the surgical insertion of inflatable implants into the penis.

It is interesting to note that a man can have an orgasm even without an erection. Therefore sex play can be quite satisfying even in the impotent. (See Sexual desires disorders)

Coping with premature ejaculation

Premature ejaculation is quite common especially in young men. You can help him to overcome this in a number of ways:

- Avoid the male dominant position, many men find this position quite challenging. They will perform better with the female dominant position or the spoon position.

- Pre sex masturbation can in many cases improve your mate's prowess. Let him try it, he might like it.

- Try the squeeze method; ask him to tell you when he is about to lose control then let him withdraw and squeeze the shaft of the penis firmly, when his sexual tension subsides let him continue, repeat this as often as possible.

- You can apply local anaesthetics to his glans; there are many brands on the market. These will desensitize the head of the penis and increase his prowess. If used with a condom the results can be quite gratifying.

- Finally learn the art of Tantric sex. This teaches the man to really appreciate intimacy without the anxiety of having to prove his virility and sexual capability.

I trust that these newfound skills will help you to overcome these sexual obstacles which often dampen the quality of gratification.

Bibliography

1. Cox, T. (1999). *Hot Sex: How To Do It*. New York: Bantam.

2. McCarthy, B. (2003). *Rekindling Desire: A Step By Step Program To Help Low-sex and No-sex Marriages*. Abingdon, United Kingdom: Routledge.

3. Nelson, J. (2009). *Let's Get It On: A Novel*. New York, New York: Amistad Press (Imprint of HarperCollins Publishers).

The Joys of Solo Sex

Woody Allen reminds us that — "having sex is like playing bridge. If you don't have a good partner, you'd better have a good hand".

So, get ready for a roller coaster ride as I introduce you to the joys of solo sex.

For most readers even the mention of solo sex induces acute anxiety and feelings of guilt, because most of us have been enculturated to think that solo sex is immoral and a threat to our health. Let me therefore unravel this mysterious taboo for you.

Liberating masturbation

Masturbation also called self love, solo sex, self pleasure and onanism is the self-stimulation of the genitals to achieve sexual arousal and pleasure, usually to the point of orgasm. The history of masturbation is filled with moral condemnation and scientific inaccuracies regarding its negative effects. Around 1712, an anonymous doctor published a text entitled: *Onania; or, The Heinous Sin of Self Pollution, and all its Frightful Consequences*. The text warned against the dangers of defiling your own body, and offered a series of cures including amputation of the penis as a way to cure the habit in compulsive males. [1] As recently as the late nineteenth century, medical doctors condemned masturbation as inimical to mental health. Both corn flakes and Graham crackers were developed in an effort to curb masturbatory impulses in young boys. [2]

Between 1856 and 1932, the U.S. patent office approved 33 patents for anti-masturbation devices. The release of Alfred Kinsey's two groundbreaking surveys of *Sexual Behaviour in the Human Male*, published in 1948 and *Sexual Behaviour in the Human Female*, published in 1953, helped to defray many of these well established beliefs.[3] [4]

In 1974, Betty Dodson, considered by many to be the grandmother of masturbation, published *Liberating Masturbation: A Meditation on Self Love* which further helped to de-stigmatize solo sex. [5] [6] Masturbation is now regarded as a normal, healthy sexual activity that is pleasant, fulfilling, acceptable and safe. It is only considered a problem if it is compulsive, inhibits sexual activity with a partner, is done in public, or causes significant distress to the person.

Religion and self love

Many Christians strongly believe that self love is immoral because in their opinion, sex should primarily be for procreation and in the absence of a desire for procreation is narcissistic. They also insist that the *Bible* specifically prohibits onanism or masturbation. This objection relates to the story of Onan in the Old Testament (Genesis 38:8 and 9). Onan was told to copulate with his deceased brother's childless widow according to the custom of the Hebrews, but he failed to follow the order and spilled his seed. An act that was deemed to be a great sin at that time with a punishment of death.

In his book, *The Sexual Man*, Dr. Archibald Hart revealed the results of a survey of some 600 Christian men, on the topic of masturbation: [7]

- 61 per cent of married Christian men masturbate
- 82 per cent of these have self sex on an average of once a week
- 10 per cent have solo sex with self five to ten times per month
- 6 per cent, more than 15 times per month
- 1 per cent, more than 20 times a month
- 13 per cent of Christian married men said they felt it was normal

From the above studies, it is obvious that masturbation is widely practiced among the clergy and the laity and the high incidence of solo sex among the married men is instructive. I am firmly of the belief that the church should seriously rethink its position on masturbation since it is widely practiced among church goers and is a highly recommended form of safe sex.

Myths about masturbation

Solo sex has been a human activity plagued with myths over the years; but we do know that masturbation does not cause:

- Blindness
- Feeble mindedness
- Madness
- Physical decrepitude
- Sexual perversion
- Reduced sexual function
- Neurotic disorders
- The growth of hair on your palms
- Acne

- Sexually transmitted diseases.
- Low sperm count

Who masturbates?

The prevailing belief by many is that masturbation is primarily a male dominated activity and that women rarely masturbate; but in 2002, Pinkerton published a study of undergraduate college students which revealed that: 98 per cent of men and 44 per cent of women reported having ever masturbated, the men reported masturbating an average of 12 times per month, while the women reported an average of 4.7 times per month.[8] In another study also done in 2002 by Robinson et al of African-American women aged 15 to 64, 62 per cent reported that they had masturbated at some point during their lives. [9] Laumann et al in his study in 1994, also reported that about 60 per cent of men and 40 per cent of women reported masturbating in the past year and that nearly 85 per cent of men and 45 per cent of women who were living with a sexual partner reported masturbating in the past year. He also discovered that 35 per cent of American men aged 18-39 do not masturbate while 37 per cent masturbate sometimes, and 28 per cent one or more times per week. [10] The study, done by Janus and Janus in 1993, revealed that 53 per cent of men and 25 per cent of women masturbated for the first time by ages 11 to 13 and that only 5 per cent of men and 11 per cent of women have never masturbated. [11]

So there you have it, both sexes enjoy solo sex, even though men do enjoy it more.

Why do people masturbate?

Self love has been shown to have the following benefits:

Sexual benefits

By exploring your own body through masturbation, you can determine what is erotically pleasing to you and can share this with your partner.

It is a safe sex practice that carries no risk of sexually transmitted infection and unwanted pregnancy.

It allows persons to express their sexuality by themselves and is valuable if, for example, they don't have a partner or if sex with their partner isn't possible.

It is a useful treatment for sexual dysfunction such as premature ejaculation and anorgasmia.

If you have specific nonsexual handicaps that prevent you from easily acquiring partners such as a small stature, physical deformity or a crippling disability, you may be able, in spite of these handicaps, to lead an active sex life through masturbation.

Health benefits

Sexual arousal and orgasm in solo sex triggers the release of oxytocin which has been shown in studies to be a potent analgesic (pain reliever) for headaches, menstrual cramps and muscle aches. It also promotes feelings of affection and nurturing and helps to reduce stress levels.

Sex encourages the release of testosterone, (which strengthens bones and muscles) and DHEA (a hormone that is important in the function of the body's immune system).

In women, oestrogen levels increase during arousal, enhancing her overall health. Endorphins are released during an orgasm and retards depression. It also improves sleep and reduce cholesterol levels.

Prevention of cancer

Giles in a ground breaking study in 2003 has shown that the more you ejaculate between the ages of 20 and 50, the less likely they are to develop prostate cancer. [12]

Improved emotional health

Autoerotic behaviour has been shown to:

- Enhance well being

- Relieve anxiety, self-doubt and depression

- Be useful as a shame-attacking and guilt-attacking homework assignment in rational-emotive therapy (RET) and other forms of cognitive-behaviour therapy

If you practice solo sex, the usual principles of personal hygiene must always be followed, namely, clean hands and fingernails, and the stimulation should not be too vigorous. Women should never insert anything sharp, breakable or anything that cannot be easily removed, into their vagina and should not share toys due to the risk of STDs.

I will end with a quotation from Dr. Joycelyn Elders, M.D., former Surgeon General of the U.S. 'Masturbation, practiced consciously or unconsciously, cultivates in us a humble elegance - awareness that we are part of a larger natural system, the passions and rhythms of which live on in us. Sexuality is part of creation, part of our common inheritance, and it reminds us that we are neither inherently better nor worse than our sisters and brothers. Far from evil, masturbation just may render heavenly contentment in those who dare.'

References

1. Unknown author (June 1986). *Onania, or the Heinous Sin of Self Pollution and All Its Frightful Consequences in Both Sexes Considered (Marriage, Sex, and the Family in England, 1660-1800)*. Abingdon, United Kingdom: Taylor & Francis.

2. Kellogg, J. H. (1888). T*reatment for Self-Abuse and Its Effects: Plain Facts for Old and Young.* Burlington, Iowa: F. Segner & Co.

3. Kinsey, A., Pomeroy, W. B. & Martin, C. E. (1948). *Sexual Behavior in the Human Male.* Bloomington, Ind.: Indiana University Press.

4. Kinsey, A. C. (1953). *Sexual Behavior in the Human Female.* Philadelphia: WB Saunders.

5. Dodson, B. (1976). *Liberating Masturbation: A Meditation on Self Love.* New York: Dodson.

6. Dodson, B. (1996). *Sex For One: The Joy of Selfloving.* New York: Crown Trade Paperbacks.

7. Hart, A. D. (1994). *The Sexual Man.* Dallas: Word Pub.

8. Pinkerton, S. D., Bogart, L. M., Cecil, H. & Abramson, P. R. (2003). *Factors Associated With Masturbation in a Collegiate Sample. Journal of Psychology & Human Sexuality, 14*(2-3), 103-121.

9. Robinson, B. E., Bockting, W. O. & Harrell, T. (2003). *Masturbation and Sexual Health. Journal of Psychology & Human Sexuality, 14*(2-3), 85-102.

10, Laumann, E. O., Gagnon, J. H., Michael, R. T. & Michaels, S. (1994). *The Social Organization of Sexuality: Sexual Practices in the United States.* Chicago: University of Chicago Press.

11. Janus, S. S. & Janus, C. L. (1993). *The Janus Report on Sexual Behavior.* New York: John Wiley & Sons.

12. Giles, G. G., Severi, G., English, D. R., McCredie, M. R. E., Borland, R., Boyle, P. & Hopper, J. L. (2003). *Sexual Factors and Prostate Cancer. BJU International, 92*(3), 211-216.

Bibliography

13. Allison, S. (2001). *Tickle Your Fancy: A Woman's Guide to Sexual Self-pleasure.* San Francisco: Tickle Kitty Press.

14. Cornog, M. (2003). *The Big Book of Masturbation: From Angst to Zeal.* San Francisco: Down There Press.

Part 4 - SEXUAL DISORDERS

Part four of this book will describe for you the common male and female sexual disorders. I hope the information gleaned from these pages will enable you to identify these problems and equip you with the tools to overcome them.

Penis Stress
Does Size Really Matter?

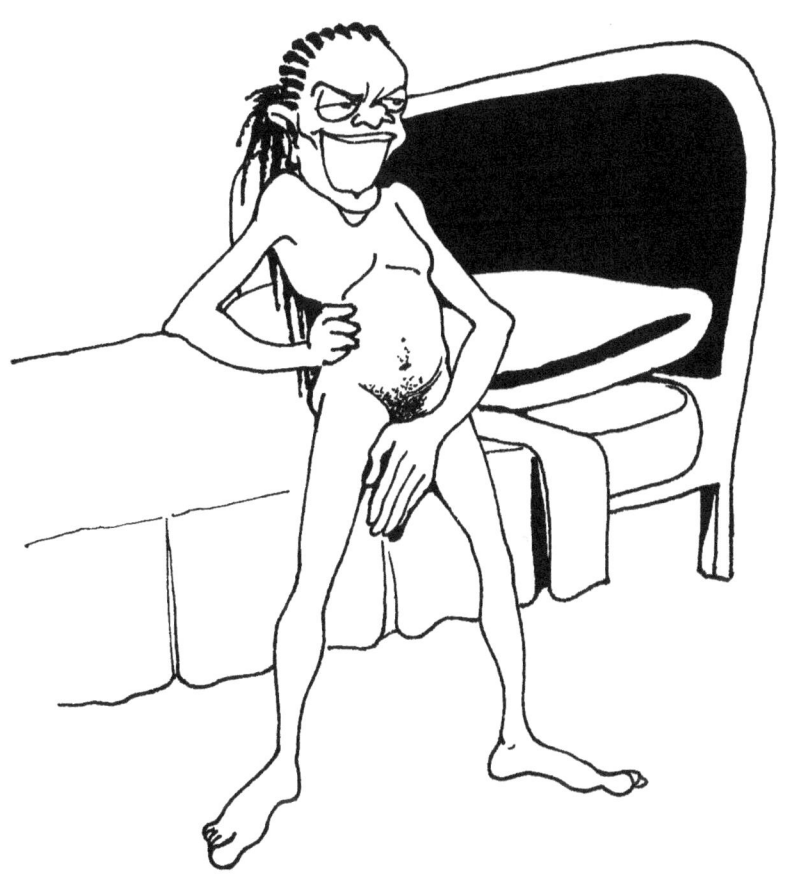

Does size really matter? Are you plagued with feelings of doubt about your masculinity due to your perceived impression of the size and shape of your member? Turn the page and get ready to be de-stressed.

A symbol of masculinity

I was recently consulted by a male patient who was planning to get married, but was absolutely petrified at the prospect, because in his mind he was not well endowed and would not be able to satisfy his spouse. He was suffering from a classic case of penis stress, a condition which is quite common in our macho society. This chapter should allay all the fears of men who are overly concerned about penis size.

The penis, particularly in its erect state, is a symbol of masculinity and in many cultures, it has come to symbolize attributes such as largeness, strength, endurance, ability, courage, intelligence, knowledge, dominance over men, possession of women and a symbol of loving and being loved.

There is compelling evidence that prehistoric cave dwellers attributed the symbolic values of strength and power to penile size, as well as those of virility and fertility. The male is often troubled by concerns that his penis is not large enough to satisfy his partner or himself. His penis size, shape, length, girth and appearance can be a cause for happiness or severe distress and can lead a man to go to extreme lengths to try to change its appearance. He often tries many methods, devices, pills, and exercises in the hope of enlarging it.

Here are some classical examples:

- Until the sixteenth century, men in the Topinama tribe of Brazil encouraged poisonous snakes to bite their penises to enlarge them for six months

- Wandering holy men in India or Sadhus are known to attach weights to their penises to elongate them

- Kayak men in Borneo pierce the glans of their penis and insert items into the holes to stimulate their partner

- Many men buy a plethora of potions and lengthening devices from the internet to enhance their virility

If a man is overly concerned about the size of his penis it is called the *small penis syndrome (SPS)*, or *locker room syndrome*. This is defined as an anxiety about the genitals being observed, directly or indirectly (when clothed) because of concern that the flaccid penis length and/or girth is less than the normal for an adult male, despite evidence from a clinical examination to counter this concern.

Urologist Kevan R. Wylie, et al, reviewed the literature on penis size in the June 2007, issue of the Urology Journal *BJU International*. He analyzed the findings of more than 50 international research projects on penile size and small penis syndrome carried out since 1942. Their findings were:

- Twelve studies which measured the penises of 11,531 men, discovered that average erect penises ranged from 14-16 centimetres (5.5 to 6.2 inches) in length and 12-13 centimetres (4.7 to 5.1 inches) in girth
- Sixty six per cent of men said their penis was average sized, 22 per cent said large and 12 per cent said small
- Eighty five per cent of women were satisfied with their partner's penile size, but only 55 per cent of men were satisfied
- Men with a larger penis both in length and circumference, have a better body image and genital image and have a feeling of greater sexual competence
- Ninety per cent of women prefer a wide penis to a long one
- Small penis syndrome is much more common in men with normal sized penises than those with a small or micropenis with a flaccid length of less than seven centimetres (2.7 inches)

There was little evidence of racial differences, with the exception of one Korean study where the men had smaller than average-sized penises. [1] Well, the jury is now out, most men are average and black men (sorry guys) are not more endowed than other races and contrary to what men believe, women prefer width rather than length. A well beloved myth has now been blown away.

What causes the small penis syndrome?

Penis envy

Sixty three per cent of men complaining of small penises said their anxieties started with childhood comparisons with an elder sibling a friend, or even his father and 37 per cent blamed erotic images viewed in their teenage years.

Relationships with others

Fears and anxieties about penile size might also arise after the breakdown of a relationship, or after derogatory or malicious remarks made by a partner during sexual activities. The denigrating remarks of other men might also have a profound effect on a man's self image.

Developmental issues

There is some evidence that for those men with poorly developed and small testicles, the problem might be accentuated, as there is no upward and forward lift to the penis, and so the genital bulge is minimal.

Psychiatric disorders

SPS might be part of a body dysmorphic disorder (BDD) which is a fixation on an imaginary flaw in the physical appearance resulting in embarrassment and fear of being scrutinized or mocked. SPS is also seen in certain psychiatric disorders such as obsessive-compulsive disorder, social phobia, anxiety and depression.

Obesity

In men who are overweight the penis cannot be seen with the abdominal overhang or the presence of a significant suprapubic fat pad causes the penis to be partly buried.

How is SPS treated?

It is recommended that the initial approach to a man who has SPS is a thorough urological, psychosexual, psychological and psychiatric assessment. Conservative approaches to therapy should be the initial interventions in all men namely:

Education — which gives the man some reassurance about the condition and his symptoms.

Mirror work — in which the patient is asked to look at himself undressed in front of a full-length mirror. By doing so, he will observe the penis in the way that he would see other men. The penis looks longer and larger than when observed from above.

Psychological therapies — whether the penis is actually small or just perceived to be small, cognitive behavioural therapy (CBT) can be useful in building confidence and counteracting negative thoughts.

Physical treatment options — could be pursued if the above does not work but their effectiveness is not guaranteed. However some men experience psychological benefits from using them. They are:

- Vacuum devices

- Penile extenders

- Stretching devices
- Penoscrotal rings
- Hot towels and wraps

Penis exercise program — (jelqing or 'penis milking') is an ancient Arab penile massage technique that forces blood into the penis to facilitate its growth in length and girth.

Medications — sometimes indicated such as: the selective serotonin re-uptake inhibitors (SSRIs) for depression, anxiolytics for anxiety and anti-psychotics for delusional BDD. Testosterone therapy is only of value in men with micropenis.

Surgery — there are four surgical options:

- Penis lengthening surgery - division of the suspensory ligament that attaches the penis to the pubic bone is the procedure that has been most commonly described for flaccid penile lengthening.
- Penis widening: this method involves injection of silicone, PMMA (polymethylmethacrylate) microspheres, and other materials into the penis and scrotum, to achieve girth enlargement.
- Liposuction or suprapubic lipectomy is potentially valuable in men with a significant suprapubic fat pad, thereby making a partly buried penis appear more prominent.
- Several techniques to augment the glans penis have been tried; a common one is injecting the glans with hyaluronic acid gel.

Please note that the results of surgery are poorly documented and significant complications can occur.

For all you men out there with 'small penis syndrome' please remember that women are much more interested in a man's personality and looks than the size of his penis. It doesn't matter how long or how short your penis is, because the vagina is so well designed. You see, the vagina of a woman who hasn't had a child is only a mere seven point five centimetres (3 inches) long when she's not sexually excited. The figures for women who have had children only vary slightly and even when she is aroused, her vagina usually extends only to a length of about ten centimetres (4 inches). But it will lengthen by 150 per cent or even 200 per cent to accommodate a man with a large member if necessary. So, if you think you are too small, why don't you ask your partner for her expert opinion?

References

1. Wylie, K. R. & Eardley, I. (2007). *Penile Size and the 'Small Penis Syndrome'.* BJU International, 99(6), 1449-1455.

Bibliography

2. Chen, J., Gefen, A., Greenstein, A., Matzkin, H., & Elad, D. (2000). *Predicting Penile Size During Erection.* International Journal of Impotence Research, 12(6), 328-333.

3. Rosario, V. (2010). *Mels van Driel, Manhood: The Rise and Fall of the Penis.* Social History of Medicine, 23(3), 687-688.

4. *Dangers of Sexual Enhancement Supplements.* Retrieved April 2012, from http://www.medscape.com/viewarticle/562177

5. *Do big penises hurt?* Retrieved April 2012, from http://www.askmen.com/dating/dzimmer/17_love_answers.html

6. McKee, A. (2004). *Does Size Matter? Dominant Discourses About Penises in Western Culture.* Cultural Studies Review, 10(2), 168-182.

7. Eisenman, R. (2001). *Penis Size: Survey of Female Perceptions of Sexual Satisfaction.* BMC Women's Health, 1(1), 1.

8. Fisch, H., Baskin,K. (2008). *Size Matters: The Hard Facts About Male Sexuality That Every Woman Should Know.* Pittsburg: Three Rivers Press.

9. Friedman, D.M. (2001). *A Mind of Its Own: A Cultural History of the Penis.* New York: The Free Press.

10. Wessells, H., Lue, T. F. & McAninch, J. W. (1996). *Penile Length in the Flaccid and Erect States: Guidelines For Penile Augmentation.* The Journal of Urology, 156(3), 995-997.

Erectile Dysfunction
How to Rise to the Occasion

Do you have difficulty rising to the occasion? Are you plagued with doubts about your virility? If the answer is yes, the next chapter is a must read. This chapter explores the challenges caused by impotence and points you to the many treatment options which are available.

How common is erectile dysfunction?

Of all the male sexual disorders, erectile dysfunction, or ED, takes pride of place in my practice. Interestingly, many of my patients willingly divulge this information on gentle probing and most admit that it is a source of major stress for them and their spouses. So what is ED?

Erectile dysfunction, (ED), is also known as impotence and is defined as the inability to achieve or sustain an erection for satisfactory sexual activity causing personal distress.

The incidence of the disorder increases with age according to the *Massachusetts Male Aging Study*, which revealed that chronic ED affects about 5 per cent of men in their forties and 15-25 per cent of men by the age of 65. Transient ED and inadequate erection affect as many as 50 per cent of men between the ages of 40 and 70. [1]

Population studies conducted in the Netherlands by Helgason et al, in 1996, found that some degree of erectile dysfunction occurred in 20 per cent of men between ages 50 to 54, and in 50 per cent of men between ages 70 to 78. [2]

What causes erectile dysfunction?

The causes of ED are many and varied as outlined below:

Disorders of the nervous system — such as spinal cord and brain injuries, Parkinson's disease, Alzheimer's disease, multiple sclerosis, and stroke.

Mental disorders — such as depression, schizophrenia, panic disorder, and generalized anxiety disorder.

Psychological factors — like stress, anxiety, guilt, depression, low self-esteem, and fear of sexual failure.

Hormonal disorders — low levels of the hormone testosterone, hypogonadism and tumours of the pituitary gland.

Arterial disorders — peripheral vascular disease, hypertension (high blood pressure).

Penile disorders — Peyronie's disease (bent penis).

Surgery — surgery of the colon, prostate, bladder, or rectum may damage the nerves and blood vessels involved in erection.

Aging — the aging process alone can cause erectile dysfunction in some men, because it decreases the compliance of the tissues in the shaft of the penis.

Lifestyle — alcohol and drugs, obesity, cigarette smoking, substance abuse, (marijuana, heroin, cocaine, and alcohol) contribute to erectile dysfunction. Alcoholism, in addition to causing nerve damage, can lead to atrophy (shrinking) of the testicles and lower testosterone levels.

Diabetes mellitus — erectile dysfunction tends to develop 10-15 years earlier in diabetic men than among non-diabetic men. This occurs due to atherosclerosis (hardening of the arteries), nerve damage or myopathy (muscle diseases).

Medications — medicines that can cause erectile dysfunction include many used to treat high blood pressure, antihistamines, antidepressants, tranquilizers, and appetite suppressants.

How is erectile dysfunction diagnosed?

Your doctor will thoroughly explore your medical history to determine if your ED is caused by a physical disease or is related to a psychological disorder. He will then perform a detailed physical examination to identify signs of hormonal problems (hypogonadism characterized by small testicles, lack of facial hair and enlarged breasts), poor circulation and penile deformity. He will then perform a battery of tests depending on his findings. Other tests of erectile function might be requested if deemed necessary. These tests assess erectile function by examining the blood vessels, nerves, muscles, and other tissues of the penis and the pelvic region.

What are the treatment options available for erectile dysfunction?

Your doctor will decide on the best treatment options for you.

Lifestyle changes — He will review your drug history and remove any potentially offending drugs from your drug schedule. Lifestyle improvements will also be strongly recommended such as: quitting smoking, exercising regularly, losing excess weight, maintaining a well balanced diet, curtailing excessive alcohol consumption, controlling hypertension and optimizing blood glucose levels in patients with diabetes.

Testosterone replacement treatment (TRT) — if you are suffering from andropause confirmed by laboratory blood testing, which revealed a low testosterone level, your doctor might recommend TRT if you are a suitable candidate.

Several testosterone delivery methods exist as outlined below:

- **Injections** — also called depot esters (Depo-Testosterone) are injected deeply into the muscles once every 2 weeks; these injections are safe and effective
- **Patch** — non-genital skin patch (Androderm) and genital skin patch (Testoderm). These patches which contain testosterone are applied each night to your back, abdomen, upper arm, thigh or scrotum
- **Gel (Androgel; Testim)** — you rub testosterone gel into your skin on your lower abdomen, upper arm or shoulder. As the gel dries, your body absorbs the testosterone
- **Gum and cheek (buccal cavity)** — Striant, a small putty-like substance which delivers testosterone through the natural depression above your top teeth where your gum meets your upper lip
- **Oral** — taking testosterone orally is not recommended for long-term hormone replacement. Testosterone taken by mouth may cause liver problems, raise your cholesterol and increase your risk of heart disease.

The drawbacks of TRT are, frequent or persistent erections (priapism), nausea, vomiting, jaundice, fluid retention and ankle swelling. Additionally, polycythemia (excess red blood cells), heart failure, precipitation or worsening of sleep apnea (difficulty breathing at night), prostate enlargement and liver damage. Body hair may increase while scalp hair recedes, and acne may worsen. Breast enlargement can also develop as testosterone can be converted to oestrogen via the enzyme aromatase.

Who should not get testosterone replacement treatment?

TRT should not be given to men with carcinoma of the breast, known or suspected carcinoma of the prostate, known hypersensitivity to TRT's, heart, kidney or liver disease, sleep apnea, severe benign prostatic hyperplasia and elevated levels of prostate-specific antigen (PSA).

Selective enzyme inhibitors — are now easily available for ED namely: Sildenafil (Viagra), Vardenafil HCl (Levitra), Tadalafil (Cialis) and Yohimbine. These drugs may be taken up to once daily to treat ED.

Patients taking nitrate drugs (used to treat chest pain) and those taking alpha-blockers (used to treat high blood pressure and benign prostatic hyperplasia) should not take selective enzyme inhibitors. Common side effects of selective enzyme inhibitors include: headache, reddening of the face and neck (flushing), indigestion, and nasal congestion, nausea, dyspepsia, diarrhea, and abnormal vision (seeing a bluish hue). Vardenafil and Tadalafil may cause muscle aches and back pain, which usually resolve on their own within 48 hours.

There have been rare reports of priapism (prolonged and painful erections lasting more than 6 hours) with the use of oral selective enzyme inhibitors. Selective enzyme inhibitors may also be associated with a potential risk for sudden hearing loss.

Yohimbine — improves erections for a small percentage of men. It stimulates the parasympathetic nervous system, which is linked to erection, and may increase libido. It is necessary to take the medication for six to eight weeks before determining whether it will work or not.

Intracavernosal injections — medications can be injected directly into the shaft of the penis to attain and maintain erections. Even though such injections can be effective, they are not widely used because the injections are painful, there may be scarring of the penis, and there is a risk of developing priapism.

Intraurethral suppositories — prostaglandin E1 can be inserted in a pellet (suppository) form into the urethra to attain erections.

Vacuum devices — are simple mechanical tools that allow a man to develop an erection suitable for sexual intercourse. Vacuum devices work by bringing more blood into the penis and then trapping it with a rubber O-ring which maintains the erection until removed. It should be left in place for no longer than 25 to 30

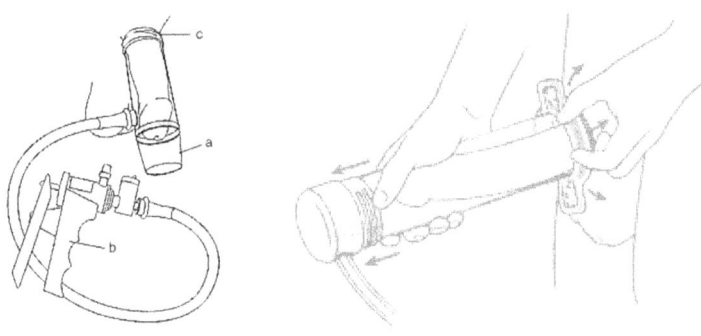

ERECTILE DYSFUNCTION

minutes.

Pictured on the previous page are the necessary components: (a) a plastic cylinder, which covers the penis; (b) a pump, which draws air out of the cylinder; and (c) an elastic ring, which, when fitted over the base of the penis, traps the blood and sustains the erection after the cylinder is removed.

Surgery — If all the above fails, surgery is sometimes recommended. The options usually offered are to implant a device that causes the penis to become erect; to reconstruct arteries in order to increase the flow of blood to the penis, or to block veins that drain blood from the penis. Here are some pictures which explain how the penile implant works.

Physical Medicine — Kegel exercises increase pelvic blood flow and muscle tone. Aerobic exercise and weight training will support the cardiovascular system, increase overall energy, and promote relaxation while at rest.

PENILE IMPLANT

With an inflatable implant, erection is produced by squeezing a small pump (a) implanted in the scrotum. The pump causes fluid to flow from a reservoir (b) residing in the lower pelvis to two cylinders (c) residing in the penis. The cylinders expand to create the erection

Psychotherapy — Psychologically based impotence can be treated using techniques that decrease performance anxiety associated with intercourse.[1]

You no longer have to suffer silently if you have ED. Visit your doctor today. He will design a treatment plan to suit your needs.

References

1. Feldman, H. A., Goldstein, I., Hatzichristou, D. G., Krane, R. J. & McKinlay, J.B. (1994). *Impotence and its Medical and Psychosocial Correlates: Results of the Massachusetts Male Aging Study. The Journal of Urology, 151*(1), 54-.61.

2. Helgason, A. R., Adolfsson, J., Dickman, P., Arver, S., Fredrikson, M., GÖTHBERG, M. & Steineck, G. (1996). Sexual Desire, Erection, Orgasm and Ejaculatory Functions and Their Importance to Elderly Swedish Men: A Population-based Study. *Age and ageing, 25*(4), 285-291.

Bibliography

3. Lewis, R.D., Hatzichristou, D.G., Laumann,E., McKinlay, J.B. (2000). *Epidemiology and Natural History of Erectile Dysfunction: Risk Factors Including Iatrogenic and Ageing.*

4. Jardin, G. Wagner, S. Khoury, F., Giuliano, I. Goldstein, & H. Padma-Nathan (Eds.). *Recommendations of the First International Consultation on Erectile Dysfunction, Co-sponsored by the World Health Organization* (WHO) (pp 21–51). Plymouth: Health Publication Ltd,

5. Kendirci, M., Nowfar, S. & Hellstrom, W. J. (2005). *The Impact of Vascular Risk Factors on Erectile Function.* Drugs of Today, 41(1), 65.

6. Korenman, S. G. (2004). *Epidemiology of Erectile Dysfunction. Endocrine, 23*(2), 87-91.

7. "Male Sexual Dysfunction Epidemiology (2006)". Retrieved April 2012, from http://www.health.am/sex/more/male_sexual_dysfunction_epid/

8. Meuleman, E. J., Donkers, L. H., Robertson, C., Keech, M., Boyle, P. & Kiemeney, L. A. (2001). *Erectile Dysfunction: Prevalence and Effect on the Quality of Life; Boxmeer Study. Nederlands tijdschrift voor geneeskunde, 145*(12), 576.

When Love Hurts

Overcoming the Challenge of Painful Sex in Men and Women

Erectile dysfunction is now behind you, but love hurts. This section will ensure that your "pains are o'er and you will sigh no more". - Gilbert

Painful sex in men

Sex is essentially a pleasurable activity for most men, but regretfully, it can at times be painful, and a source of profound distress. Many of my patients in fact have become secondarily impotent due to fear of pain. Painful sex affects about five per cent of men. [1] Men experience pain during sex due to physical or psychological reasons.

The primary psychological causes are:
- Anxiety and guilt
- Post ejaculatory pain syndrome (a rare condition)

The usual physical causes are:
- Trauma from the dangling string of an intrauterine contraceptive device
- Infection or inflammation of the head (glans) of the penis, the urethra or prostate
- A curved penis which is called Peyronie's disease
- Vigorous intercourse (hard core sex) which tears the delicate tissue under the glans of the penis called the frenulum or in some instances even fractures (breaks) the penis

How is this diagnosed?
Your doctor will take a thorough medical history, perform a pelvic and rectal examination and do comprehensive laboratory and radiological investigations to identify the cause.

How is it treated?
Your treatment depends on the underlying cause of your pain and may include: psychotherapy and medical treatments for any underlying infections. Peyronie's disease can be corrected with surgery.

A fractured penis is a medical emergency which requires urgent surgical treatment.

Painful sex in women

Many women have difficulty achieving an orgasm during regular intercourse and this anorgasmic state is aggravated by moderate to severe pain often due to an overzealous and insensitive lover. Regretfully, in our culture, a woman's expression of pain is often interpreted as a pleasurable outburst, however, most women can enjoy fulfilling, pain free sex once the cause has been identified and treated.

Painful sex affects about 15 per cent of sexually active women.[1] Because of obvious anatomical differences, women are more prone to experiencing pain than men and in my practice, painful intercourse is the second most prevalent sexual disorder that I treat. Painful intercourse is for many women a difficult subject to discuss and many suffer silently due to fear of rejection or offending their partner. The medical term for painful intercourse is dyspareunia. This is defined as persistent or recurrent genital pain during or after sexual intercourse, that is not caused exclusively by lack of lubrication or by vaginismus, and causes marked distress or interpersonal difficulty. The word is derived from the Greek word, dyspareunos, which means *difficulty mating or badly mated.* Dyspareunia can be caused by psychological or physical reasons.

The primary psychological causes are:

- Deep underlying sexual phobias
- Strong religious hang ups about sex
- Fear of pain
- A past history of sexual abuse
- Vaginismus (a condition which is characterized by involuntary spasm of the muscles of the pelvic floor, making sex quite painful or impossible).

The usual physical causes can be superficial or deep

Superficial pain can be caused by: infection or irritation of the external genitalia or vulva called vulvitis due to irritation from soaps, detergents, sanitary pads, female hygienic products, yeast, herpes and other sexually transmitted diseases. Vigorous or rough sex can also tear the delicate lower part of the vagina called the fourchette.

Deep pain is caused by rough sex which results in forceful contact of the penis against the cervix, the uterus or the ovaries which might be in the pelvic floor. Other causes are genitourinary disorders such: as endometriosis, pelvic inflammatory disease, uterine prolapse, a retroverted uterus (bent backwards), uterine fibroids, cystitis, irritable bowel syndrome, hemorrhoids (piles), ovarian cysts, chronic cervicitis and pelvic congestion.

How is it diagnosed?

Your doctor will take a thorough medical history, perform a pelvic and rectal examination and do comprehensive laboratory and radiological investigations to identify the cause.

How is it treated?

Your treatment depends on the underlying cause of your pain and may include:

Improved hygiene habits — avoid or discontinue the use of: perfumed soaps, douching, vaginal perfumes, bubble baths, scented or tinted toilet papers, panty liners or tight synthetic undergarments such as panty hoses

Switch positions — try the female dominant position (woman on top) during sex. Women usually have more control in this position, so you may be able to regulate penetration to a depth that feels comfortable

Improve communication — talk about what makes you feel good and what does not

Longer foreplay — can help to stimulate your natural lubrication and you can reduce pain by delaying penetration until you feel fully aroused

Use lubricants — a water-based lubricant, such as K-Y jelly can make sex more comfortable

Treating underlying conditions — if an infection or medical condition is contributing to your pain, treating the underlying cause may resolve your problem

Vaginal dilators and oestrogen — can alleviate vaginal strictures (an abnormally tight vagina)

Oestrogen therapy — using creams, tablets or flexible vaginal rings can enhance lubrication

Desensitization therapy — is a critical tool to learn vaginal relaxation exercises and (Kegel exercises). Discuss this with your doctor

Counselling or sex therapy — might be necessary for those afflicted with psychological dyspareunia.

Don't suffer silently. Dyspareunia is an eminently treatable condition. If you cannot enjoy sex due to pain, seek help from a health professional and begin to experience the true joy that sex brings.

References

1. Laumann, E. O., Gagnon, J. H., Michael, R. T. & Michaels, S. (1994). *The Social Organization of Sexuality: Sexual Practices in the United States.* Chicago: University of Chicago Press.

Bibliography

2. Bachmann, G., Lobo, R. A., Gut, R., Nachtigall, L. & Notelovitz, M. (2008). *Efficacy of Low-dose Estradiol Vaginal Tablets in the Treatment of Atrophic Vaginitis: A Randomized Controlled Trial. Obstetrics & Gynecology, 111*(1), 67-76.

3. Goldstein, S.W., Arleque, L. (2007). *When Sex Isn't Good: Stories & Solutions of Women With Sexual Dysfunction.* Bloomington, IN: Universe, Inc.

4. Goldsmith, M. (1995). *Painful Sex A Guide To Causes, Treatments and Prevention.* Canada: HarperCollins.

5. Graziottin, A. (2008). *Dyspareunia and Vaginismus: Review of the Literature and Treatment. Current Sexual Health Reports, 5*(1), 43-50.

Premature Ejaculation
Quick on the Draw

Many men have no problem with erectile dysfunction or pain, but are too quick on the draw. As you read on, I will provide some solutions help you to manage this dilemma.

What is premature ejaculation?

I have seen many young men over the years who have been affected by premature ejaculation and whose self esteem have been shattered because they are not as virile as other men. Prior to coming to see me, they had tried a variety of herbal drinks—roots tonics, stone, chiney brush, horse tonics, gungo, medina, spanish fly, etc in a desperate attempt to delay ejaculation. Delayed ejaculation has become almost an obsession among Jamaican youth, who are influenced by the strong persuasive lyrics of the local dance hall culture, which admonishes them to prove their virility by a display of prolonged staying power affectionately called daggering.

On the other hand, a lot of women are quite dismissive of men who suffer from premature ejaculation and describe them as having a *weak back* or being a *rabbit*. I once had a patient who developed suicidal ideation after he was harshly criticized by his girlfriend who called him a *'wotless bwoy'*. This section is therefore a must read for men who are *quick on the trigger*.

How common is premature ejaculation?

Around 30 per cent of men experience PE at some time in their life. [1] In October 2007, the International Society for Sexual Medicine *(ISSM)* gathered the world's leading sexual health experts to develop an evidence-based definition of premature ejaculation. The ISSM has defined premature ejaculation as:

a) a male sexual dysfunction characterized by ejaculation which always, or nearly always, occurs prior to or within about one minute of vaginal penetration

b) inability to delay ejaculation on all or nearly all vaginal penetrations

c) negative personal consequences, such as distress, bother, frustration and/or the avoidance of sexual intimacy. [2]

In a four-week study appearing in the May 2005 issue of *The Journal of Sexual Medicine,* Donald L. Patrick evaluated 1,587 men and the researchers reported that men who suffer from premature ejaculation (PE) had an average intravaginal ejaculatory latency time (IELT) of 1.8 minutes, compared to 7.3 minutes in men who did not. [3] Premature ejaculation is classified as either primary; if you've had the problem for as long as you've been sexually active, or secondary; if you developed the condition after having had satisfying sexual relationships in the past.

What causes premature ejaculation

Primary premature ejaculation — can be caused by your genes or psychological reasons.

Genetic causes

The rapidity of ejaculation in men was found to be genetically determined by Neuropsychiatrist Marcel Waldinger and Pharmacological Researcher Paddy Janssen of the Utrecht University who studied 89 Dutch men with premature ejaculation. They discovered that those who climaxed too soon during intercourse had a version of a gene that controls the hormone serotonin, which determines the rapidity of ejaculation. They also discovered that premature ejaculating fathers had a higher probability of having sons with that problem too. [4]

Psychological causes are:

- **Conditioning** — many doctors believe that early sexual experiences influence future sexual behaviour. So, if a teenager conditions himself to ejaculate quickly, to avoid being caught while masturbating, or having sex, then it might be difficult to break this habit

- **Medical problems** — is common if you have a medical concern that causes you to feel anxious during sex, such as a heart problem

- **Guilt** — can increase your tendency to rush through sexual encounters

- **A traumatic sexual experience at an early age** — such as child abuse may lead to life-long performance anxiety

- **Your upbringing** — some men, who have had a strict upbringing, where sexual activity is only considered appropriate in certain circumstances, such as after marriage, may find it difficult to relax during sex

Secondary premature ejaculation — can be caused by psychological or physical factors.

Psychological causes:

Performance anxiety is often the main issue at the start of a new sexual relationship, or where a man has had previous problems with sexual performance. Conflicts or sexual incompatibility in relationships are also psychological causes.

Physical causes

Diabetes, hypertension, an under-active thyroid gland, excessive drinking, inflammation and infection of the prostate or urethra, nervous system damage due to surgery, trauma and withdrawal from narcotics are some of the major physical causes. The use of a drug called Trifluoperazine (Stelazine), used to treat anxiety and other mental health problems is another physical cause of premature ejaculation.

What are the complications?

Very early ejaculation, occurring prior to entry into the vagina may be the cause of infertility and marital disharmony

How is premature ejaculation diagnosed?

Your doctor will diagnose premature ejaculation based on a comprehensive sexual history, a thorough physical examination and appropriate laboratory investigations.

How is it treated?

Treatment options for premature ejaculation include self help techniques, sexual therapy, medications and psychotherapy.

1. Self-help techniques

- Masturbating an hour or two, before you have sex
- Using a thick condom to help decrease sensation
- Taking a deep breath in order to briefly shut down the ejaculatory reflex
- Having sex with your partner on top
- Contraction of your PC muscles when you think you are about to ejaculate

2. Sexual therapy

- **Couples Therapy** — if you are in a long term relationship, you may benefit from couples therapy. Couples are encouraged to explore any issues that may be affecting their relationship and given advice on how to resolve them. They are also shown techniques that can help the man unlearn the habit of premature ejaculation. The two most popular techniques are the *'squeeze'* technique and the *'stop-and-start'* technique.

- **The squeeze technique** — this technique involves sexual stimulation until the man recognizes that he is about to ejaculate. At that point, the man or his partner gently squeezes the end of the penis for several seconds, withholding further sexual stimulation.

- **The stop and start technique** — this involves sexual stimulation until the man recognizes that he is about to ejaculate, the stimulation is then stopped for about thirty seconds and then resumed. The sequence is repeated until ejaculation is desired.

3. Medical therapy

- **Topical anaesthetic creams** — topical aesthetic creams containing lidocaine or prilocaine will dull the sensation on the penis to help delay ejaculation. It is applied a short time before intercourse. These creams are wiped off when your penis has lost enough sensation to help you delay ejaculation.

- **Anti-depressants** — your doctor may prescribe one of several antidepressants such as Sertraline (Zoloft), Paroxetine (Paxil) or Fluoxetine (Prozac) to help delay ejaculation. Recently researchers at the University of Minnesota have shown that the drug Dapoxetine is a safe and effective drug treatment.[5] If the timing of your ejaculation doesn't improve, your doctor may prescribe the tricyclic antidepressant Clomipramine (Anafranil).

4. Psychotherapy

This is also called talk therapy and is a useful adjunct to the above approaches especially in patients with severe emotional and relationship difficulties.

References

1. Laumann, E. O., Gagnon, J. H., Michael, R. T., & Michaels, S. (1994). *The Social Organization of Sexuality: Sexual Practices in the United States.* Chicago: University of Chicago Press.

2. Sharlip, I. D., Hellstrom, W. J. & Broderick, G. A. (2008). *The ISSM Definition of Premature Ejaculation: A Contemporary, Evidence-based Definition. The Journal of Urology,* 179(4), 340.

3. Patrick, D. L., Althof, S. E., Pryor, J. L., Rosen, R., Rowland, D. L., Ho, K. F. & Jamieson, C. (2005). *Original Research — Ejaculatory Disorders: Premature Ejaculation: An Observational Study of Men and Their Partners. The Journal of Sexual Medicine,* 2(3), 358-367.

4. Janssen, P. K., Bakker, S. C., Rethelyi, J., Zwinderman, A. H., Touw, D. J., Olivier, B. & Waldinger, M. D. (2009). *Serotonin Transporter Promoter Region (5-HTTLPR) Polymorphism is Associated With the Intravaginal Ejaculation Latency Time in Dutch Men With Lifelong Premature Ejaculation. The Journal of Sexual Medicine,* 6(1), 276-284.

5. Hellstrom, W., Althof, S., Gittelman, M., Steidle, C., Ho, K. F., Kell, S., & Nilsson-Neijber, A. (2005). *Dapoxetine For the Treatment of Men With Premature Ejaculation (PE): Dose-finding Analysis. Southern Medical Journal,* 98(10), S40-S41.

Sexual Desire Disorders
Sexual Anorexia

Whereas men are often challenged by premature ejaculation, both sexes have to cope with a common sexual conundrum; the variance between male and female sexual desire. To quote Mignon McLaughlin 'Desire is in men a hunger, in women only an appetite.'

Read on as we try to resolve this issue.

Sexual anorexia

I was the co-host of a show on a local radio station in Ocho Rios, Jamaica in May 2010, and the theme for the night was sexual anorexia. A most unsettling theme since it suggested that there were men and women out there with no appetite for sex and its attendant social and relational consequences. Surprisingly, many listeners to the program called in to ask for help to overcome this problem. I hope this section will provide some insight to all those who are challenged by this malady.

The sex drive or libido refers to an individual's urge or desire to engage in sexual activity. On the other hand inhibited sexual desire (ISD), sometimes called frigidity, sexual aversion, sexual apathy, sexual anorexia or hypoactive sexual desire, refers to a *low level of sexual desire and interest manifested by absence of sexual fantasies, thoughts, and/or desire for, or receptivity to, sexual activity, which causes personal distress*. ISD disorder may be lifelong or acquired, generalized (global) or situational (partner-specific).

How common is sexual anorexia?

It occurs in 30 per cent of women and in 15 per cent of men.[1] ISD may be a primary condition where the person has never felt much sexual desire or interest, or it may have occurred secondarily when the person who formerly had sexual desire, no longer has any interest. Low sexual desire is often the barometer of the emotional health of the relationship and may cause a partner to feel hurt and rejected, resulting in feelings of resentment and disharmony. It is interesting to note that the opposite of ISD is hyper sexuality, which is the desire to engage in human sexual behaviour at a level high enough to be considered clinically significant.

It is characterized by a debilitating need for frequent genital stimulation which, once achieved, may fail to result in the expected long-term emotional or sexual satisfaction.

Male/female discrepancy in sex drives

A man's libido is greatest during adolescence but lowers after age 50 when his testosterone level drops. A woman's sexual peak on the other hand is between her thirties and forties and lowers, like men in her fifties. Richard Driscoll, a marriage therapist in Knoxville, Tennessee and author of *Intimate Masquerades: A Survival Guide for Those Who Know Too Much,* discovered that the average American couple married five years has sex only once or twice a week, and that half of all marriages experience some discrepancy in desire at some point with men consistently having a greater sex drive than women. Interestingly, about one in five women reported that their husbands had turned them down for sex, while half of all men said their wives had turned them down. [2]

Is it really true that men think about sex every seven seconds?

This is a figment of a few guys' imagination. Being awake for 17 hours per day, for example, would mean you have sexual thoughts more than 8,742 times a day. That doesn't leave much time for anything else now, does it?

This myth was debunked by Edward Laumann et al in 1994, in a study called *The Social Organization of Sexuality: Sexual Practices in the United States*. The study revealed that the majority of males between ages 18 to 59 in the U.S report that they think about sex at least once a day. One third think of it several times a day, but only 25 per cent of females report thinking about it every day. He also discovered that men, on average, take four minutes from the point of entry until ejaculation, while women usually take around ten to eleven minutes to reach orgasm. Additionally, among men in a stable sexual relationship, 75 per cent report that they always have an orgasm, but only 26 per cent of the women reported having an orgasm with their partner. [1]

This is further compelling evidence that men really do have sex on their mind a lot of the time and also find sex more enjoyable than women. Couples therefore need to develop greater empathy and deeper understanding of each other's sexual needs and conditions in order to achieve sexual harmony.

What can dampen your sex drive?

Many factors can reduce one's sex drive as shown below:

Interpersonal relationships

The most common cause of ISD seems to be relationship problems in which one partner does not feel emotionally intimate or close to the other. Other common factors are communication problems, sexual boredom, power struggles and conflicts, and a lack of time together without the company of others.

Sociocultural influences

Inhibited sexual desire may also be associated with a very restrictive upbringing concerning sex, negative attitudes toward sex, traumatic sexual experiences such as sexual abuse, inadequate education and conflict with religious, personal or family values.

Psychological factors

A number of psychological factors influence the libido; these include:

- Loss of privacy
- Distraction
- Environmental stressors such as prolonged exposure to elevated sound levels or bright light
- Depression
- Stress or fatigue
- Paranoia
- Body image issues
- Sexual performance anxiety
- Aging

Unhealthy Lifestyles

Such as obesity, under nutrition, alcoholism, smoking and drug abuse can seriously dampen your desire.

Medications

Many medications can affect the libido for example: The birth control pill, antidepressants, tranquilizers and blood pressure medications.

Medical Conditions

A plethora of medical conditions can also influence your libido namely:

- **Hypogonadism** — a medical term for a defect of the reproductive system which results in impaired function of the gonads (ovaries or testes) with low testosterone output.
- **Prolactinoma** — a tumour of the pituitary gland which secretes prolactin.
- **Sexual anhedonia** — a rare variant of ISD seen in the male, in which the patient experiences erection and ejaculation, but no pleasure from orgasm.

Sexual dysfunctions such as:

- Painful intercourse (dyspareunia) is more common in women than in men, but may be a deterrent to genital sexual activity in both sexes.
- Inability to have an orgasm (anorgasmia)
- Erection problems (impotence)
- Retarded ejaculation

Physical illnesses

The medications taken for some illnesses may also contribute to ISD, particularly when they produce fatigue, pain, or general feelings of malaise. Some typical examples are:

- Depression, as caused by the pills called SSRI's used to treat it.
- The hormonal changes of menopause
- Cardiovascular disease and hypertension
- Endometriosis
- Fibroids
- Thyroid disorders
- Tumours of the pituitary gland (which controls most hormone production, including sex hormones)
- Surgery (hysterectomy: removal of the uterus and ophorectomy: removal of the ovary)

Taking care of others

"One of the most intriguing obstacles to desire is caretaking," says Esther Perel, a couples and family therapist in New York City, and author of *Mating in Captivity: Reconciling the Erotic and the Domestic*. "Caretaking makes you think about others, while desire hinges on your being able to think about yourself and your own needs." She concludes that desire is rooted in autonomy, freedom, and selfishness. If you can't be selfish, you can't have an orgasm. [3]

Treatment

Treatment must be individualized to the factors that may be inhibiting sexual interest. Currently, there is no approved drug or pharmacological treatment for ISD and psychotherapy has proved to be only minimally effective. If the cause is related to a medical condition, therapy is directed toward the cure or amelioration of that condition such as genitourinary infections, improvement in diabetes control, avoidance of substance abuse and medications that may be potentially responsible.

Therapy should also be directed towards other accompanying sexual disorders such as erectile dysfunction.

- In cases where insufficient testosterone is suspected as a possible cause, serum androgen levels should be tested. A testosterone level less than 300 nanograms per decilitre in males and less than ten nanograms per decilitre in females, indicates a need for supplemental replacement therapy.

- If the cause is determined to be of an interpersonal nature, couples therapy may be beneficial.

- Tricyclic antidepressants (TCAs) or monoamine oxidase inhibitors (MAOIs) may help in the treatment of accompanying depression or panic symptoms.

- A recent study has reported that almost a third of non-depressed women with ISD responded favourably to therapy with sustained release tablets of bupropion hydrochloride. The women on bupropion noted improvement in sexual function across a variety of psychometric domains. Over 70 per cent reported being definitely satisfied with treatment compared to less than 10 per cent of those on placebo. [4]

Sex for most couples, either bonds their relationship or creates a wedge that gradually drives them apart. When one partner is significantly less interested in sex than their companion, professional help is recommended before the relationship becomes strained.

I hope this chapter would have provided for you some critical insights into the way forward to overcoming the barriers to a satisfying sex life.

References

1. Laumann, E. O., Gagnon, J. H., Michael, R. T., & Michaels, S. (1994). *The Social Organization of Sexuality: Sexual Practices in the United States.* Chicago: University of Chicago Press.

2. Driscol,R. & Davis, N. A. (2006). *Intimate Masquerades: A Survival Guide for Those Who Know Too Much.* Akron, OH: Westside Publishing Co.

3. Perel, E. (2006). *Mating in Captivity: Reconciling the Erotic and the Domestic.* New York: Harper Collins.

4. Safarinejad, M. R., Hosseini, S. Y., Asgari, M. A., Dadkhah, F. & Taghva, A. (2010). *A Randomized, Double-blind, Placebo-controlled Study of the Efficacy and Safety of Bupropion for Treating Hypoactive Sexual Desire Disorder in Ovulating Women. BJU International, 106*(6), 832-839.

The Elusive Female Orgasm

We will now move on to a very emotional topic - The elusive orgasm. This chapter will answer Sigmund Freud's question - "What does a woman want?"

Sex is a chore

Besides painful intercourse, disorders of orgasm is one of the most common female sexual disorders seen in my practice. Many women do not know what an orgasm is and usually fail to experience one during a lifetime of intimacy. One of my patients has been sexually active since she was seventeen and forty three years later, she is still wondering what all the fuss is about. It is really hard for most men to admit this, but for many women sex is a chore.

During the sexual act, they are just mere spectators and the euphoria that they so desperately want and which their partner seems to experience effortlessly, is for them an elusive dream. But they genuinely want to please their partner. They were told that true sexual satisfaction is only achieved when you have an orgasm. Many men voice profound disappointment when their partner fails to 'come'. So, to placate them, many women fake it!

What is an orgasm?

An orgasm also called sexual climax, apoplexy, coming, consummation and the little death is derived from the Ancient Greek (orgasmos) from (orgao) "to swell with moisture".

It is the conclusion of the plateau phase of the sexual response cycle, and may be experienced by both males and females. An orgasm is characterized by intense physical pleasure, controlled by the involuntary or autonomic nervous system.

Orgasm and sexual satisfaction

A 1990 study called the *National Survey of Sexual Attitudes and Lifestyles*, conducted by Kaye Wellings et al using a random sample of 20,000 British people aged 16-59, revealed that: [1]

- 48.75 per cent of men agree that orgasm is necessary to male sexual satisfaction

- 43.3 per cent of women agree that orgasm is necessary to male sexual satisfaction

- 37.45 per cent of men agree sex cannot be readily satisfying for women without orgasm

- 28 per cent of women agree that sex without orgasm is not readily satisfying for them

In 1994, another paper entitled: *The Social Organisation of Sexuality* conducted by Laumann et al revealed that [2]:

- 75 per cent of men in partnerships always have an orgasm with their partner
- 28.65 per cent of women always have an orgasm with their partner
- Men's estimates of how often their partners had an orgasm was 15 per cent higher than the real figures. 24.1 per cent reported difficulty achieving an orgasm

Many other studies have shown that only about 30 per cent of women regularly reach orgasm by penile-vaginal intercourse alone. It is obvious that there is a large pool of frustrated women out there and many men are unaware of how unfulfilled their partners are. I have generated the ire of many women when I suggest to them that based on these studies, nature seems to have tipped the balance unfairly towards men, who really find sex far more gratifying than women and whose sex drive far outstrip the fairer sex; sorry ladies.

Anorgasmia

When a woman has difficulty reaching an orgasm it is called anorgasmia, frigidity or female orgasmic dysfunction.

There are four types namely:

- **Primary** — orgasm has never been achieved
- **Secondary** — orgasm has been achieved in the past
- **Absolute** — orgasm is impossible in all situations
- **Situational** — orgasm is impossible only in certain situations

Fake orgasms

Women fake orgasms for a variety of reasons namely:

Sociocultural influences — such as sexual taboos and a strict religious upbringing

Sexual double standards — which stipulate that, women are supposed to be submissive

Low self-esteem — poor judgement of oneself

Emotional difficulties — such as anxiety, stress, depression and unresolved feelings towards a traumatic sexual experience as in sexual abuse or rape

Unresolved resentment — a partner who has primary or secondary difficulty in achieving an erection

Fears about pregnancy or STDs

Same sex orientation — some women would rather be with a partner of the same sex.

Physical factors — drugs (anti-depressants etc) injuries to the back, nerve damage (as in spinal cord injuries); or systemic disease (diabetic neuropathy, multiple sclerosis, etc).

What are the physical signs of an orgasm? Or how to detect a faker

An orgasm in women is preceded by erection of the clitoris and increased vaginal lubrication. As a woman nears orgasm, the clitoral glans moves inward under the clitoral hood, and the labia minora (inner lips) become darker.

Rhythmic muscle contractions — occur in the outer third of the vagina, the uterus and anus. The first muscle contractions are the most intense, and occur at a rate of about 1 per second. As the orgasm continues, the contractions become less intense and occur at a more random rate. A mild orgasm may have 3-5 contractions, an intense orgasm 10-15

A sex flush — a reddening of the skin over much of the body due to increased blood flow to the skin

Female ejaculation — emission of a spray of fluid from the urethra during orgasm occurs in some women

The facial expression — of a woman may indicate that she is in pain when she is having a pleasurable orgasm. The entire body may become momentarily rigid at the peak of orgasm

Involuntary actions — including muscular spasms in other areas of the body and vocalizations (the emission of erotic sounds)

The clitoris re-emerges — after orgasm from under the clitoral hood, and returns to its normal size, usually within ten minutes

After the climax her breasts and nipples are very sensitive to touch.

Heavy breathing, rapid heartbeat and sweating usually accompany the final orgasm.

How do you overcome anorgasmia?

Let us now explore some possible solutions:

Improve communication — it is important that you learn to communicate your feelings and also to communicate how you like your body to be touched. Try to build up a vocabulary with your partner that is easy to use.

Change your sex position — we recommend the female-above position for penile-vaginal intercourse, as it may allow for greater stimulation of the clitoris by the penis or symphysis pubis or both, and it allows the woman better control of movement.

Try bridging — if, for example, the woman is readily orgasmic with manual stimulation, but not with penile-vaginal thrusting, she is encouraged to combine those two regularly until her body has learned to associate high levels of excitement and orgasm with penile-vaginal thrusting.

Use marital aids — sex toys can be an easy way to achieve your first orgasm and help you learn what feels good, you can also integrate it into lovemaking. But do not rely on it indefinitely, because it may decrease your ability to fantasize and cause jealousy or resentment from your partner if they are unable to satisfy you without a toy.

Try solo sex — learn how to give yourself an orgasm through masturbation. Include healthy fantasies with your masturbatory therapy. Masturbating helps you to learn just exactly which pressures and rhythms you need in order to bring you to orgasm.

Indulge in sensate focus — sensate focus is designed to increase communication between partners. Each person gets the opportunity to slowly explore touching their partner's body, listening to their partner as he or she tells what feels best.

Practise pelvic exercises — tighten your legs and thighs to increase myotonia (muscle tension) which aides in triggering orgasm and do regular Kegel exercises.

Help your partner last longer by using premature ejaculatory therapy if needed, such as the "squeeze/release" and "stop/go" techniques.

Sex therapy — is useful for those women who have severe anorgasmia and major psychological issues.

The problem with faking it is that your partner will never find out how to really please you, since you appear to be quite happy with his sexual prowess. Faking ensures that sex is all about orgasm, rather than intimacy and could seriously undermine your relationship. So stop faking it and experience the ecstacy of the moment.

References

1. Wellings, K., Field, J., Johnson, A. M., Wadsworth, J. & Bradshaw, S. (1994). *Sexual Behaviour in Britain: The National Survey of Sexual Attitudes and Lifestyles.* New York, NY: Penguin Books.

2. Laumann, E. O., Gagnon, J. H., Michael, R. T., & Michaels, S. (1994). *The Social Organization of Sexuality: Sexual Practices in the United States.* Chicago: University of Chicago Press.

Bibliography

3. Delaney, S. M., and McCabe, M. P. (1988). Secondary Anorgasmia in Women: A Treatment Program and Case Study. *Sex. Marital Ther.* 3,165-190.

4. Wadsworth, J., Field, J., Johnson, A. M., Bradshaw, S., & Wellings, K. (1993). Methodology of the National Survey of Sexual Attitudes and Lifestyles. *Journal of the Royal Statistical Society: Series A (Statistics in Society)*, 156(3), 407-421.

Part 5 - SEXUAL TABOOS

Part 5 of this book addresses sexual taboos; that aspect of sexuality that perturbs many of us, that leaves many unanswered questions in our minds. As you read on I hope your fears will be allayed.

Sex In The Elderly

Malcolm Muggeridge argues that "sex is unnecessary in the case of the young, inconvenient in the case of the middle aged and unseemly in the old." This archaic point of view will be debunked in this section.

A taboo subject

During early 2010, I was consulted by an agitated patient who wanted me to talk to her elderly father who was recently widowed and was now busily courting someone as a prelude to a new marriage. The cause for this agitation was really a sense of embarrassment that her father could even be entertaining the thought of having sex, at his age!!

I also had an elderly male patient who was in his late seventies and experiencing erectile dysfunction due to diabetes and was now unable to satisfy the needs of his wife, who was of a similar age. She had become so annoyed with him that she had stopped cooking his meals and was hinting at the possibility of divorcing him. These two examples I just cited sent me back to the literature, because I also had some biases based on our West Indian culture which really regards sex between the elderly as gross, inappropriate and wrong. However while the human body does impose limits on the maximum age for reproduction, sexual activity can in fact be performed or experienced well into the later years of life. We have sex for several reasons. The primary motivation is reproduction, but sex also promotes intimacy and commitment between two people regardless of age.

Older people have a difficult task in coming to terms with their decline in physical attributes, sexual potency and attractiveness. So, inevitably they withdraw from sex or sexual contact.

Many studies have been done to shed some light on sex in the elderly and below is a brief summary of some of the most important ones.

1. A study in Finland in 1990, found that more than half of 50 residents in a nursing home did not consider it proper for older people to have an active sex life; 25 per cent felt that sexual needs and desires were sinful and shameful. Fewer than a quarter of the respondents were prepared to talk to the staff about sexual matters. [1] Other factors besides social constraints can have a negative impact on sexuality such as: a dysfunctional relationship, physical fatigue and disabilities, psychological problems and economic woes.

2. According to a survey relating to urogenital ageing in 2,045 people aged between 55 and 85, they found that no more than 11 per cent were affected at any one time; but of that group, 73 per cent were sexually inactive. Of the 11 per cent affected, only one third sought professional advice, whereas 36 per cent resorted to over-the-counter remedies and 33 per cent did not seek help This confirms the strong aversion to sexuality of many women as they age.[2]

3. A study of 59 healthy post-menopausal women aged 60-70 by Bachmann in 1990, reported that 66 per cent were coitally active and 34 per cent were abstinent. The active group reported more sexual interest, greater sexual satisfaction and on pelvic examination were noted to have less genital atrophy. [3] A study by Gramegna in 1998, on Chilean women reported that only 40 per cent of women over 60 were sexually active. [4]

How do women adapt sexually following the loss of their marital partner?

Interestingly, the increasing age of a widow was associated with less unhappiness with loss of marriage-related activities. What the older woman missed most could be expressed as non-sexual heterosexual activity, such as the social company of a man. [5] A study of 81 healthy married men aged 60-71 with no physical illness, no psychopathology and no marital problems found that 36 per cent of the sample suffered from erectile failure. Ageing was associated with a decline in the frequency of sexual intercourse and an increase in the frequency of masturbation.[6]

A sample of 319 men, aged 50-80 who were surveyed by a postal questionnaire, revealed that physiological potency for men aged 50-59, 60-69 and 70-80 amounted to 97 per cent, 56 per cent and 51 per cent, respectively. Among the oldest men (70-80 years) 46 per cent reported orgasm at least once a month.[7] Brahler et al in 1994, surveyed a group of 450 elderly men and women who still had a partner, and found that 65 per cent of people aged 61-70 and 33 per cent of those aged over 70 engaged in sexual activity. [8] In a study in Massachusetts, 15 per cent of 70-year-old men were completely impotent and 34 per cent moderately impotent. The problem was associated with a significant number of physical and medication problems. [9]

Does the elderly masturbate?

Seventy two per cent of men and 40 per cent of women over the age of 65 engage in occasional masturbation. [10]

Types of sexual dysfunction

Helgasson, in his study in 1996, concluded that, 'Sex is important to elderly men.' Even among the 70-80-year-olds, an intact sexual desire, erection and orgasm are common and it is considered important to preserve them.' He concluded

240

that, 'sexual function should be considered in the clinical assessment of elderly men.'[14] The sexual dysfunction survey by Laumann in the USA in 1999, involved 1410 men and 1749 women aged 18–59, of whom 79 per cent took part. In women, 32 per cent complained of a lack of interest in sex, 26 per cent of an inability to achieve orgasm and 16 per cent of pain during intercourse.

Of the men, 31 per cent complained of premature ejaculation, 18 per cent of performance anxiety and, in the 50 to 59 year-old age group, erectile failure was present in 18 per cent.

Low sexual desire was associated with general unhappiness, and sexual dysfunction was strongly associated with unsatisfactory personal relationships. [11]

Stacy Tessler Lindau, in a paper published in the *New England Journal of Medicine* in August 23, 2007, reported the prevalence of sexual activity, behaviours, and problems in a national probability sample of 3005 U.S. adults (1550 women and 1455 men) 57 to 85 years of age. It revealed that the prevalence of sexual activity declines with age, yet a substantial number of men and women engaged in vaginal intercourse, oral sex, and masturbation even in the eighth and ninth decades of life. Nearly one in seven men reported taking medication to improve sexual function.

About one quarter of sexually active older adults with a sexual problem reported avoiding sex as a consequence.

The prevalence of sexual activity declined with age: 73 per cent among respondents who were 57 to 64 years of age, 53 per cent among respondents who were 65 to 74 years of age and 26 per cent among respondents who were 75 to 85 years of age. The most prevalent sexual problems among women were low desire (43 per cent), difficulty with vaginal lubrication (39 per cent), and inability to climax (34 per cent). Among men, the most prevalent sexual problem was erectile dysfunction (ED) (37 per cent).[12]

Another study by Laumann in 2009, reported that 'many men and women in the United States report continued sexual interest and activity into middle age and beyond. But, although a number of sexual problems are highly prevalent, few people seek medical help.' [13]

There you have it, the elderly are for more interested in sex than we thought and despite the understandable problems of the later years are quite busy in the bedroom.

Physiological changes in men and women as they age

Physiological changes in men as they age are secondary to declining levels of testosterone; which has been shown to decline 0.4-0.8 per cent, per year after the age of 50. [14]

The decreased hormone levels results in:

- Atrophy (shrinkage) of the sexual organs over time and this includes: thinning of the pubic hair, laxity of the scrotal tissues, atrophy of the perineal muscles, loss of collagen and muscle mass tissue and weight gain

- Decreased sex drive

- Erectile dysfunction (delay in achieving and maintaining a full penile erection). There is also a need for more manual stimulation to achieve an erection

- Decline in intensity of orgasm and in the propulsive force of ejaculation

- The volume of the ejaculate may be reduced by 50 per cent. The *plateau* phase, or period between erection and ejaculation, is prolonged. The refractory period, or time interval before erection is able to be achieved again, can be quite long, as much as a week in very elderly men

- Sex drive and performance vary widely between individuals of the same group and the maintenance of sexual activity depends on many factors such as regular sexual activity, the presence of a willing sexual partner, the absence of a major physical illness and the quality of the relationship

Physiological changes in women as they age are secondary to declining secretions of oestrogen after the menopause, which result in:

- Thinning of the pubic hair

- Shrinkage of the cervix, uterus and the lips of the vagina (the labia)

- The walls of the vagina become less elastic. The canal atrophies (shrinks) and the vaginal length and width decrease

- The thinning of the vaginal mucosa (inner lining) and the reduced lubrication may lead to dyspareunia (painful sex) and bleeding during intercourse

- There is also laxity of the perineal muscle, which can cause prolapse of the uterus.

- The clitoris can become highly sensitive
- Another important consequence of this sex steroid starvation is a loss of sex drive or sexual anorexia
- Many women complain that orgasmic contractions have become painful and the loss of elasticity in breast tissue and loss of breast dimensions can be quite demoralizing

The causes of sexual disorders in the elderly

Numerous factors can contribute to the sexual slump as you age. They include the biological changes of ageing, negative cultural expectations, medical or surgical problems, the effects of drugs, and mental illnesses such as depression, psychosis and dementia.

Physical disorders — ageing is associated with an increase in the prevalence of chronic illnesses, in the number of prescribed drugs and also in the likelihood of surgical procedures which may have unpleasant physical and psychological after effects. In addition, there may be damage to the blood supply of the genitalia and impairment of the pulmonary and cardiovascular systems.

Illnesses — some illnesses that contribute to sexual problems in old age include cardiovascular problems, particularly hypertension, peripheral vascular disease, diabetes mellitus, renal failure, chronic lung diseases, cancer, arthritis, neurological problems and the post-op effects of various operations such as prostatectomy, hysterectomy, mastectomy and various 'ostomies'. [16]

Coronary artery disease — coronary artery disease may lead to chest pain with sexual activity, or fear of having a heart attack during sex.

Chronic lung disease — chronic lung disease can lead to breathlessness.

Arthritis — arthritis may impair the ability to use some positions for sex.

Prostatectomy — the effects of prostatectomy on sex function have been well studied. According to one study, prostatectomy is associated with major erectile failures in 12 per cent and absent ejaculation in 24 per cent of cases. [17]

Cancer — the sexual dysfunction found in prostate cancer patients is primarily due to the effects of treatment, with radical prostatectomy carrying the highest risk.[18] Finasteride, which is used in prostatic enlargement, is associated with loss of libido, erectile failure and reduced volume of ejaculate in 5-6 per cent of men.[19] Some older persons may find that embarrassment over the loss of a breast, or the presence of a colostomy bag or some other apparatus, may inhibit free sexual expression, especially with a new partner.

Stroke and dementia — illnesses that result in disability, such as stroke and dementia, invariably lead to important changes in sexual behaviour.[20] Changes in sexuality after a stroke are often due to a change in role function because of the increased dependency of the afflicted partner.[21]

Mental disorders — the most common mental disorders affecting older people are depression, dementia, delusional disorders and delirium. Sexual behaviour may change significantly in depression, [22] and dementia. [23] Delusional disorder may be associated with pathological jealousy, which may cause severe distress to the other partner as well as endangering his or her well-being. Sexual problems may be further aggravated in this group of patients by the use of psychoactive agents.

Pharmacological agents and sexual dysfunction

There is a large body of literature on the sexual side-effects of antidepressant drugs. All types of antidepressants, including monoamine oxidase inhibitors, tricyclics and selective serotonin re-uptake inhibitors (SSRIs) have been implicated in a variety of sexual problems affecting libido, arousal and ejaculation. It is likely that as much as 50 per cent of patients treated with SSRIs may develop sexual dysfunction. [24]

Occasionally, patients treated with SSRIs may report increase in sexual desire. The drugs implicated here are Trazodone, Bupropion and, occasionally, Benlafaxine, Paroxetine and Fluoxetine. Trazodone is the drug most frequently associated with priapism.[25] This has also been reported with Phenothiazines, Putyrophenones and Benzisoxazoles.[26] Antipsychotic drugs have a predominantly depressant effect on sexual function through their effects on the dopaminergic system. Non-psychotropic medication may also have a negative influence on sexuality. Anticonvulsants, antihypertensives, H_2 blockers and thiazide diuretics, as well as Cimetidine, Digoxin and Metoclopramide are known to cause erectile dysfunction. [27] [28]

A recipe for successful love making in the later years

As you get older your desire for sex may be undiminished, but your capabilities may be compromised. The advice given below should help you to overcome these difficulties:

Take it easy — remember that sexual arousal takes longer and requires more manual stimulation.

Take your time during foreplay — take all the time that you often didn't have in your younger days to pleasure each other or yourself.

Communicate — share what makes you feel good with your partner

Use your senses — take time to explore in great detail all the tactile, visual, auditory, and even olfactory aspects of being intimate

Set the right mood — take your time to set the stage for this special experience – experiment with lighting, music, candles, oils, perfumes, and incense. Try a new location

Here are some suggestions for the older woman:

- **Lubrication** — to avoid irritation of the vagina or painful intercourse, make adequate lubrication part of your routine. An over-the-counter lubricant such as K-Y jelly can be quite helpful.

- **Vaginal estrogens** — some women with extreme vaginal dryness and irritation may benefit from a short course of vaginal estrogens.

- **Psychotherapy** — if you feel overwhelmed by sexual challenges or your relationship has become stormy, see a sex therapist.

Here are some thoughts for the older man:

- **Get a check-up** — please visit your doctor for a comprehensive physical examination and appropriate investigations to identify many treatable medical conditions that may cause impotence. If you are taking medications and think that one of them may be impairing your sexual performance, discuss it with your doctor.

- **Be patient** — please remember that more stimulation is required to achieve an erection as you get older.

- **For men with heart disease** — men who have heart disease may be quite concerned about whether sex will put too much strain on their heart, and many men who have had a heart attack or heart surgery wonder if they will ever be able to resume sexual activity. Relax! Most men can resume sexual activity within two to four weeks after a heart attack.

- **Testosterone** — if you would like to be more sexually active, but your libido is impaired, you might benefit from testosterone, caution here! Many men cannot, or should not take testosterone, your doctor will advise you.

- **Treatment for erectile dysfunction (ED)** — first-line medications for the treatment of ED are readily available and safe. Your doctor will prescribe a suitable one for you.

- **Other treatment options** — if erectile dysfunction drugs are not an option for you, there are other medications that can be tried. Some involve application into the urethra, or injection into the penis. Some men benefit from a vacuum pump device to aid in getting an erection, and others may choose the surgical implantation of a penile prosthesis.

- **Psychotherapy** — if you feel overwhelmed by sexual challenges or your relationship has become stormy see a sex therapist.

Positions to Try

Experiment with different positions if you are challenged by pain, strength, or endurance. Some options are:

- The spoon position in which both partners lie on their sides, the woman with her back to the man.

- The woman lies on her back and the man at a right angle to her on his side. The person with less strength or endurance lies on her/his back, with the stronger partner kneeling above.

Remember you can still achieve full sexual gratification in your golden years if you inform yourself of the challenges which accompany aging and approach intimacy with compassion, gentility and respect for your partner.

References

1. Paunonen, M., & Häggman-Laitila, A. (1990). Sexuality and the Satisfaction of Sexual Needs. A Study on the Attitudes of Aged Home-nursing Clients. *Scandinavian Journal of Caring Sciences, 4*(4), 163.

2. Barlow, D. H., Cardozo, L. D., Francis, R. M., Griffin, M., Hart, D. M., Stephens, E., & Sturdee, D. W. (1997). Urogenital Ageing and its Effect on Sexual Health in Older British Women. *BJOG: An International Journal of Obstetrics & Gynaecology, 104*(1), 87-91.

3. Bachmann, G. A. (1990). Sexual Issues at Menopause. *Annals of the New York Academy of Sciences, 592*(1), 87-94.

4. Gramegna, G., Blümel, J. E., Roncagliolo, M. E., Aracena, B., & Tacla, X. (1998). Patterns of Sexual Behavior in Chilean Women. *Revista médica de Chile, 126*(2), 162-168.

5. Malatesta, V. J., Chambless, D. L., Pollack, M., & Cantor, A. (1988). Widowhood, Sexuality and Aging: A Life Span Analysis. *Journal of Sex & Marital Therapy, 14*(1), 49-62.

6. Weizman, R. & Hart, J. (1987). Sexual Behavior in Healthy Married Elderly Men. *Archives of Sexual Behavior, 16*(1), 39-44.

7. Feldman, H. A., Goldstein, I., Hatzichristou, D. G., Krane, R. J. & McKinlay, J. B. (1994). Impotence and its Medical and Psychosocial Correlates: Results of the Massachusetts Male Aging Study. *The Journal of Urology, 151*(1), 54-61.

8. Brahler, E. & Unger, U. (1994). Sexual Activity in Advanced Age in the Context of Gender, Family Status and Personality Aspect. *Zeitschrift für Gerontologie, 27*, 110-115.

9. Feldman, H. A., Goldstein, I., Hatzichristou, D. G., Krane, R. J. & McKinlay, J. B. (1994). Impotence and its Medical and Psychosocial Correlates: Results of the Massachusetts Male Aging Study. *The Journal of Urology, 151*(1), 54-56.

10. Bretschneider, J. G. & McCoy, N. L. (1988). Sexual Interest and Behavior in Healthy 80-to 102-year-olds. *Archives of sexual behavior, 17*(2), 109-129.

11. Laumann, E. O., Paik, A. & Rosen, R. C. (1999). Sexual Dysfunction in the United States. *JAMA: The Journal of the American Medical Association, 281*(6), 537-544.

12. Lindau, S. T., Schumm, L. P., Laumann, E. O., Levinson, W., O'Muircheartaigh, C. A. & Waite, L. J. (2007). A Study of Sexuality and Health Among Older Adults in the United States. *New England Journal of Medicine, 357*(8), 762-774.

13. Laumann, E. O., Glasser, D. B., Neves, R. C. S., & Moreira, E. D. (2009). A Population-based Survey of Sexual Activity, Sexual Problems and Associated Help-seeking Behavior Patterns in Mature Adults in the United States of America. *International Journal of Impotence Research, 21*(3), 171-178.

14. Helgason, A. R., Adolfsson, J., Dickman, P., Arver, S., Fredrikson, M., Göthberg, M. & Steineck, G. (1996). Sexual Desire, Erection, Orgasm and Ejaculatory Functions and Their Importance to Elderly Swedish Men: A Population-based Study. *Age and ageing, 25*(4), 285-291.

15. Seidman, S. N., & Walsh, B. T. (1999). *Testosterone and Depression in Aging Men. American Journal of Geriatric Psych, 7*(1), 18-33.

16. Feldman, H. A., Goldstein, I., Hatzichristou, D. G., Krane, R. J.& McKinlay, J. B. (1994). Impotence and its Medical and Psychosocial Correlates: Results of the Massachusetts Male Aging Study. *The Journal of Urology, 151*(1), 54-61.

17. Thorpe, A. C., Cleary, R., Coles, J., Reynolds, J., Vernon, S., & Neal, D. E. (2008). *Written Consent About Sexual Function in Men Undergoing Transurethral Prostatectomy. British Journal of Urology, 74*(4), 479-484.

18. Helgason, A. R., Adolfsson, J., Dickman, P., Arver, S., Fredrikson, M., Göthberg, M. & Steineck, G. (1996). Sexual Desire, Erection, Orgasm and Ejaculatory Functions and Their Importance to Elderly Swedish Men: A Population-based Study. *Age and ageing, 25*(4), 285-291.

19. Gormley, G. J., Stoner, E., Bruskewitz, R. C., Imperato-McGinley, J., Walsh, P. C., McConnell, J. D. & Ng, J. (1992). *The Effect of Finasteride in Men with Benign Prostatic Hyperplasia. New England Journal of Medicine, 327*(17), 1185-1191.

20. Boldrini, P., Basaglia, N. & Calanca, M. C. (1991). *Sexual Changes in Hemiparetic Patients. Archives of Physical Medicine and Rehabilitation, 72*(3), 202.

21. Burgener, S.& Logan, G. (1989). *Sexuality Concerns of the Post-Stroke Patient. Rehabilitation Nursing, 14*(4), 178-181.

22. Feldman, H. A., Goldstein, I., Hatzichristou, D. G., Krane, R. J. & McKinlay, J. B. (1994). Impotence and its Medical and Psychosocial Correlates: Results of the Massachusetts Male Aging Study. *The Journal of Urology, 151*(1), 54-61.

23. Haddad, P. M. & Benbow, S. M. (1993). *Sexual Problems Associated With Dementia: Part 1. Problems and Their Consequences. International Journal of Geriatric Psychiatry, 8*(7), 547-551.

24. Ellison, J. M. (1998). *Antidepressant-induced Sexual Dysfunction: Review,*

Classification, and Suggestions For Treatment. Harvard Review of Psychiatry, 6(4), 177-189.

25. Warner, M. D., Peabody, C. A., Whiteford, H. A., & Hollister, L. E. (1987). *Trazodone and Priapism. Journal of Clinical Psychiatry,* 48(6), 244-245.

26. Patel, A. G., Mukherji, K. & Lee, A. (1996). *Priapism Associated With Psychotropic Drugs. British Journal of Hospital Medicine,* 55(6), 315-319.

27. O'Keefe, M., & Hunt, D. K. (1995). *Assessment and Treatment of Impotence. Medical Clinics of North America,* 79(2), 415-434.

28. Guay, A,T. (1995). *Erectile Dysfunction—Are You Prepared to Discuss It? Postgrad Med.,* 97:127–143.

Bibliography

29. Mims, C. (2003) *Love & Old Age: Breaking the Taboo of Sex and the Elderly.* Brighton, East Sussex, UK: Book Guild.

30. Segraves, R.T. & Segraves, K.,B.(1995). *Human Sexuality and Aging.* J *Sex Education Therapy,* 21: 88-102.

Sex In The Disabled

This section really touches on a delicate subject —
"sex in the disabled". We will explore the challenges they face and offer some innovative solutions.

Are disabled persons asexual?

For those of us who are comfortable with our own sexuality very little thought is given to those among us who; despite a physical disability; are sexual beings with needs like all of us. I shudder to think of the loneliness, the frustration and isolation these people must feel. This chapter therefore, should be a wake-up call for both the disabled and the able bodied.

Many persons are born with a disability or afflicted with one later in life. Do these individuals have sexual needs, fantasies or the desire to form committed relationships and have children? Disabled persons often feel unattractive and isolated and find it difficult to be sexually expressive. They assume that sexual intimacy is no longer possible due to sensation loss in their genitals, their altered physical appearance or impaired mobility.

This chapter will provide for you a comprehensive overview of the sexual challenges faced by the disabled and offer some solutions to assist them to circumvent these difficulties.

What is a disability?

The term *disabled person* means, any person unable to ensure by himself or herself, wholly or partly, the necessities of a normal individual and/or social life, as a result of deficiency, either congenital or not, in his or her physical or mental capabilities. It is a condition or function judged to be significantly impaired relative to the usual standard of an individual or group. The term is used to refer to individual functioning: including physical impairment, sensory impairment, cognitive impairment, intellectual impairment, mental illness and various types of chronic diseases.

Three dimensions of disability are recognized in *The International Classification of Functioning, Disability and Health (ICF)* namely:

- Impairment of body structure and function
- Activity restrictions
- Participation restrictions

Rights of the disabled

The United Nations general assembly resolution 3447 (XXX) of December 9, 1975 Declaration on the Rights of Disabled Persons stipulated that, disabled persons have the inherent right to respect for their human dignity. Disabled persons, whatever the origin, nature and seriousness of their handicaps and disabilities, have the same fundamental rights as their fellow-citizens of the same age, which implies first and foremost the right to enjoy a decent life, as normal and full as possible.

Types of disabilities

Types of disabilities include various physical and mental impairments that can hamper or reduce a person's ability to carry out his day to day activities. Below is a summary of the more common disabilities.

Mobility and physical impairments

Persons with mobility and physical impairments include a varied group of individuals. Some use crutches or walkers to move about due to muscular, bone, or joint disorders, while others use prosthetics due to limb amputations or congenital absence of an arm or leg. Persons who use wheelchairs do so due to paralysis caused by parkinsonism, a stroke, spinal cord injury, muscular or bony disorders, limb amputations, multiple sclerosis, cerebral palsy, spina bifida etc.

The disability could affect the upper limb, the lower limb, manual dexterity or there might be disability in co-ordination with different organs of the body, such as the bladder and the bowel.

Parkinsonism — is a neurological syndrome characterized by tremor, hypokinesia, (decreased bodily movement), rigidity, and postural instability due to lesions of a part of the brain called the basal ganglia.

Multiple sclerosis (MS) — is a degenerative disease affecting the central nervous system. MS causes scarring of nerve fibres and leads to such symptoms as arm and leg weakness, numbness, double vision and impaired coordination and movement.

Stroke — is a disease that affects the arteries leading to and within the brain. A stroke occurs when a blood vessel that carries oxygen and nutrients to the brain is either blocked by a clot or bursts, leading to damage to the central nervous system resulting in: weakness of the face, arm, and/or leg on one side of the body, numbness in the face, arm, and/or leg on one side of body, inability to understand spoken language, inability to speak, inability to write and so on.

A spina bifida — is a birth defect in which the spinal cord is malformed and lacks its usual protective skeletal and tissue coverings; resulting in physical disability mobility difficulties, learning disability, lower limb paralysis and occasionally complete paralysis.

Spinal cord disability

A spinal cord injury (SCI) can sometimes lead to lifelong disabilities. This kind of injury mostly occurs due to severe accidents. The injury can be either complete or incomplete. In an incomplete injury, the messages conveyed by the spinal cord is not completely lost, so the person still has limited sensation and ability to move the limbs. Whereas a complete injury results in a total loss of sensation and paralysis of the limbs below the lesion.

Trauma is the most common cause of spinal cord disease. In civilian life, this can be a result of motor vehicle accidents, recreational injuries (e.g. diving, boating) and construction injuries.

Quadriplegia (or tetraplegia) — refers to the state where a person is impaired in all four extremities (usually a cervical spinal injury).

Paraplegia — refers to the state where the impairment is limited to the lower extremities (usually a thoracic or lumbar injury).

Head injuries - brain disability

A disability in the brain occurs due to a brain injury. The magnitude of the brain injury can range from mild to moderate to severe. There are two types of brain injuries: Acquired Brain Injury (ABI) and Traumatic Brain Injury (TBI). The causes of traumatic brain injury are mainly caused by external forces applied to the skull. TBI results in emotional dysfunctioning and behavioural disturbance.

Vision disability

A visually impaired person could be partially-sighted, low-vision, legally blind, or totally blind.

Partially-sighted means the person has some form of visual disability that may require special education. Low-vision usually is used to refer to persons who experience a more severe loss of vision that is not necessarily limited to distance vision. Persons with low-vision may be unable to read a newspaper at an average distance with eyeglasses or contacts, and may need large print or Braille. Persons who are legally blind have less than 20/200 vision in their better eye, or a very limited field of vision, often 20 degrees at its widest point. Persons who are totally blind are unable to see and often use Braille or other non-visual forms of media.

Hearing disability

Hearing disabilities include people that are completely or partially deaf (*Deaf* is the politically correct term for a person with hearing impairment). People who are partially deaf can often use hearing aids to assist their hearing. Deafness can be evident at birth or occur later in life from several biologic causes, for example meningitis can damage the auditory nerve or the cochlea.

Deaf people use sign language as a means of communication. Hundreds of sign languages are in use around the world. In linguistic terms, sign languages are as rich and complex as any oral language, despite the common misconception that they are not real languages.

The impact of disabilities on sexuality

Neurological diseases

Lesions in the brain, spinal cord, and peripheral nerves which regulate sexual functions can diminish a person's libido and ability to become sexually aroused, as well as inhibit orgasm. Muscular weakness or spasticity may also hinder movement and mobility during sexual activity. Other factors that may affect a person's sexual functioning are their altered body shape and image, bladder and bowel incontinence, and immobility. Psychological and social factors resulting from dealing with a chronic, irreversible neurologic disease may also aggravate sexual dysfunction.

Spinal cord injuries

In spinal cord injuries above the ninth thoracic vertebra, physical stimuli can cause lubrication or erection (reflex erections). If the area of injury occurs between the tenth and twelfth thoracic vertebra, it will be difficult to lubricate or have an erection either through physical stimulation or mental imagery (psychogenic erections). But if the injury is below the twelfth thoracic vertebra, lubrication or erection can be experienced through mental imagery.

Where the spinal cord is completely severed, the skin and other structures beneath the injury will not respond to physical stimuli. If the injury is incomplete, tactile stimuli below the level of the injury may initiate arousal. Incomplete injuries result in some sensation and arousability of those parts of the skin and body parts innervated below the level of injury. Interestingly, in Berard's study, three complete quadriplegics reported arousability following breast stimulation, and two reported clitoral arousability. [1]

Sipski et al, in 1995, reported that eleven of 25 women with all levels of spinal injury were able to climax. However, only two of these women reported that the sensation of climax was the same as pre-injury; the others reported decreased or different sensations. They concluded that women with otherwise complete lesions still have some sense of deep vaginal penetration and hypothesized that the nerves coming from the cervix, upper vagina, and/or uterus sends sensations directly to the brain by passing the spinal cord. [2] Comarr and Vigue (1978), postulated that spinal cord injury victims can reach orgasm by stimulation of other erogenous areas such as the neck, ears, arms, nipples, or any area responsive to sensual touch; in other words they have a mental orgasm. They also note that women incorporate fantasy more readily than men into their sexual activity to achieve sexual stimulation and climax. Loss of reproductive capacity is often seen in patients with spinal cord injury due to ejaculatory dysfunction and poor semen quality particularly sperm motility.[3] [4]

Parkinson's disease/Parkinson's syndrome

One report of a study including 14 women, stated that 70 per cent of the women had decreased sexual interest, 67 per cent had difficulty with arousal, 75 percent had decreased frequency of orgasm since the onset of parkinsonism, and 38 per cent were anorgasmic. [5] Wermuth and Stenager (1995) reported that seven of ten young women with Parkinson's disease (ages 36-56) had decreased libido, and eight of ten had a decrease in sexual activity since the onset of the disease. [6] In male patients, hypersexuality (HS), erectile dysfunction and problems with ejaculation were found.

Multiple sclerosis

In MS, men may experience erectile dysfunction, loss of ejaculatory force, loss of sex drive, and diminished capacity for orgasm. However, the occurrence of sexual dysfunction in women with MS has been documented in several studies, with the incidence ranging from 50 to 70 per cent The most common complaints were of fatigue, loss of libido, and decreased genital sensation with impairment of genital engorgement on physical stimulation.[7][8] [9] [10] Many other studies have concluded that sexual dysfunction correlates highly with the presence of bladder and/or bowel symptoms.[11] [12] [13]

Strokes (cerebrovascular accidents)

In 1999, Juha T. Korpelainen et al conducted a study in Finland which assessed sexual functioning among stroke patients and their spouses. 192 stroke patients and 94 spouses were evaluated. A majority of the stroke patients reported a marked decline in all the measured sexual functions such as libido, coital frequency, erectile and orgastic ability, and vaginal lubrication, as well as in their sexual satisfaction. The spouses also reported a significant decline in their libido, sexual activity, and sexual satisfaction as a consequence of a stroke. [14] R. Aloni in his study in 1994, assessing sexual function in post-stroke female patients, also reported that the most prominent sexual finding was decline in desire. [15]

Spina bifida

The nerve damage in spina bifida that affects urinary and bowel functions may also affect sexual functioning. Touch sensation in both sexes may be impaired even though they may still feel the desire to have sex and can be sexually aroused. Men often complain of impairment of genital engorgement on physical stimulation (erectile dysfunction). Satisfactory erections are often possible, but there is no ejaculation. Some may benefit from electrical or mechanical stimulation to facilitate ejaculation. Females generally have less challenges with sexual dysfunction than men. Those challenged by orthopaedic deformities may have difficulty using some positions but there are many options discussed below. It is important to note however that most males and females with spina bifida are fertile. Many of the issues surrounding conception in spina bifida are due to mechanical and anatomical difficulties in conceiving rather than a lack of fertility.

Alzheimer's disease

Derouesné C, in a study in 1996, asked the spouses of 135 patients diagnosed with Alzheimer's disease to rate their sexual function. Indifference to sexual activity was reported by 70 per cent of the spouses, and sexual behavioural modifications were reported by 50 per cent. [16]

Traumatic brain injury (TBI)

TBI damages sexual functioning primarily, by direct destruction of brain tissue and secondarily by way of individual emotional responses to loss of function and faculties. Injury to the hypothalamus or pituitary gland may cause testosterone production to fall and thereby reduce desire. Conversely, injury to the frontal lobes of the cerebral cortex characteristically results in loss of restraint, which manifests itself in various forms of uninhibited and socially-inappropriate behaviour, (like masturbating in public). Injury to the left limbic region in some patients has been said to be the cause of new-onset sexual sadism. Loss of libido is the most common sexual dysfunction following TBI. Even if desire is not diminished, loss of erections or vaginal lubrication is common. A third of male TBI victims also have diminished capacity for orgasm even though they might experience pleasurable climactic sensations. Failure of ejaculation is another common dysfunction following TBI and infertility may result.

Those who have developed hemiplegia (paralysis of one side of the body) and cognitive losses (impaired memory, confusion, and an eventual inability to recognize loved ones), may become depressed and experience performance anxiety, low desire, feelings of inadequacy as a sexual being, and have difficulties in initiating a sexual encounter. Physical problems such as high muscle tone, poor balance, poor control of fine movement and tremor (ataxia) all make sexual activity more difficult. Poor control over swallowing and consequent drooling can be challenging.

Loss of sensation or feelings in various areas of the body may affect sexual enjoyment. The loss of the sense of taste and smell, which are particularly common following traumatic brain injury, may also affect sexual arousal and satisfaction.

Many of the drugs commonly prescribed after brain injury can have the side effect of erectile dysfunction in men and reduced vaginal lubrication in women.

Finally, it is not uncommon for people recovering from traumatic brain injury to become suspicious or even paranoid (a particularly strong and unshakable feeling of suspicion). [17]

The visually impaired

The visually impaired obviously will have difficulty dating and initiating new relationships. They will therefore have to use other means of communication such as verbal gesturing, speech, and touching of the hands and arms of the other person. It is obvious that initiation of sexual activity may be challenging unless proper verbal communication has been established.

The hearing impaired

The hearing impaired will have difficulty communicating with a potential partner who does not understand sign language and many individuals are unwilling to learn it.

Treatment

Treatment for sexual dysfunction in those with neurologic disease and traumatic brain injury is primarily aimed at improving genital hygiene, maximizing genital sensation, reversing medication-related side effects, and, where possible, treating or stabilizing the patient's overall medical condition to improve their sense of well being.

Communication — disabled persons must master the art of effective communication to ensure that their needs are met. Try and find out what both you and your partner desire and feel comfortable doing. Be imaginative and feel free to experiment with different types of touch, sensual massage and aromatherapy. Learn the art of Tantric sex and Kama Sutra.

Psychotherapy — with or without the partner, is frequently helpful even when organic causes for sexual dysfunction are identified. This approach is meant to help the couple deal with the loss of prior sexual functioning, develop emotional connections to support the relationship, and explore new avenues of emotional and physical exchange.

Hormone replacement therapy (HRT) — has been shown to improve the vascularity (blood supply) of vaginal tissue and increase lubricating capacity in women who have experienced menopause.[18] Oestrogen replacement given by mouth (systemic) has not been demonstrated to have a direct effect on libido,[19] but the improved overall sense of well-being brought on with hormonal balance does seem to increase sexual desire.[20] For women with difficulty in lubrication, either systemic or topical hormone replacement improves vaginal tissue integrity. Topical hormone therapy works more rapidly, and is indicated for those women who choose not to have systemic replacement due to the increased risks of cancer. [21]

Water soluble, topical preparations — can also be used for vaginal lubrication (K-Y jelly, Astroglide, Replens) They can be helpful in relieving discomfort with intercourse caused by vaginal dryness.

Androgens — have been studied as a treatment for decreased libido in women. Those placed on androgen in a study in 1985, had greater sexual desire, arousal levels, and sexual fantasies compared to placebo or oestrogen alone; but androgens did not impact on coital or orgasmic frequency. Oestrogen alone had no effect on desire, arousal, or frequency of sexual fantasies.[22]

Use of sexual aids (vibrators and dildos) — may overcome the sensory deficit in some instances by providing genital stimulation at greater intensity for women who have decreased genital sensation, or who fail to orgasm because of inadequate genital signals being sent to the central nervous system.

Concentrating tactile stimuli — to the less affected side may be beneficial. If one side of the body is less affected by the neurologic disorder than the other,

Treatment for erectile dysfunction (ED) — first-line medications for the treatment of ED are readily available and safe.

Sexual positions for the less able

Some difficulty in assuming desired positions is seen in all the above conditions. There are no positions specifically for disabled people and we recommend the following:

Mobility-impaired person with able-bodied partner — the able-bodied person can manoeuvre the impaired person's body into different positions, stimulating erogenous zones as desired. The sexual experience, whether it is kissing, touching, cuddling or oral, penile or vaginal intercourse is similar to that of two able-bodied people, even though the able-bodied person will be in charge, as he or she can move without assistance.

Mobility-impaired person with mobility-impaired partner — depending upon the severity of the impairment in each partner, some, but not all types of sexual activity may be possible. For example, kissing and touching may be easy, but penile and vaginal sex might be difficult. Oral or manual sex should then be tried if both partners are able to position their bodies as needed.

Paralyzed persons — depending upon the severity and cause of the paralysis, individuals who are totally or partially paralyzed may not be able to experience a physiological orgasm. However, stimulation of identified erogenous zones such as the neck, nipples, ears, arms or any other area that is responsive to touch could be quite gratifying. The most difficult challenge faced by the paralyzed is their inability to experience sexual release, but many are convinced that their sexual feelings have been moved into their heads and that they now have mental orgasms.

Remember: a disability does not mean a disabled sex drive. Regardless of the person's disability be it visual, hearing, mobility or paralysis, he or she has the emotional need for closeness, affection and sexual stimulation.

References

1. Berard, E. (1989). *The Sexuality of Spinal Cord Injured Women: Physiology and Pathophysioiogy.* A review. *Paraplegia, 27,* 99-112.

2. Sipski, M. L., Alexander, C. J. & Rosen, R. C. (1995). *Orgasm in Women with Spinal Cord Injuries: A Laboratory-based Assessment. Archives of Physical Medicine and Rehabilitation, 76*(12), 1097-1102.

3. Comarr, A. E., & Vigue, M. (1978). *Sexual Counseling Among Male and Female Patients with Spinal Cord and/or Cauda Equina Injury. American Journal of Physical Medicine & Rehabilitation, 57*(3), 107.

4. Komisaruk, B. R., Gerdes, C. A., & Whipple, B. (1997). *'Complete' Spinal Cord Injury Does Not Block Perceptual Responses To Genital Self-stimulation in Women. Archives of Neurology,* 54(12), 1513-1520.

5. Koller, W. C., Vetere-Overfield, B., Williamson, A., Busenbark, K., Nash, J., & Parrish, D. (1990). *Sexual Dysfunction in Parkinson's Disease. Clinical Neuropharmacology,* 13(5), 461-463.

6. Wermuth, L.& Stenager, E. (1995). *Sexual Problems in Young Patients with Parkinson's Disease. Acta Neurologica Scandinavica, 91*(6), 453-455.

7. Barak, Y., Achiron, A., Elizur, A., Gabbay, U., Noy, S. & Sarova-Pinhas, I. (1996). *Sexual Dysfunction in Relapsing-remitting Multiple Sclerosis: Magnetic Resonance Imaging, Clinical, and Psychological Correlates. Journal of Psychiatry and Neuroscience, 21*(4), 255-258.

8. Hulter, B. M., & Lundberg, P. O. (1995). *Sexual Function in Women with Advanced Multiple Sclerosis. Journal of Neurology, Neurosurgery & Psychiatry, 59*(1), 83-86.

9. Lilius, H. G., Valtonen, E. J., & Wikström, J. (1976). *Sexual Problems in Patients Suffering from Multiple Sclerosis. Journal of Chronic Diseases, 29*(10), 643-647.

10. Valleroy, M. L., & Kraft, G. H. (1984). *Sexual Dysfunction in Multiple Sclerosis. Archives of Physical Medicine and Rehabilitation, 65*(3), 125-128.

11. Barak, Y., Achiron, A., Elizur, A., Gabbay, U., Noy, S., & Sarova-Pinhas, I. (1996). *Sexual Dysfunction in Relapsing-remitting Multiple Sclerosis: Magnetic Resonance Imaging, Clinical, and Psychological Correlates. Journal of Psychiatry and Neuroscience, 21*(4), 255-258.

12. Lundberg, P. O. (1981). *Sexual Dysfunction in Female Patients with Multiple Sclerosis. Disability & Rehabilitation, 3*(1), 32-34.

13. Valleroy, M. L.& Kraft, G. H. (1984). *Sexual Dysfunction in Multiple Sclerosis.*

Archives of Physical Medicine and Rehabilitation, 65(3), 125-128.

14. Korpelainen, J. T., Nieminen, P., & Myllylä, V. V. (1999). *Sexual Functioning Among Stroke Patients and Their Spouses. Stroke, 30*(4), 715-719.

15. Aloni, R., Schwartz, J., & Ring, H. (1994). *Sexual Function in Post-stroke Female Patients. Sexuality and Disability, 12*(3), 191-199.

16. Derouesné, C., Guigot, J., Chermat, V., Winchester, N., & Lacomblez, L. (1996). *Sexual Behavioral Changes in Alzheimer Disease. Alzheimer Disease & Associated Disorders, 10*(2), 86-92.

17. Aloni, R., & Katz, S. (2003). *Sexual Difficulties After Traumatic Brain Injury and Ways to Deal With It.* Springfield, IL: Charles C. Thomas Pub. Limited.

18. Studd, J. W. W., Collins, W. P., Chakravarti, S., Newton, J. R., Oram, D., & Parsons, A. (1977). *Oestradiol and Testosterone Implants in the Treatment of Psychosexual Problems in the Post-menopausal Woman. BJOG, 84*(4), 314-315.

19. Campbell, S. & Whitehead, M. (1977). *Oestrogen Therapy and the Menopausal Syndrome. Clinics in Obstetrics and Gynaecology, 4*(1), 31-47.

20. Heiman, J.R. & Lentz, G.M. (2000). *Sexuality in the Context of Women's Heath.* In Selzer, V.& Pearse, W. (Eds.), *Women's Primary Health Care: Office Practice and Procedures* (pp. 453- 473). New York: McGraw-Hill.

21. Genazzani, A. R., & Gambacciani, M. (1999). *Hormone Replacement Therapy: The Perspectives for the 21st Century. Maturitas*, 32(1), 11-17.

22. Sherwin, B. B., Gelfand, M. M., & Brender, W. (1985). Androgen Enhances Sexual Motivation in Females: A Prospective, Crossover Study of Sex Steroid Administration in the Surgical Menopause. *Psychosomatic Medicine, 47*(4), 339-351.

Bibliography

23. Neistadt, M. E. & Freda, M. (1987). *Choices: A Guide to Sex Counseling with Physically Disabled Adults.* Malabar, Florida: Krieger.

24. Silverburg, C., Kaufman, M., & Odette, F. (2003). *The Ultimate Guide to Sex and Disability: For All of Us Who Live With Disabilities, Chronic Pain, and Illness.* Berkeley, CA: Cleiss Press.

25. Sipskl, M. L., Alexander, C. J., & Rosen, R. C. (1999). *Sexual Response in Women With Spinal Cord Injuries: Implications For Our Understanding of the Able Bodied. Journal of Sex & Marital Therapy, 25*(1), 11-22.

Voyeurism
Are You a Peeping Tom?

Let us now move on to a lighter subject; one that intrigues us rather than perturbs us - The Peeping Tom.

Wide spread distribution of sex tapes

It is quite normal to find an attractive member of the opposite sex alluring to look at and in fact with the recent dressing down of many women, so called "window shopping" is quite common. But the recent plethora and wide spread distribution of sex tapes depicting well known public figures in flagrante delicto, speaks to a latent tendency of many individuals to see others involved in erotic pursuits.

This phenomenon called non-consensual voyeurism has caused great disquiet among the victims and serious ethical and moral issues have been raised about what for many, is a gross invasion of privacy.

What is voyeurism?

This is defined as a paraphilia characterized by repetitive looking at unsuspecting people, usually strangers, who are either naked, in the act of disrobing, or engaging in sexual activity, as the method for achieving sexual excitement.

The word is derived from the French verb voir (to see) with the 'eur' suffix that translates as 'er' in English. The literal translation would then be: seer or observer.

A voyeur is also known as a peeping Tom, a name given to the fictional character, who after warnings not to do so at the pain of death, spied on the naked Lady Godiva as she rode through the town clad only in her long hair to protest against the unreasonable taxes levied by her husband on the citizens. Voyeuristic practices may take many forms, but the prototypical feature is that the voyeurs do not directly interact with the object of their voyeurism, who are often unaware that they are being observed. Instead, they observe the act from a distance by peeping through an opening or using aids such as cameras (camera phones and video cameras), mirrors, binoculars, etc.

This stimulus often becomes part of a masturbation fantasy during or after observing the event. What distinguishes voyeurism from mixoscopia (pleasure from watching others have sex), is that those being watched are unaware of the voyeur and the thrill which the voyeur experiences is enhanced by the fear of being caught.

Who is a true voyeur?

According to the mental health professional's handbook, *Diagnostic and*

Statistical Manual of Mental Disorders, two criteria are required to make a diagnosis of voyeurism: over a period of at least six months, an individual must experience recurrent, intense, sexually arousing fantasies, sexual urges, or behaviors that involve the act of observing an unsuspecting person who is naked, in the process of disrobing, or engaging in sexual activity.

The fantasies, sexual urges, or behaviors must cause clinically significant distress or impairment in social, occupational, or other important areas of functioning. Scopophilia is a synonym for voyeurism.

However the critical factor here is that unless you actively seek out these experiences, you are not a true voyeur.

Video voyeurism

In some cultures, voyeurism is considered to be a deviant act and even a sex crime. It is usually classified as a misdemeanor. As a result, legal penalties are often minor. The possibility of exposure and embarrassment may deter some voyeurs. It is also not easy to prosecute voyeurs as intent to watch is difficult to prove. In their defense statements, they usually claim that the observation was accidental. In the United Kingdom, non-consensual voyeurism became a criminal offence on May 1, 2004, under section 67 of the Sexual Offences Act 2003.

In Canada, voyeurism was declared as a sexual offence on November 1, 2005,

In the United States, video voyeurism is criminalized in nine states, and some institutions, such as gyms and schools, have banned camera phones because of the privacy issues they raise in areas like change rooms and locker rooms.

Saudi Arabia banned the sale of camera phones nationwide for a period, but revoked the ban in 2004.

South Korea requires that all camera phones sold in the country make an audible sound whenever a picture is taken.

How common is voyeurism?

Voyeurism is more common in men, but does occasionally occur in women. The onset is usually before the age of fifteen there are no reliable statistics about the incidence of voyeurism in adulthood.

The individual may become so enamored with the voyeuristic activity, that they fail to get involved in stable relationships.

What causes voyeurism?

The actual cause of voyeurism is unknown but most experts attribute the behavior to a random or accidental observation of an unsuspecting person who is naked, in the process of disrobing, or engaging in sexual activity. We do know that successive repetitions of the act tend to reinforce and perpetuate the voyeuristic behavior.

How is it treated?

For treatment to be successful, a voyeur must want to change his behavior but many are unwilling to do so and often have to be forced by court order. The treatment offered is psychotherapy, cognitive, behavioral and group therapy. There are no direct drug treatments for voyeurism.

The prognosis for eliminating voyeurism is poor, because most voyeurs have no desire to change their pattern of behavior. Since voyeurism involves non-consenting partners and is against the law in many jurisdictions, the possibility of embarrassment may deter some individuals.

How can we protect ourselves?

We must be vigilant in our daily lives to preserve our privacy and sequester ourselves from the lustful eyes of voyeurs. Legislation must be urgently put in place to curtail the activities of voyeurs, and we as citizens, must put systems in place to protect ourselves, by ensuring that all activities which we deem to be private are indeed done in private.

Bibliography

1. Alexander, L. (2007). *Voyeur*. New York, NY: Penguin group (USA) Inc.

2. Calvert, C. (2004). *Voyeur Nation: Media, Privacy, and Peering in Modern Culture*. Laguna Beach: Basic Books.

3. Baker, S. et al. (2010). *Exposed: Voyeurism, Surveillance, and the Camera Since 1870*. S. S. Phillips (Ed.). Yale/San Francisco Museum of Modern Art.

4. Tyler, A., & Bussel, R. K. (Eds.). (2006). *Caught Looking: Erotic Tales of Voyeurs and Exhibitionists*. Berkeley, CA: Cleis Press.

5. American Psychiatric Association. (1994). *Diagnostic Criteria from DSM-IV*. Amer Psychiatric Pub Inc.

6. Black, D. W. (2003). *The Shorter Oxford Textbook of Psychiatry. American Journal of Psychiatry*, 160(1), 199-b.

7. Kohut, J. J., & Sweet, R. (2000). *Real Sex: Titillating but True Tales of Bizarre Fetishes, Strange Compulsions, and Just Plain Weird Stuff*. New York: Penguin.

8. Wilson, J. F. (2003). *Biological foundations of human behavior*. Belmont: Thomson/Wadsworth.

9. Abouesh, A. & Clayton, A. (1999). *Compulsive Voyeurism and Exhibitionism: a Clinical Response to Paroxetine. Archives of Sexual Behavior*, 28(1), 23-30.

10. Furnham, A., & Haraldsen, E. (1998). *Lay Theories of Etiology and "Cure" for Four Types of Paraphilia: Fetishism; Pedophilia; Sexual Sadism; and Voyeurism. Journal of Clinical Psychology*, 54(5), 689-700.

11. Rösler, A., & Witztum, E. (2000). *Pharmacotherapy of Paraphilias in the Next Millennium. Behavioral Sciences & the Law*, 18(1), 43-56.

12. Simon, R. I. (1997). *Video Voyeurs and the Covert Videotaping of Unsuspecting Victims: Psychological and Legal Consequences. Journal of Forensic Sciences*,42(5), 884-889.

Sexual Fetishism Exposed

Many persons have found themselves in a sexual quandary, in that they are sexually attracted to materials and objects not conventionally viewed as being sexual in nature. They are afflicted by sexual fetishism. Is this really an illness? Can they be cured? Read on.

What is fetishism?

Have you ever felt a kind of magnetic attraction to an object or material that someone is wearing? I am sure you have, if you are totally honest. But most of us would not really admit to such a thing for fear of being called a freak. Well, if you are experiencing sexual attraction to materials and objects not conventionally viewed as being sexual in nature or your preference for a body part takes precedence over its owner, then you have a sexual fetish.

The term *fetishism* was first introduced by Alfred Binet in 1887.[1] It is defined as a compulsion or fixation over a period of at least six months characterised by recurrent, intense, sexually arousing fantasies, sexual urges, or behaviours involving non-living objects. The fantasies, sexual urges, or behaviours should cause clinically significant distress or impairment in social, occupational, or other important areas of functioning to be deemed a disorder. The fetishist does not limit the fetish objects to articles of female clothing used in cross-dressing or to devices designated for the purpose of genital stimulation (vibrators, dildos etc).

The fetishist focuses his attention exclusively on the object of interest usually totally ignoring the wearer even if she is a partner, whereas non-fetishists may occasionally make a particular body part or an object part of their general sexual arousal and foreplay with another person, but is not fixated on it.[2] [3]

Types of fetish objects

Inanimate object fetishes can be categorized into two types: **form fetishes** and **media fetishes**. In a form fetish, it is the object and its shape that are important, such as high-heeled shoes, drawings or photographs. In a media fetish, it is the material out of which the object is made that is important, such as silk, leather, rubber or fur.

Form fetishes

Some common form fetishes are:

Shoe fetishism — is the attribution of attractive sexual qualities to shoes or other footwear as a matter of sexual preference, and an alternative or complement to a relationship with a partner. Individuals with shoe fetishism can be erotically interested in either men's or women's shoes.

Boot fetishism — is very closely related to shoe fetishism. Many of the same sexual appeals regarded by those obsessed with high-heeled shoes apply to boots. In most cases the fetish of the boot is accompanied by a fetish for the material with which it is made. Examples could be leather, rubber, or latex.

High-heeled boots — help to elongate the calf, creating a longer-legged appearance, which is usually considered to be more sexually attractive.

Restrictive clothing — limits the wearer's movement and is commonly used for this property, particularly among those who enjoy BDSM.

Corsets — such as the training corsets and bondage corsets have also become a staple in fetish wear, particularly among dominatrices.

A hobble skirt — is a long, tight skirt, extending below the knees and often ankle length, which is so tight that it is difficult to walk in. When used as fetish clothing, it is often made of latex or PVC and sometimes corseted, to increase the restriction.

Stockings — fetishists usually find sexual partners clothed in sheer nylon or silk stockings to be sexually stimulating, or find the act of a person putting on or removing a pair of stockings arousing. Some men find it arousing to collect and wear stockings, sometimes hidden under a pair of trousers.

Uniforms fetishism — are quite common among BDSM practitioners, some of the more common uniforms in uniform fetish are those of a schoolgirl, nurse, French maid, waitress, cheerleader and Playboy Bunny. Some people also regard nuns' habits or even aprons as uniforms.

Media fetishes

Some common media fetishes are:

Fur — fetishism refers to the sexual fetishism that revolves around people wearing fur, or in certain cases, to the garments themselves.

Leather — fetishism is the name commonly used to describe a sexual attraction to people wearing leather and or to the garments themselves. The smell and the sound of leather is often an erotic stimulus for people with a leather fetish. Leather uniforms may also become a fetish.

Latex — fetishism is the fetishistic attraction to latex clothing or garments and are sometimes called rubber fetishism as latex is a type of rubber. Latex or rubber fetishists may even refer to themselves as rubberists.

PVC — fetishism is often closely associated with latex fetishism even though the two materials are quite different. PVC fetishism involves an erotic attraction to shiny plastic clothes made from polyvinyl chloride (PVC)

Spandex — fetishism is a fetishistic attraction to people wearing stretch fabrics or, in certain cases, to the garments themselves, such as leotards.

Fetishists may collect the object of their desire, and go to great lengths, including theft to acquire the right addition for their pleasure chest. In many instances the fetishists prefer objects that have already been worn.

The worn object does not serve as a symbolic reminder of the former owner, however, because it is the object that the fetishist relates to, not the person attached to it. Usually the fetishist obtain sexual excitation by kissing, fondling or tasting the object, or it is used during masturbation or with a partner to enhance sexual excitement.

The relative prevalence of different types of fetishes

AJ Chalkley and GE Powell conducted a study in 1983, in which they reviewed the files of all cases over a 20 year period which met criteria for non-transvestic fetishes in a large London teaching hospital. 48 cases were identified, and the objects of their fetishes included clothing (58.3 per cent), rubber and rubber items (22.9 per cent), footwear (14.6 per cent), body parts (14.6 per cent), leather jackets, vests, and leather items (10.4 per cent), and soft materials and fabrics (6.3 per cent). [4]

In order to determine the relative prevalences of different fetishes in the new millenium, researchers at the University of Bologna in 2007, obtained a sample of at least 5000 individuals worldwide from 381 internet discussion groups. The relative prevalences were estimated based on (a) the number of groups devoted to a particular fetish, (b) the number of individuals participating in the groups and (c) the number of messages exchanged. The study revealed that, the top body part fetish was feet and toes 47 per cent, and objects associated with feet; shoes (high heels), boots & other footwear 64 per cent, followed by costumes and jackets, 26 per cent. 150 people were turned on by hearing aids, and two had palpitations when they thought of pacemakers, 12 per cent were excited by underwear, nine per cent by coats, body fluids and body size, seven per cent felt like pulling their hair out when they saw hair, five per cent by muscles, and four per cent by genitals and body modifications such as tattooing.

Three per cent were among those excited about navels, ethnicity and breasts, and two per cent were allured by legs, buttocks, mouths, lips and teeth. Less than one percent were intrigued by stethoscopes, wristwatches, bracelets, nappies and catheters, body hair, nails, noses, ears, neck and body odour. This survey revealed that foot fetishism, foot partialism, foot worship, or podophilia is the most common form of sexual preference for otherwise non-sexual objects or body parts. It also appears that sexy shoes holds pride of place in the minds of many people around the world. [5]

I was, as you suspect, a bit sceptical about this foot issue, so I continued to search for further evidence and discovered that in August 2006, *America on Line* released a database of the search terms submitted by their subscribers. In ranking only those phrases that included the word fetish, it was found that the most common search was for feet. They concluded that women, as well as men, are likely to share a foot fetish. In fact, it is quite common for women in the 20-40 age range to include foot love in foreplay. I think the evidence is incontestable that many persons are happy to be called *foot freaks,* since they do not regard it as a compulsion or a fixation.

Causes of fetishism

The causes of fetishism (a compulsion or fixation on an inanimate object or body part that is not primarily sexual in nature), are not clearly understood. Some psychologists believe that it develops from early childhood experiences, in which an object was associated with a particularly powerful form of sexual arousal or gratification. Others suggest that the condition begins in later childhood and adolescence due to the conditioning associated with masturbation activity.

Many case studies have been published in which fetishism is said to be linked to emotional problems. They posit that a lack of parental love leads to a child projecting its affection to inanimate objects. Many argue that premature suppression of sexuality could lead to a child remaining in a transitory phase. One of Freud's defence mechanisms, displacement, is the redirection of an impulse onto a substitute target. In other words, someone who feels uncomfortable with their sexual desire for a real person may therefore use a fetish as a substitute.

Treatment

There are three possible treatments for fetishism: cognitive therapy, psychoanalysis, and medication.

Cognitive therapy

Cognitive therapy seeks to change the patient's behaviour without analyzing how and why it has shown up. It focuses on helping patients tune in to automatic thoughts that affect their mood and behaviour. As the patients become more aware of these automatic thoughts, they learn to alter irrational thoughts and resolve contradictions that lead to distress. One possible therapy is aversive conditioning. The patient is confronted with his fetish and as soon as sexual arousal starts, he is exposed to an unpleasant stimulus. Another possible therapy is a technique called thought stopping. The therapist asks the patient to think of his fetish and suddenly cries out, "Stop!", when the patient becomes aroused. After analyzing the effects of the sudden break together, the therapist will teach the patient to use this technique by himself to interrupt thoughts about his fetish.

Psychoanalysis

Psychoanalysis tries to find the traumatic unconscious experience that has caused the fetish. Bringing this unconscious knowledge to a conscious state and, by enabling the person to work out the trauma rationally and emotionally, may relieve the person from the problem. There are various techniques available for the analyzing process, including talk therapy, dream analysis and play therapy. This type of treatment is rarely used in fetishism.

Medication

Pharmaceutical treatment consists of various forms of drugs that inhibit the production of the sex steroids, testosterone and oestrogen, thus reducing sexual desire.

Some experts deem fetishism as an obsessive-compulsive disorder, and have used serotonin re-uptake inhibitors and dopamine blockers for controlling paraphilias that interfere with a person's ability to suppress perverse thoughts. If you have a fetish which is causing great turmoil in your life, you must seek the help of a sex therapist to normalize your sexuality and become mainstream again. [6] [7]

References

1. Binet, A. (1887). "Du fétichisme dans l'amour" (Fetishism in love) in: *Revue Philosophique, 24*, 143–167.

2. Lowenstein, L. F. (2002). *Fetishes and Their Associated Behavior. Sexuality and Disability*, 20(2), 135-147.

3. De Silva, W. P. (1999). *Sexual Variations. BMJ, 318*(7184), 654-656.

4. Chalkley, A. J., & Powell, G. E. (1983). *The Clinical Description of Forty-eight Cases of Sexual Fetishism. The British Journal of Psychiatry,* 142(3), 292-295.

5. Scorolli, C., Ghirlanda, S., Enquist, M., Zattoni, S., & Jannini, E. A. (2007). *Relative Prevalence of Different Fetishes. International Journal of Impotence Research,* 19(4), 432-437.

6. Shiah, I., Chao, C. Y., Mao, W. C. & Chuang, Y. J. (2006). *Treatment of Paraphilic Sexual Disorder: The Use of Topiramate in Fetishism. International Clinical Psychopharmacology,* 21(4), 241-3.

7. Lorefice, L. S. (1991). *Fluoxetine Treatment of a Fetish. Journal of Clinical Psychiatry, 52*(1), 41.

8. Bruckner, A. (2010). *Illustrated Foot Sex: Footjobs & Foot Fetishism.* Brian Phillippe.

Bibliography

9. Fernbach, A. (2002). *Fantasies of Fetishism: From Decadence to the Post-human.* Edinburgh, United Kingdom: Edinburgh University Press.

10. Kaplan, L. J. (2006). *Cultures of Fetishism.* New York NY: Palgrave Macmillan.

11. Kaplan, L. J. (1991). *Female Perversions: The Temptations of Emma Bovary* (p. 9). New York: Doubleday.

12. Krips, H. (1999). *Fetish: An Erotics of Culture.* Ithaca:Cornell University Press.

13. Kunzle, D. (1982). *Fashion and Fetishism: A Social History of the Corset, Tight-Lacing, and Other Forms of Body-Sculpture in the West.* Totowa, Lanham: Rowman and Littlefield.

14. Scott, P. (2004). *The Fetish Fact Book.* London, United Kingdom: Virgin Books.

15. Steele, V. (1995). *Fetish: Fashion, Sex & Power.* Oxford: Oxford University Press.

Kinky Sex
The Pleasure of Pain

World renowned sex therapist Alfred Kinsey insists that 'the only unnatural sex act is that which you cannot perform.'

Do you agree with him?
Are you into vanilla sex or do you like kinky sex?
This chapter will clear the air.

Power play

I have not met many persons who have admitted to being involved in BDSM or kinky sex, perhaps for good reason, since this lifestyle is really not widely accepted by most West Indians. However, I do know that there are a few kinky ones among us and I will use this section to uncover their secrets.

The term BDSM describes the activities between consenting partners that contain sadistic and masochistic elements. It is the collective term for a group of related sexual preferences and is a form of *power play,* where power dynamics are used as part of the erotic experience. It includes bondage and discipline (B & D), dominance and submission (D & S), and sadism and masochism (S & M).

BDSM is also referred to as power exchange or the lifestyle. The term *vanilla* refers to normative (non-kinky) sex and relationships, the vanilla world being mainstream society outside of the BDSM subculture. The term comes from vanilla ice cream which is considered the default flavour. In the past, many activities and fantasies related to BDSM were regarded by psychiatrists as pathological and deemed a mental disorder. However, The DSM-IV *Diagnostic and Statistical Manual of Mental Disorder* asserts that 'The fantasies, sexual urges, or behaviours must cause clinically significant distress or impairment in social, occupational, or other important areas of functioning' and the activity must be the sole means of sexual gratification for a period of six (6) months, or involve a violation of consent for sexual sadism or masochism to be considered a mental disorder. [1]

BDSM apparently releases a plethora of pleasure hormones which reinforce the behaviour such as endorphins, serotonin and melatonin, epinephrine and nor epinephrine.

How prevalent is BDSM?

A study in 1953, revealed that 12 per cent of females and 22 per cent of males reported erotic response to a SM story and 55 per cent of females and 50 per cent of males reported having responded erotically to being bitten. [2] Another study in 1983 discovered that 5 to 10 per cent of the U.S. engage in SM for sexual pleasure on at least an occasional basis and that 11 per cent of men and 17 per cent of women reported trying bondage. [3] In 1987, a study of 178 male and 47 female self-identified sadomasochists, determined that the most common activity was spanking. The second most common behaviour was bondage. Approximately two-thirds of the participants had experienced humiliation, whipping, and fetishism. Acutely painful and semi-permanent or permanent forms of body modification such as tattoos (6.8 per cent), branding (10.1 per cent), and piercing (14.7 per cent) were also reported. [4]

In 1993, it was reported that 14 per cent of men and 11 per cent of women have had some sexual experience with sadomasochism. [5] Finally, according to a 2005 Durex survey of 317,000 people in 41 countries, about 20 per cent of the surveyed people had at least once used masks, blindfolds or other bondage utilities and five per cent explicitly connected themselves with sadomasochism. Interestingly, BDSM practitioners are usually well educated, wealthy yuppies in the age range 20-40. [6]

What is a BDSM scene?

BDSM participants often refer to their activity as play, with an individual play session called a *scene*.

In these scenes, one of the party voluntarily gives up control or authority. BDSM practitioners make a clear distinction between consensual BDSM and sexual abuse. It is important that the process is voluntary and that whoever is giving up control is willing to perform the tasks that are asked of them. This is illustrated in the expression *safe, sane and consensual,* which means that the participants are aware of the dangerous nature of what they are doing, that what they are doing is sensible, they are in a right frame of mind and that full informed consent has been given by everyone. In general, it must be possible for the consenting partner to withdraw his or her consent at any given time, for example, by using a safe word that was agreed on in advance. Failure to honour a safe word is considered the most serious misconduct that can take place in BDSM and can even change the sexual consent situation into a crime.

The common myths about BDSM are:

- Dominants are naturally cruel people
- Submissives are naturally weak-willed doormats
- Submissives are attempting to re-live childhood abuse
- Women who are into D/s are nymphomaniacs, or indiscriminate sex partners
- Dominance is a case of role-reversal with people who have much power and responsibility in real life often preferring a submissive role

Bondage/Discipline

In the practice of bondage and discipline, physical restriction and psychological restraint are used to facilitate obedience, servitude, training, and punishment. Studies among BDSM practitioners in the U.S. have shown that about half of all men find the idea of bondage to be erotic; many women do as well.

Typical bondage activities are:

- Immobilization
- Intricate Japanese rope bondage
- Binding the partner by tying their appendages together
- Spreading the appendages and fastening them with chains to a St. Andrews cross or spreader bars
- Psychological bondage
- Breast/chest bondage - the act of tying female breasts etc
- Mummification
- Tightly corseting the submissive

The term discipline describes the use of rules and punishment to control overt behaviour such as: chaining, public humiliation, kneeling, cloistered in cells & closets, etc.

Dominance and submission

Dominance and submission (also known as D&s, Ds or D/s) is a set of behaviors, customs and rituals relating to the giving and accepting of dominance of one individual over another in an erotic or lifestyle context. Those who take the superior position are called dominants, top or doms (male) or dommes (female), while those who take the subordinate position are called submissives or bottom or subs (male or female). A switch is an individual who plays in either role. Two switches together may negotiate and exchange roles several times in a session.

Dominatrix is a term usually reserved for a female professional dominant who dominates others for pay. Some people maintain a special room or area, called a dungeon, which contains special equipment (shackles, handcuffs, whips, queening stools and spanking benches or a Berkley horse, for example) used for play scenes, or they may visit a BDSM club that maintains such facilities.

D/s activities may include:

- Spanking
- Domestic servitude or consensual slavery
- Enforced chastity of the submissive,
- Brown showers
- Golden showers
- Erotic humiliation
- Forced dressing
- Chauffeuring
- Food play
- Verbal humiliation
- Forced nudity
- Forced servitude
- Pup play
- Boot worship,
- Forced feeding
- Forced bed wetting
- Rope bonding, etc
- Fetishes-such as: foot/shoe/boot worship
- Animal play-where one partner takes the role of owner/caretaker and the other takes the part of a pet or animal

(See glossary for descriptions of these activities.)

Sadomasochism

Sadomasochism is described as a preference for sexual activity which involves the infliction of physical or psychological pain, humiliation, or bondage. If the subject prefers to be the recipient of such stimulation this is called masochism; if the provider, sadism. Often an individual obtains sexual excitement from both sadistic and masochistic activities. The terms *sadism* and *masochism* are derived from the names of the Marquis de Sade and Leopold von Sacher-Masoch, based on the content of the authors' works. The German psychiatrist Richard von Krafft-Ebing introduced these terms into the medical terminology in his work, *Neue Forschungen auf dem Gebiet der Psychopathia Sexualis (New Research in the Area of Psychopathy of Sex)* in 1890.[7]

Sadomasochistic practices are also varied and may include:

- Abrasion
- Caning
- Anal torture
- Needle play
- Fire play
- Water torture
- Tit torture
- Wax play
- Branding
- Gunplay
- Impact play
- Knife play
- Bruising
- Sensation play
- Genitotorture
- Hairbrush spanking

- Hair pulling
- Piercing
- Biting
- Breast whipping
- Face slapping
- Hot oil
- Asphyxiation
- Ball stretching
- Flame play
- Tattooing
- Ice play
- Electrocution using the TENS Unit or the violet wand

(See glossary for descriptions of these activities.)

BDSM can be dangerous

BDSM can be dangerous so practitioners must be advised of the following risks:

- Top's disease or the tendency for some dominants to develop a sense of infallibility or omnipotence
- Physically or mentally abusive dominant partner
- Self-hating submissives
- Dominant partners who violate the trust relationship by attempting to isolate the sub from society or monetarily exploit the submissive
- Unstable dominant partners or subs who, through act or threat of calling public attention to the other's private life and their relationship, can cause financial or personal hardship
- Emotionally unstable or manipulative subs or dominant partners seeking more from the relationship than the other as a human being can give

If you are into BDSM please remember SSC (Safe, Sane and Consensual) which mean that the participants are aware of the dangerous nature of what they are doing; that what they are doing is sensible; they are in a right frame of mind and that full informed consent has been given by everyone.

References

1. American Psychiatric Association. (2000). *Diagnostic and Statistical Manual of Mental Disorders: DSM-IV-TR.* 4th ed. Washington, DC: American Psychiatric Association.

2. Kinsey, A. C., Pomeroy, W. B., Martin, C. E., & Gebhard, P. H. (1953). *Sexual Behavior in the Human Female.* Philadelphia: W. B. Saunders Company.

3. Lowe, Walter. *The Playboy Readers' Sex Survey.* 1983.

4. Moser, C., & Levitt, E. E. (1987). An Exploratory-descriptive Study of a Sadomasochistically Oriented Sample. *Journal of Sex Research,* 23(3), 322-337.

5. Janus, S. S., & Janus, C. L. (1993). *The Janus Report on Sexual Behavior.* New York: John Wiley & Sons.

6. *Research-Face Of Global Sex 2005.* Retrieved January 23, 2012 from http://ebookbrowse.com/research-face-of-global-sex-2005-pdf-d159917745

7. Krafft-Ebing, R. V. (1892). *Psychopathia Sexualis, with Special Reference To Contrary Sexual Instinct: A Medico-legal Study,* Trans. Charles Gilbert Chaddock. Philadelphia: F.A. Davis.

Bibliography

8. Moore, H. T. (1917). *Pain and Pleasure.* New York: Moffat, Yard and Company.

9. Moser, C. (2002). Are Any of the Paraphilias in DSM Mental Disorders? *Archives of Sexual Behavior,* 31, 490–491.

10. Spengler, A. (1983). Manifest Sadomasochism of Males. Results of an Empirical Study. In T. Weinberg & G. W. Levi Kamel (Eds.), *S and M: Studies in Sadomasochism* (pp. 57–72). Buffalo, NY: Prometheus Books.

11. Schmidt, C. W., Schiavi, R., Schover, L., Segraves, R. T., & Wise, T. N. (1998). DSM-IV *Sexual Disorders: Final Overview.* In T. A. Widiger, A. J. Frances, H. A. Pincus, R. Ross, M. B. First, W. Davis, & M. Kline (Eds.), *DSM-IV Sourcebook* (Vol. 4, pp. 1087–1095). Washington, DC: American Psychiatric Association.

12. Bradford, J. M. W., Boulet, J., & Pawlak, A. (1992). *The Paraphilias: A Multiplicity of Deviant Behaviours. Canadian Journal of Psychiatry,* 37, 104–108.

13. Breslow, N., Evans, L., & Langley, J. (1985). On the Prevalence and Roles of Females in the Sadomasochistic Subculture: Report of an Empirical Study. *Archives of Sexual Behavior,* 14, 303–317.

14. Breslow, N., Evans, L., & Langley, J. (1995). On the Prevalence and Roles of Females in the Sadomasochistic Subculture: Report of an Empirical Study. In T. S. Weinberg (Ed.), *S & M studies in Dominance and Submission* (pp. 249–267). Amherst, NY: Prometheus Books.

15. Hilliard, R. B., & Spitzer, R. L. (2002). *Change in Criterion for Paraphilias* in DSM-IV-TR [Letter]. *American Journal of Psychiatry*, 159, 1249.

Pornography
A Blessing or a Curse?

Pornography is distributed using a variety of media — printed literature, photos, sculptures, drawings, paintings, animations, sound recordings, films, videos, or video games and the internet. Can it cause sexual aberrant behaviour? Is it addictive? Let us guide you through the uncharted seas of pornography.

The display of overt sexual matter

The debate about the pros and cons of pornography has been raging for decades. But one must admit that in this post modern era, the usual constraints which existed in the past are rapidly whittling away, and porn is now accessible to all and sundry. We must therefore take a critical look at this aspect of sexuality and join in the debate. Pornography is described as the display of overt sexual matter which excites the viewer. It is also called porn or porno. The word is from the Greek porne (whore) and graphien (write), and describes writings by/or about whores. The origins of porn are obscure but it was widely used by the Greeks and Romans, in songs and paintings and was quite common in ancient Eastern cultures.

There are many different kinds of pornography namely:

Soft porn — describes pictures or movies that show people who may or may not be naked, but who are posed in a sexy manner; the women posing in these pictures are called cheesecake and the men called beefcake.

Hard porn — depicts pornographic pictures or movies which show people having sex.

Hardcore porn — depicts sexual acts which are violent or degrading.

Child pornography — depicts any film or photo that shows children being used for a sexual act.

Internet pornography — is pornography that is distributed by means of various sectors of the Internet, such as websites, peer-to-peer file sharing, or Usenet newsgroups.

Porn can also be described as amateur, fetish, orientation-based; (gay, lesbian, bisexual); race-oriented (e.g. Asian, Black, Latino, interracial) and voyeur pornography (e.g. hidden camera, upskirt etc).

Pornography is distributed using a variety of media — printed literature, photos, sculpture, drawing, painting, animation, sound recording, film, video, or video game and the internet.

Who watches porn?

The statistics speaks for itself:

- Pornography in the United States is now a multibillion-dollar business
- In 2002, 4 billion porn videos were sold and 11,300 hard core films were released
- The average age at which an adolescent first views a porn magazine is 13
- In 2003, there were 1.3 million porn websites
- More than 20,000 images of child porn are posted on the net each week
- 77 per cent of online visitors to adult sites are men

A study in 1999 by Cooper, A., et al, called *'Sexuality on the Internet: From Sexual Exploration to Pathological Expression',* reported that:

- Only 8 per cent of men and women using the Internet for sexual reasons reported significant problems typically associated with compulsive disorders
- The average time spent on the Internet for non-academic and nonprofessional purposes was 38 hours per week
- Males make up two thirds of users of sexually explicit internet sites and account for 77 per cent of on-line time
- 51 per cent of women reported they never download sexual material[1]

In 2005, a study published in *Sexuality and Culture* revealed that:

- 14 per cent of people reported having never used a sexually explicit website ever
- 25 per cent of men reported visiting a pornographic site in the previous 30 days
- 4 per cent of women reported visiting pornographic sites in the same timeframe [2]

Mitchell, K. J., et al in another study in 2005, determined that overuse, pornography, infidelity, and risky behaviour are among the most frequently treated internet-related problems by mental health professionals. [3] Yoder, V.C, et al, in a paper titled *'Internet Pornography and Loneliness: An Association',* revealed that half of all spending on the Internet is estimated to be related to sex. US porn revenues have been estimated to exceed the combined revenues of companies like ABC, CBS, and NBC. [4] Wolak, J. et al, in 2007, surveyed adolescent internet users (10-17 years old) and found that 42 per cent had been exposed to internet pornography in the past year, with 66 per cent of those exposures reported as unwanted. Only boys ages 16-17 reported more wanted exposures than unwanted exposures to internet pornography.[5] In 2002, Kinsey Institute surveyed 10,453 respondents who were asked 'Why do you use porn?' The results are quite interesting. 72 per cent did it for physical release while 69 per cent went solo to arouse themselves or their partners, 54 per cent indulged in this pastime out of curiosity, 43 per cent to enhance their sexual fantasies and 38 per cent to distract themselves. [6]

The data clearly suggests that porn usage is entrenched in most cultures and is used either for physical release or to promote arousal and the Internet now has pride of place as the main source for porn

Religion and porn

Many religious groups discourage their members from viewing or reading pornography, and support legislation restricting its publication. For them, sex should be primarily for procreation and they believe that porn induces erotic thoughts which cause one to lust. They also argue that it is addictive and leads to self destructive behaviour. What does the literature say about Christians and porn?

In 2006, the world's most visited Christian website, (http://www.christianet.com), conducted a survey asking site visitors eleven questions about their personal sexual conduct. There were one thousand responses to the poll and the poll results indicate that '50 per cent of all Christian men and 20 per cent of all Christian women are addicted to pornography,' said Clay Jones, founder and president of Second Glance Ministries, whose ministry objectives include providing people with information which will enable them to fully understand the impact of today's societal issues. Sixty per cent of the women who answered the survey admitted to having significant struggles with lust, 40 per cent admitted to being involved in sexual sin in the past year, and 20 per cent of the church-going female participants struggle with looking at pornography on an ongoing basis.[7]

A national coalition survey of pastors in Seattle, in 2000, revealed interestingly that: out of 81 pastors surveyed (74 males, 7 females), 98 per cent had been exposed to porn and 43 per cent intentionally accessed a sexually explicit website.[8]

Patrick Means in his book, *Men's Secret Wars*, reveals a confidential survey of evangelical pastors and church lay leaders. The surprise findings were that 64 per cent of these Christian leaders confirm that they are struggling with sexual addiction or sexual compulsion including, but not limited to the use of pornography, compulsive masturbation, or other secret sexual activity. [9] In March of 2002, Rick Warren's (author of the *Purpose Driven life)*, pastors.com website conducted a survey on porn use of 1351 pastors. His findings revealed that, 54 per cent of the pastors had viewed internet pornography within the last year, and 30 per cent of these had visited within the last 30 days. [10]

As with masturbation, the church's influence seems to be waning and the research begs for a more rational and understanding approach to be adopted. Lets us look now at the pros and cons, and you be the judge.

The opponents of porn believe that:

- Pornography 'eroticizes' the domination and humiliation of women
- It diminishes male sensitivity to women's legal rights including the right to withhold consent to sex
- It is harmful to female actors and in general to all women
- It perpetuates gender stereotypes and promotes violence against women
- Prolonged use of pornography could encourage kinky sex
- It increases the acceptance of the use of coercion in sexual relations and reinforces sexual and cultural attitudes that encourage rape and sexual harassment
- Causes decreased satisfaction of participants with their sex lives and partners
- Desensitizes men and women to normal sexual stimulus
- It encourages recreational sex thus undermining the institution of marriage
- It promotes promiscuity especially in teenagers
- It can provoke intense jealousy in one or both spouses

The proponents of porn believe that:

- The wide availability of pornography may reduce crimes by giving potential offenders a socially accepted way of regulating their own sexuality by practising solo sex.

- Pornography may serve as a safety valve, preventing violence against women by serving as a form of fantasy and as safe sex.

- It can stimulate desire during foreplay.

- Couples can use it to gain a better understanding of human sexuality and the wide array of sexual expressions that are possible.

Hard core materials should be restricted

The advent of very liberal views about porn now pose a clear and present danger to our children. Adequate steps must be put in place to prevent children being used for porn or being exposed to it at an age when they are most impressionable. Hard core materials should be restricted to adult book stores, mail orders and parent controlled cable channels. The widespread availability of porn on the sidewalks and in mainstream stores should be discouraged.

Protecting children from watching porn on the net is a real challenge and we recommend the installing of web filters and blocking software in schools, homes and internet cafés. Commercially available web filters available are Net Nanny, Safe Eyes, Cybersitter, Cyberpatrol, Filter Pack, Net Mop, Wise Choice Net and others. As you can see, there are many sides to the porn story; let your conscience be your guide.

References

1. Cooper, A., Scherer, C. R., Boies, S. C. & Gordon, B. L. (1999). *Sexuality on the Internet: From Sexual Exploration to Pathological Expression*. Professional Psychology: Research and Practice, 30(2), 154-164.

2. Buzzell, T. (2005). *Demographic Characteristics of Persons Using Pornography in Three Technological Contexts*. Sexuality & Culture, 9(1), 28-48.

3. Mitchell, K. J., Becker-Blease, K. A. & Finkelhor, D. (2005). *Inventory of Problematic Internet Experiences Encountered in Clinical Practice*. Professional Psychology: Research and Practice, 36(5), 498-509.

4. Yoder, V. C., Thomas, B. & Kiran, A. (2005). *Internet Pornography and Loneliness: An Association?*. Sexual Addiction & Compulsivity, 12(1), 19-44.

5. Wolak, J., Mitchell, K., & Finkelhor, D. (2007). *Unwanted and Wanted Exposure to Online Pornography in a National Sample of Youth Internet Users*. Pediatrics,119(2), 247-257.

6. PBS Frontline. *"American Porn," Do You Use Porn? A Survey from the Kinsey Institute*. Retrieved April 2012, from http://www.pbs.org/wgbh/pages/frontline/shows/porn/ etc/surveyres.html

7. *Are Evangelicals Addicted to Porn?*. Retrieved May 2012, from http:// www.christiannews.christianet.com/1154951956.htm

8. *A National Coalition Survey of Pastors in Seattle*. Retrieved May 2012, from http://www.blazinggrace.org/cms/bg/pornstats

9. Means, P. A. (1999). *Men's Secret Wars*. Grand Rapids: Fleming H. Revell Company.

10. *Rick Warren Survey*. Retrieved May 2012, from http://www.blazinggrace.org/cms/bg/pornstats

Bibliography

11. McElroy, W. (1995). *XXX: A Woman's Right to Pornography*. Gordonsville, Virginia: St. Martin's Press.

12. Light, J. (2002). *The Art of Porn: An Aesthetics for the Performing Art of Pornography*. New York, NY: Julian's Books.

Part 6 - SAFER SEX

Sex can be a source of great pleasure but as you are aware, unsafe sexual practices are indeed quite risky. Part six of this book affords you the opportunity to pause and reflect on the risks of unsafe sex and the benefits of safer sex

SAFER SEX

How To Keep It Sexy And Safe

Are you familiar with the practices that are designed to reduce the risk of infections during sexual intercourse? If not then this section is a must read for you.

A harm reduction strategy

Safe sex (also called safer sex or protected sex) is a set of practices that are designed to reduce the risk of infection during sexual intercourse to avoid developing sexually transmitted diseases (STDs). On the other hand, unsafe sex refers to engaging in sexual intercourse without the use of any barrier contraception or other preventive measures against STDs. Safe sex became a buzz word in the late 1980s, as a result of the AIDS epidemic. Promoting safe sex is now a critical component of sex education. Safe sex should be regarded as a harm reduction strategy. Please note that safe sex is about risk reduction, not risk elimination. Sexual contact is the most common route of HIV transmission.

At the end of 2008, an estimated 240,000 people were living with HIV and AIDS in the Caribbean. Some 20,000 people were newly infected during 2008, and there were 12,000 deaths due to AIDS. In two countries in this region; the Bahamas and Haiti; more than two per cent of the adult population is living with HIV. Higher prevalence rates are found only in sub-Saharan Africa, making the Caribbean the second-most affected region in the world. Half of adults living with the virus are women. AIDS is now one of the leading causes of death in some of these countries, with Haiti being the worst affected. An estimated 7,500 lives are lost each year to AIDS in Haiti, and thousands of children have been orphaned by the epidemic.

Overall, the main route of HIV transmission in the Caribbean is heterosexual sex. Much of this transmission is associated with commercial sex, but the virus is also spreading in the general population, especially in Haiti. Sex between men is also a major factor in some countries' epidemics. Cultural and behavioural patterns (such as early initiation of sexual acts, and taboos related to sex and sexuality), gender inequalities, lack of confidentiality, stigmatization and economic need are some of the factors influencing vulnerability to HIV and AIDS in the Caribbean. In Jamaica, in 2007, the number of persons living with HIV/AIDS was 27,000. The prevalence rate in the 15-49 age group was 1.6 per cent and the deaths due to AIDS in 2007, was 1,400.

Researchers consistently detect HIV in blood, semen and cervical secretions of infected persons. Infectious HIV exists in saliva, tears and urine; however, it has only been recovered from these fluids at extremely low titers, therefore, saliva, tears, and urine are unlikely sources of HIV transmission. Infectious HIV has also been isolated in breast milk, and transmission from HIV-infected mothers to nursing infants is well documented. Breast milk is not commonly encountered during sexual intercourse. However, should you accidentally or intentionally come in contact with HIV-infected breast milk during sex; care should be taken to avoid contact with your eyes and mouth.

Let us now describe various sexual practices and the associated risks of HIV infection:

No-risk practices — these sexual activities cannot transmit HIV:

- Self-masturbation
- Touching, massaging, hugging, caressing
- Social (dry) kissing
- Any type of sexual intercourse between partners who are certain that they are un-infected
- Using one's own sex toys (without sharing of any toys that contact body fluids)

Extremely low-risk practices — these activities carry a small (based on case reports) or theoretical risk of HIV transmission between partners of unlike or unknown HIV serostatus:

- French (wet) kissing.
- Mutual masturbation (if no cuts on hands, and no ulcers or lesions on genitals of either partner)
- Vaginal sex with a male or female condom (with proper use, including putting latex or polyurethane condom in place before any penetration)
- Fellatio with condom (with latex condom placed on penis before oral contact)
- Cunnilingus with dental dam (with latex dam placed over vaginal area before oral contact)
- Contact with urine (only with intact skin, avoiding contact with mouth)

Low-risk practices — epidemiologic studies have found these sexual activities to have a low probability of HIV transmission between partners of unlike or unknown HIV serostatus:

- Fellatio without condom (risk of HIV infection to insertive partner is extremely low, risk to receptive partner is increased if ejaculation occurs in mouth.)
- Cunnilingus without a latex dam.
- Vaginal penetration with the hand with latex gloves.

High-risk practices — these sexual activities carry the highest risk, based on epidemiologic studies of transmitting HIV between partners of unlike or unknown HIV serostatus:

- Vaginal intercourse without a male or female condom.
- Anal intercourse.
- Anal penetration with the hand (fisting) or other rectal trauma.

Safe sex techniques:

To minimize the risk of STD's and HIV, a variety of safe sex techniques are suggested:

Abstinence

The only effective way to avoid the risks associated with sexual contact is to abstain from sexual activity entirely; this will eliminate the chances of contracting STDs and HIV.

Monogamy

Monogamy practised faithfully, is very safe (as far as STDs and HIV are concerned) when your partner is non-infected.

Solo sex

A solitary sexual activity including phone sex (mutual masturbation at a distance with the aid of technology, and cybersex) is relatively safe. However, some practices such as self-bondage and autoerotic asphyxia, (see glossary) are made considerably more dangerous by the absence of people who can intervene if something goes wrong. Masturbation is safe, as long as contact is not made with other people's discharged body fluids.

Non-penetrative sex

A range of sex acts, sometimes called 'outercourse' can be enjoyed by lovers with significantly reduced risks of infection and no risk of pregnancy. Non-penetrative sex (also known as outercourse) is sexual activity without vaginal and possibly oral penetration, as opposed to intercourse. No bodily fluids should be exchanged.

There are many options for non penetrative sex as outlined below:

- **Auxiliary intercourse** — where a man rubs his penis in his partner's armpit, also known as bagpiping
- **Frottage** — any form of consensual sexual rubbing, whether naked or clothed
- **Handsex** — stimulating genitals with the hand
- **Foot sex** — stimulating genitals with the feet
- **Intercrural sex** — also known as interfemoral intercourse, where a man places his penis between the partner's thighs
- **Mammary intercourse** — when a man rubs his penis between a woman's breasts
- **Mutual masturbation** — rubbing of the genitals
- Oral stimulation of the male or female nipples.

Limiting fluid exchange

Various devices are used to avoid contact with blood, vaginal fluid and semen during sexual activity:

- **Male condoms** — cover the penis during sexual activity. They are most frequently made of latex, but can also be made out of polyurethane. Polyurethane is thought to be a safe material for use in condoms, since it is nonporous and viruses cannot pass through it.
- **Female condoms** — are inserted into the vagina prior to intercourse.
- **A dental dam** — (originally used in dentistry) is a sheet of latex used for protection when engaging in oral sex. It is typically used as a barrier between the mouth and the vulva during cunnilingus.
- **Medical gloves** — may be used as a dental dam during oral sex, or to protect the hands during mutual masturbation. Hands may have invisible cuts on them that may admit pathogens that are found in the semen or the vaginal fluids of STD infectees.
- **Dildos or other sex toys** — are another way to avoid contact with blood and semen during sex-play.

Other precautions

For those who are not monogamous, reducing the number of sexual partners, particularly anonymous sexual partners, should reduce potential exposure to STDs.

Communication

Communication with one's sexual partner(s) makes for greater safety. Before initiating sexual activities, partners should discuss what activities they will and will not engage in, and what precautions they will take. This can reduce the chance of risky decisions being made in the throes of passion. Refraining from the use of recreational drugs, including alcohol, before and during sexual activity can protect against associated risks such as reduced inhibitions, decreased immune response, impaired judgment, and loss of consciousness. For persons sexually active with a number of partners, it is important that they get regular check-ups from a doctor and be tested periodically for STDs. In the absence of a vaccine, practising safe sex is the only effective means we have at our disposal to halt the spread of HIV and STDs. The options I have described are many and varied; discuss them with your partner and have a safe and satisfying sex life.

Bibliography

1. Fulbright, M. Y. K. (2003). *The Hot Guide to Safer Sex: The Ideas You Want, the Information You Need to Keep It Sexy and Safe When You're "Doin the Deed".* Alameda, California: Hunter House publishers.

2. Violet Blue. (2007). *The Modern Safer Sex Guide.* Retrieved January 23,2013, from http://www.tinynibbles.com/blogarchives/2007/11/the-modern-safer-sex-guide-free-download.html

3. Violet Blue. (2008).Open Source Sex Ed: The Complete E book Guide To Sex available at http:// www.digitapub.com/open-source-sex-ed-the-complete-ebook-guide-to-sex-ebook/.

4. Westheimer, R. K. (1992). *Dr. Ruth's Guide to Safer Sex.* New York, New York: Warner Books.

The Mysterious Condom

Abstinence, fidelity and condom usage are the cornerstone of safe sex practices. This ubiquitous item called the condom has now assumed pride of place in the fight against HIV/AIDS and deserves more detailed attention; so get ready to learn more about the mysterious condom.

Rubbers, Prophylactics, Safes, Protection, and Jimmies

The humble little condom now has pride of place in the fight against HIV and STDs and has continued to play its original role as a contraceptive device. But, did you know that the condom can also be a source of fun in sex play? It can significantly enhance the sexual experience for both partners, as well as be used as a useful adjunct in premature ejaculation and erectile dysfunction. Most users are also unaware of the varied types available on the market and their specific usages. The most common problem encountered by users of condoms is breakage due to poor application technique. This chapter will therefore paint a completely new picture of the condom and help you to choose wisely when you need this little gadget.

A condom is a device used during sexual intercourse. It is put on a man's erect penis or inserted in the vagina and physically blocks ejaculated semen from entering the body of a sexual partner. It is also known as: rubbers, prophylactics, safes, protection, and jimmies. Condoms have been used for at least 400 years. Since the nineteenth century, they have been one of the most popular methods of contraception in the world. The first rubber condom was produced in 1855. Latex (rubber suspended in water) was invented in 1920. The first polyurethane condom was introduced in the 1990s and the first custom sized-to-fit condom, called *They Fit* was introduced in 2003.

When do you use condoms?

Condoms are recommended for the prevention of pregnancy and sexually transmitted infections (STIs). They have been shown to be effective in reducing infection rates in both men and women. The condom when used properly prevents the transmission of HIV. According to a 2000 report by the National Institutes of Health, correct and consistent use of latex condoms reduces the risk of HIV/AIDS transmission by approximately 85 per cent. They can be used with a local anaesthetic to treat premature ejaculation and since they compress the outer veins of the penis, may be helpful for men who have difficulty maintaining an erection.

What are they made of?

Condoms are usually made from latex, but some are made from other materials such as polyurethane, lamb intestine and polyisoprene.

Latex condoms — have good elastic properties and may be stretched in excess of 800 per cent before breaking, but they can cause latex allergy and have to be stored and packaged carefully to avoid degradation of the latex.

Polyurethane condoms — tend to be the same width and thickness as latex condoms but are better than latex in a number of ways, in that they conduct heat better than latex; are not as sensitive to temperature and ultraviolet light and so have less rigid storage requirements and a longer shelf life, can be used with oil-based lubricants are less allergenic than latex, and do not have an odour.

Polyisoprene condoms — are made from a synthetic version of natural rubber latex but are more expensive. They have the advantages of latex in that they are softer and more elastic than polyurethane condoms without the protein which is responsible for latex allergies.

Lambskin condoms — are made from lamb intestines. They have a greater ability to transmit body warmth and tactile sensation, when compared to synthetic condoms, and cause less allergies. However, there is an increased risk of transmitting STIs compared to latex because of pores in the material.

Types

Condoms are made in different lengths, widths and shapes. Most have a reservoir tip but some have a plain tip. They may have straight sides, fit snugly to the penis or flared (wider over the head of the penis), colored or tinted, transparent or opaque, dry, powdered or lubricated with either a silicon-based or water-based lubricant. Some use a spermicide such as nonoxynol-9.

A number of different types are available, namely:

Desensitizing condoms — which delay orgasm by desensitizing the penis using a climax control lubricant. This is in a bead form and is released by body heat after the condom is rolled onto the penis so that the male genitals are desensitized with virtually no loss of sensation for the partner

Non-lubed condoms — are used for microphone covers, gun covers, and ultrasound machines and so on. They are also used with warming or flavoured lubricants

Night light condoms — glows-in-the-dark

Ribbed condoms — textured with ribs or bumps, which can increase sensation for both partners

Warming condoms — are made of thinner latex, which helps to heighten sensation. They contain a warming lubricant which heats up during sexual intercourse

Edible condoms — are for novelty use only; they do not provide any type of protection against pregnancy or sexually transmitted infections

Pleasure shaped condoms — have enlarged, pouch-like tips which allow for more friction, because the extra latex stimulates the nerve endings at the tip of the penis

French tickler condoms — fit over the penis and are available in various styles of nodules, nubs, ridges and shapes that provide stimulation by tickling the inner walls of the vagina. These condoms are considered to be novelty types, so they do not prevent pregnancy or disease

Tingling pleasure condoms — contain a safe spearmint tingling lubricant as well as a minty scent. These condoms are formulated to provide an intense, tingling experience for both partners

Kiss of mint condoms — are non-lubricated and are coated with a mint flavoured powder that provides a sweet spearmint taste

Female condoms — also known as femidoms are larger and wider than male condoms but equivalent in length. They have a flexible ring-shaped opening, and are designed to be inserted into the vagina. They also contain an inner ring which aids insertion and helps keep the condom from sliding out of the vagina during sex

What are the disadvantages of condoms?

- Many men and women feel that the condom reduces the pleasure of sex
- Some men are unable to maintain an erection after putting on a condom
- The friction caused by the condom may reduce female stimulation which can make sex less enjoyable or uncomfortable
- The man must withdraw his penis immediately after ejaculation
- Pre-planning is required; in other words you must have a condom before sex is contemplated
- One to two per cent of women and men are allergic to latex
- The spermicide—nonoxynol-9— used in some condoms is a chemical that some people are allergic to, the resultant irritation will make you more

vulnerable to HIV infection

- Condoms may slip off the penis after ejaculation

- Latex degradation can occur due to improper storage, exposure to oil based or petroleum based products or age

How do you use a condom?

You need to use a new condom every time you have sexual intercourse. Never use the same condom twice. Put the condom on after the penis is erect and before any contact is made between the penis and any part of your partner's body. Open the condom package at one corner being careful not to tear the condom with your fingernails. Make sure the package and condom appear to be in good condition, and check for the expiry date. Pinch the air out of the condom tip with one hand and unroll the condom over the penis with the other hand. Roll the condom all the way down to the base of the penis, and smooth out any air bubbles, since air bubbles can cause a condom to break. Withdraw before the penis softens, and hold the condom against the base of the penis while you pull out, so that the semen doesn't spill. Dispose of the condom properly.

See figure below.[2], [3], [4], [5]

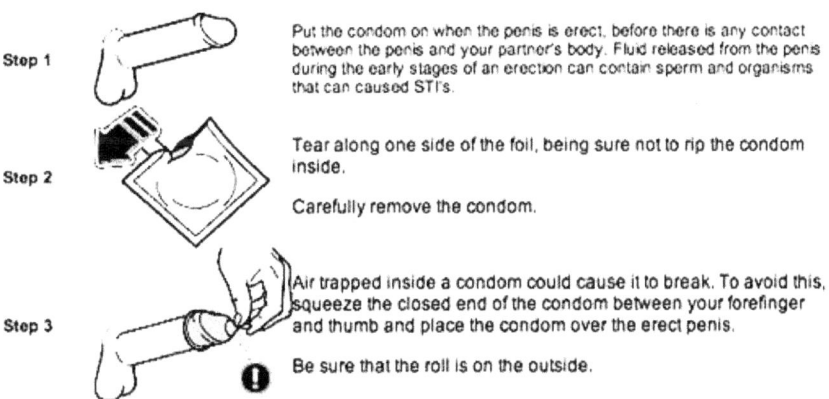

Pictogram of steps detailing proper use of a condom

| THE MYSTERIOUS CONDOM

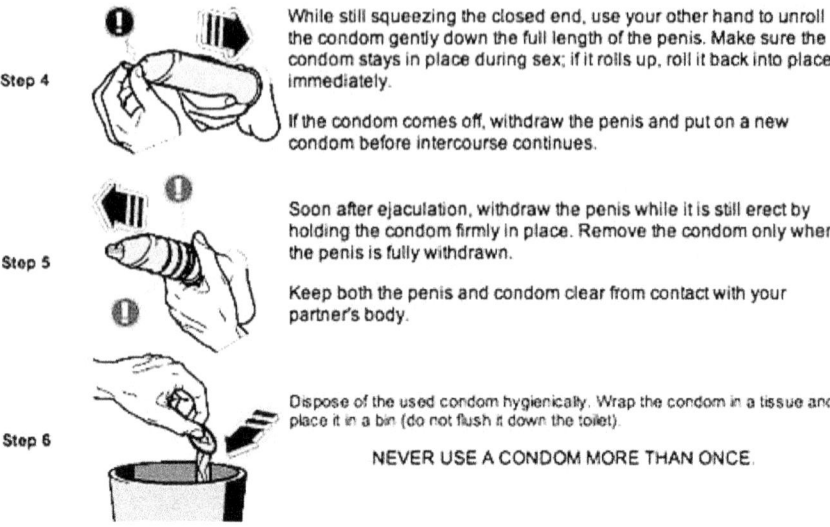

Step 4 — While still squeezing the closed end, use your other hand to unroll the condom gently down the full length of the penis. Make sure the condom stays in place during sex; if it rolls up, roll it back into place immediately.

If the condom comes off, withdraw the penis and put on a new condom before intercourse continues.

Step 5 — Soon after ejaculation, withdraw the penis while it is still erect by holding the condom firmly in place. Remove the condom only when the penis is fully withdrawn.

Keep both the penis and condom clear from contact with your partner's body.

Step 6 — Dispose of the used condom hygienically. Wrap the condom in a tissue and place it in a bin (do not flush it down the toilet).

NEVER USE A CONDOM MORE THAN ONCE.

Pictogram of steps detailing proper disposal of a condom

Please note that double bagging, that is using two condoms at once, increases the risk of condom failure. In this era of HIV safer sex by using condoms is the only way to significantly minimize your risk of contracting STIs and HIV.

References

1. *Scientific Evidence on Condom Effectiveness for Sexually Transmitted Disease (STD) Prevention (2000).* Retrieved January 23, 2013, from http://www.niaid.nih.gov/about/organization/dmid/documents/condom report.pdf

Bibliography

2. Allen, P. (2008). *Condom: One Small Item, One Giant Impact.* Oxford, United Kingdom: New Internationalist Publications Ltd.

3. Collier, A. (2007). *The Humble Little Condom: A History.* Amherst: Prometheus Books.

4. Griffin, G. M. (1993). *The Condom Encyclopedia.* Los Angeles, CA: Added Dimensions.

5. Sweeney, M. M., & Grisman, R. K. (2005). *Condom Sense: A Guide to Sexual Survival in the New Millennium.* Bristol: Lantern Books.

Part 7 - SEX THERAPY

The final section of this book will provide for you an overview of the role of the sex therapist and how this professional can help you to deal with all the sexual challenges we have discussed so far and motivate you to explore new avenues of experience in your love life.

Sex Therapy
A New Beginning

A sex therapist is a licensed mental health professional who has obtained specialized training in the evaluation and treatment of sexual disorders

Well readers, we have come to the end of our journey through what, for many of you, has been a sexual maze. I trust that your understanding of your own sexuality has been significantly enhanced and you are now well on your way to a fulfilling sexual life.

Now, as you may recall, at the end of each chapter I recommended that you seek medical attention if, despite your best efforts, the sexual disorder or relationship challenge persisted. Therefore pay careful attention to the advice given below and renew your sexuality.

When depression, anxiety or substance abuse are predominant, you will be referred to a psychotherapist.

If your primary problem is one of a weak pelvic floor, a physical therapist is needed. When pain impacts seriously on your sexuality, then a pain specialist should be consulted. If the sexual problems stems from a disorder of the genital tract a gynecologist or urologist is the preferred provider. If you have a number of co-morbid problems such as hypertension, diabetes, hypercholesterolemia, heart disease, respiratory (lung disorders) or musculoskeletal disorders you should be referred to an internist. But, if the problem is purely sexual or due to relationship issues you need to see a sex therapist.

Who is a sex therapist?

A sex therapist is a licensed mental health professional who has obtained specialized training in the evaluation and treatment of sexual disorders.

When do you consult a sex therapist?

- When relationship issues are the main cause of sexual disorders

- When lifelong or acquired problems are diagnosed, such as erectile dysfunction (ED), premature ejaculation, anorgasmia (inability to have orgasms), painful sex, problems with penetration, arousal disorders, sexual addiction etc

- When sexual rehabilitation is recommended such as sensate focus exercises, the use of vaginal dilators, the eros clitoral therapy device etc

- When sexual problems develop after an illness or surgery

How are you evaluated?

The therapist will do a comprehensive psychosexual evaluation which involves:

An intake interview — in which the therapist determines to what extent the problem is related to sexual attitudes, performance anxiety or is it related to relationship issues, a medical problem or psychological issues. He will also want to know if it only occurs with specific partners (situational) or under all circumstances (global).

Assessment of the chief complaint — you will be asked to describe your symptoms namely: when did they begin, under what conditions do they occur, how your partner responds and what motivated you to seek help.

Sexual status examination — the therapist will try and create a video of your sex life. You will be asked to divulge all the intimate details of your sex life: such as the time of day and location. Who initiates sex? How does your partner respond? What is your sexual behavior (preferred sexual positions, preference for peno-vaginal, manual or oral stimulations)? Can you have an orgasm? What activity facilitates this? What are your fantasies? How does the sexual disorder affect you emotionally? Is it just experienced with your present partner or with others? And so on.

Medical history — this discuses illnesses, surgeries, and medications along with assessment of drug use, over the counter medications and prescription medications.

Psychiatric history — this focuses on previous or existing emotional problems and treatment as well as a brief family history of psychiatric problems.

Family history — this concentrates on relationships in the home during childhood and adolescence and the patient's perception of the intimate relationship of parents.

Sexual history — this includes a description of sexual learning and modeling as well as accounts of sexual experiences with and without partners. Any unwanted sexual experiences such as rape, incest and sexual abuse will be explored.

Relationship history — how the relationship began, how the partner feels about each other, how is it different from previous experiences, any problems with intimacy, communication and control issues, future plans about children, marriage etc.

Treatment techniques

The therapist utilizes a variety of techniques that are tailored to the needs of the patient or couple such as:

Bibliotherapy — assigned reading of appropriate books and viewing of videotapes.

Education and reframing — the patient is educated about various aspects of sexuality and helped to restructure or reframe their concept of sexuality. The therapist also helps the couple to become more immersed in a sexual experience, and to become comfortable with a variety of sexual fantasies and experiences rather than being mere spectators. They are also encouraged to set up dates or time to be together and to take risks in initiating intimate activity, while at the same time giving permission for the other to reject such advances as long as it is done in a supportive way.

Sensate focusing — you are taught the art of sensual touching, thus enabling you to explore your spouse's body and discover new aspects of your own sexuality and deepen intimacy.

Tantric sex — you are taught erotic rituals which focus on exchanging pleasures, awakening the senses and allow couples to communicate deeply, physically and emotionally.

Eros clitoral therapy — you might be asked to purchase a small device designed to improve clitoral arousal through the induction of mechanical engorgement and use it in structured home work.

Cognitive therapy, psychodynamic therapy, play therapy and dream analysis — can be used for all disorders which have a strong psychological component.

Treatment of specific dysfunctions – typical examples are:

- Self-help techniques and couples therapy using the squeeze or the stop start technique for premature ejaculation
- Dilator and desensitization therapy for vaginismus (involuntary spasm of the vaginal muscles)
- PC exercises for anorgasmia
- Psychotherapy for erectile dysfunction (ED) and vaginismus
- Couples therapy for desire disorders

Sex therapy broadens the couples' approach so that sexual practices become more varied, creative and exciting, anxiety about specific practices is reduced and the needs of both members are met.

I am sure I have piqued your curiosity in human sexuality and you will continue to explore new avenues of experience in your love life. Always accept the sexual side to your persona and enjoy the happiness and improved health that good sex brings.

Bibliography

1. Hawton, K. (1985). *Sex Therapy: A Practical Guide*. Oxford: Oxford University Press.

2. Kaplan, H. S. (1988). *The Illustrated Manual of Sex Therapy*. Abingdon, United Kingdom: Routledge.

3. Kaplan, H. S. (1974). *New Sex Therapy: Active Treatment of Sexual Dysfunctions* (Vol. 1). Abingdon, United Kingdom: Routledge.

4. Keesling, B. (2006). Sexual Healing: *The Completest Guide to Overcoming Common Sexual Problems*. Alameda, CA: Hunter House Publishers.

5. Keesling, B. (1990). *Sexual Healing: A Self-help Program to Enhance Your Sensuality and Overcome Common Sexual Problems*. Alameda, CA: Hunter House Publishers.

6. Leiblum, S. R. (Ed.). (2006). *Principles and Practice of Sex Therapy*. New York: Guilford Press.

GLOSSARY

A

Abrasion: Dictionary term meaning a wearing, grinding, or rubbing away by friction. In BDSM play this would see also stimulating the surface of the body with abrasive materials such as rough silk, leather, sandpaper, brushes, etc.

Abstinence: Not engaging in any sexual behaviour with another person.

Anal intercourse: A sexual act involving the insertion of a penis in, or external stimulation of, another person's anus.

Anal beads: A set of strung beads used to insert into the anus to stimulate the anal nerves as foreplay or to cause orgasm.

Anal play: In this practice, the anus may be penetrated with either beads, ice, dildos, anal plugs, penis, or fist. Rimming the anus with a finger or toys stimulates the nerves which can create a more intense orgasm. Inserting and playing with one's prostate gland (males) will cause increased orgasm.

Anal plug: A specially designed dildo for use in the anus that is shaped in a way so that it will not fall out. Most commonly inserted and left in the anus for a given amount of time. Also used for rectum training to stretch out the anus and get one accustomed to having something in their rectum.

Anal Sex: Any sexual activity involving the anus. Examples are: rimming (oral), butt / anal plugs, dildos and penile penetration.

Animal role playing: Games in which one or more partners, usually the bottom, takes on the role of an animal. Most common is probably a dog, or puppy boy / girl, though horses are also popular. The person playing the anima, may imitate animal behaviour, wear items such as collars, leads, bridles and so on, or carry out tasks associated with animal behaviour.

Aphrodisiac: A food, drink, medication, or sometimes a thought that intensifies sexual desire.

Aromas: Play which involves the use of certain aroma therapy to induce relaxation. Also referred to as poppers. In some instances these can be volatile compounds whose vapors cause temporarily increased heart and breathing rates, muscle relaxation, and a rushing feeling in the head. These types of play are popular in the gay and rave scenes, and often used in an S/M context. There are some dangers associated with their use.

Asphyxiation: Commonly referred to as breath control, refers to play involving control of or restriction of air and / or oxygen to the brain. Any form of stopping breathing freely including choking, smothering and hoods with tubes, sacks, plastics, is asphyxia. Sometimes used to cause a more intense orgasm. Other examples would be strangling, which is compression of the neck or throat area to prevent oxygen to the brain; suffocation involves reducing the level of oxygen available to breathe; hanging where the body is suspended by the neck (remember, all these games are extremely dangerous, either alone or with a partner, and may cause DEATH)

B

Ball stretching: Play which involves a type of penile constraint attached to weights, in order to provide a variety of sensations including discomfort and pain, while stretching the testicles and scrotum.

Bathroom use control: Scenes where the dominant restricts or takes control over the submissive's bodily functions through the use of techniques such as catheterization, enemas, diapers, rubber pants, and possibly golden showers. Examples in play: house training a puppy, age play, and golden shower play.

BDSM: Acronym for bondage, domination, sadism, masochism. It typically involves the use of physical restraints that limit a person's range of motion, the infliction and reception of pain, and the playacting of submissive and dominant roles.

Beating: Striking the body with various objects or the hand. Typically administered as punishment in connection with childhood punishments. For example, the dominant may administer a beating to an unruly submissive.

Biting: Scenes involving the biting of the skin to induce pain. Safety note: Although certain types of nibbling/biting are quite safe, extreme biting causing breaking/bleeding of the skin is not recommended and can be dangerous if not carefully done.

Blindfolds: Play which involves temporarily blocking the submissive's sense of sight. This type of play is essential when everyday objects are used to give unexpected sensations. Blindfolds come in many forms, from the more expensive leather (full-head type) to the inexpensive handkerchiefs, scarves, bandages. Safety Note: Do not make the blindfold too tight as to put pressure on the eyeballs. Although some people take blindfolding in stride, it can have unpredictable psychological effects and be extremely frightening for some people.

Body Dysmorphic Disorder (BDD): which is a fixation on an imaginary flaw in the physical appearance resulting in embarrassment and fear of being scrutinized or mocked

Boot worship: The practice of play involving a fetish for boots / shoes. Commonly used for domination and humiliation practices (i.e. licking or cleaning of the Dominant's boots, shoes or bare feet).

Bondage: The restriction of a person's bodily movements for erotic reasons using fastenings of various types or textures. Also used in S/M practices though with a heavier pretence.

Examples; rope, cuffs, chains, and other restraining apparatus.

Breast/chest bondage: The restriction/bondage of the woman's breast/ chest area for erotic reasons using various types of fastenings (i.e., rope, scarves, etc.).

Breath Control: Refers to play involving control of or restriction of air and/ or oxygen to the brain. Other examples would be strangling, which is compression of the neck/throat area to prevent the flow of oxygen to the brain. Suffocation involves reducing the level of oxygen available to breathe; hanging where the body is suspended by the neck (remember, all these games are dangerous to play, either alone or with a partner).

Branding: Making a permanent or semi-permanent scar on the skin by burning it with a hot metal object, as practised on livestock. Seen by some as body art, this technique can be carried out safely; however, it is still likely to be intensely painful. Can also use temporary tattoos or markers. Used by dominants to mark their property; not for the novice.

Breast whipping: Whipping of the woman's/submissive's chest area using a variety of items which include: floggers, whips, cat tails, paddles, for erotic purposes.

Brown showers (Scat): The practice of play involving a fetish for including human (or animal) faeces. Although this type of play can be safe if done correctly, it is not recommended for those faint of heart!

Bruising: A condition which may occur as a result of pinching or striking. Care should be taken to avoid bruising.

C

Caning: Mostly made of bamboo, this whip is by far the most painful. Care should be used, as the welts from caning are slow to rise, and blood can be accidentally drawn if not in constant monitoring. Caning should be limited to the fleshy part of the buttocks, and nowhere else on the body. This can be very dangerous, and is not for the novice.

Chains: A strong metal type of bondage material used in bondage scenes. Chains are less flexible and potentially more dangerous than other types of bondage material. Note: Always make sure you observe metal bondage rules and choose a chain and equipment that will withstand heavier strain.

Chauffeuring: Requiring one's submissive to chauffeur them around physically in vehicles or other types of transportation.

Chastity: A synonym for abstinence.

Condom: A flexible sleeve, used to cover an erect penis to prevent conception. Many Roman Catholic and conservative Protestants teach that they are relatively or completely ineffective at preventing conception or infection from AIDS or other STDs. Public health specialists, physicians, human sexuality specialists teach that, properly used, they are quite effective at preventing infection or conception.

Come: Verb: to have an orgasm Noun: Ejaculated sperm.

Copulation: Penile-vaginal sexual activity, making love.

Cognitive therapy: Psychological therapy in which the major focus is altering and changing irrational beliefs through a type of Socratic dialogue and self-evaluation of certain illogical thoughts. Conditioning and learning are important components of this therapy.

Corsets: A lingerie / binding type device worn to restrict the chest area and make the waist smaller. Worn by early nineteenth century women as a form of formal dress to make one's self more appealing to the opposite sex.

Couples therapy: Is a means of resolving problems and conflicts that couples have not been able to handle effectively on their own. It involves both partners sitting down with a trained professional to discuss their thoughts and feelings. The aim is to help them gain a better understanding of themselves

Cunnilingus: A form of oral sex involving the stimulation of a woman's clitoris.

Cyberskin: Is a thermal plastic elastomer and feels like real skin. It is made from ingredients on the FDA approved lists and does not contain phthalates, polyvinyl chloride (PVC), heavy metals or latex.

D

Desensitization (systematic): Is a type of behavioural therapy used in the field of psychology to help effectively overcome phobias and other anxiety disorders. More specifically, it is a type of Pavlovian therapy / classical conditioning therapy.

E

Ejaculate: verb: The act of expelling semen from the penis. Noun: Semen itself.

Enforced Chastity: In BDSM / S/M circles, meaning the banning or physically preventing one from achieving orgasm or any form of genital stimulation. A means of domination over one's submissive. A device (lockable) panty-type which when worn prevents any type of genital stimulation. See also — Chastity belt.

Erection: The growth in length, diameter and rigidity of a penis as caused by sexual excitement. Sometimes used to refer to the swelling of a clitoris or nipples.

F

Face slapping: Involves play where a moderate amount of slapping of the face is used for humiliation / control. This play can be dangerous if an eye is struck.

Fantasy abandonment: Play which involves the fantasy of abandonment. Possibly leaving the submissive in a deserted area or public area for a short period of time to exert control and punishment.

Fantasy rape: Scenes where the dominant fulfils a submissive's fantasy of rape. Note: This type of play can become quite emotional for the submissive, so use extreme care when performing this type of play. After care is extremely important.

Fantasy rape (Gang): Involves the same type of play with the exception of scene being performed by a group. A sexual fantasy also called an erotic fantasy may be defined as a mental imagery, a thought or long, drawn-out story which passes through our mind principally during sexual activity either coital or masturbatory, often resulting in orgasm..

Fellatio: Oral sex involving the stimulation of a penis with a mouth and/or tongue.

Fisting (anal / vaginal): Play which involves placing or attempting to place the entire hand (or even both hands) in the rectum / vagina. The hand is only formed into a fist, and once fully inserted, requires an extreme gentleness, care and patience. Involves moving of the fist in and out of the orifice and can be a dangerous technique if not performed correctly. Proper study should be done, before attempting such and after care is extremely important. This form of play is dangerous.

Flame play: Play which involves the use of fire in scening. It should be noted here that using any type of fire / flame during scening is quite dangerous and could result in permanent scarring / burning of the body. Use extreme care when using fire in scenes, as this is extremely dangerous and should not be done by a novice.

Food play: Where the dominant controls amount and type of food allowed to be consumed by the submissive. This includes liquid intake as well.

Foot worship: The practice of play involving a fetish for feet. Commonly used for domination and humiliation practices (i.e., licking / cleaning of the dominant's feet).

Forced bed wetting: Forcing the submissive to purposely urinate in the bed. Most commonly used as a form of control / humiliation and in age play scenes.

Forced dressing: Forcing the submissive to dress however the dominant sees fit, whether publicly or privately. Used generally for humiliation.

Force-feeding: A technique by which the dominant controls the submissive's eating habits. Used to fatten up submissives or in age play games.

Forced masturbation: Scenes where the submissive is forced to perform masturbation in front of/for the dominant or others as a form of erotic / sensual play or humiliation.

Forced nudity: A scene which involves forcing one's submissive to remain nude either privately or publicly. Generally as a form of control / humiliation. Note: In some areas, this is illegal in public.

Forced servitude: A form of play involving the submissive acting as a servant / maid to the dominant. May be played out in public or in private as a form of humiliation.

G

Gag: To restrict the use of the mouth by inserting a gag, in various textures (i.e. cloth, leather, ball gag, etc.). When using gags, it is important to remember that these only be worn for short periods of time. This form of play can be dangerous.

Gender: The definition of a person as male or female. It is sometimes based on the shape of their sexual organs. Other times, it is based on the presence of X and/or Y chromosomes in each cell of the body. Sometimes it is based on the individual's own feelings.

Golden shower: Play which involves urinating on one's submissive or vice versa.

Gun play: Scenes involving the use of firearms. It should be noted here: gun play is a dangerous form of play and should not be entered into lightly. Serious consequences could occur from such play and it is not recommended, It is also considered illegal.

H

Hairbrush spanking: Play which involves the use of a hairbrush to inflict pain on the buttocks. Commonly used in naughty boy / girl scenes for punishment.

Hair pulling: Pulling of one's hair for the purpose of pain / humiliation. Used often in heavy scening.

Hand jobs: Using the hands to perform sexual gratification on a man's penis. Stroking of the penis to facilitate orgasm.

Heterosexual: General definition: A sexual orientation in which a person is sexually attracted only to persons of the opposite gender. They may or may not act on their attraction. Religious conservatives: A behaviour in which a person engages in sexual activity only with members of the opposite gender.

High heels: Along with boots, these are the most fetished items around. They combine the discomfort and pain of wearing them with the damage they can inflict when used as weapons. Some scenes may involve wearing, licking, cleaning, etc.

Hot oils: The use of warmed oils for massaging or various other uses for erotic type play. Be careful of oil temperature before applying to another's skin. Test on your own forearm first. This form of play can be dangerous.

Hot Wax: The process of using hot wax in scening. The wax most commonly used are candles and can be used on various parts of the body for erotic stimulation. Some types of wax, beeswax for instance, have a tendency to become extremely hot during burning and should always be used carefully to prevent permanent burning / scarring of the skin. Note: not for the novice, as this form of play is extremely dangerous.

Humiliation: To humiliate the submissive by requiring them to perform things they normally would not do, most commonly in public (i.e., wearing revealing clothing; having sex in public; playing out puppy, boy / girl scenes, etc.).

Hypnotism: To place someone in a trance-type state, and offer suggestions into certain types of behaviour. Safety note: This form of play is not for the novice.

I

Ice play: ice used on nipples or genital areas for desensitization of senses or nerves.

Immobilization: Any form of bondage technically immobilizes someone; however, this term is usually used for extreme forms of bondage where the submissive literally cannot move a muscle. Not recommended for long periods of time, and is dangerous.

Intricate (Japanese) Rope Bondage: A very complex form of bondage that is also quite beautiful to not only see but witness being performed. The submissive is also bonded in such a way as to allow easy access / removal of the device at any time.

K

Knife Play: Cutting the surface of the skin with sharp objects, generally a knife, for the thrill, sensation, or pain. To also create decorative scars. The same basic precautions apply as with other types of blood play. Remember to stay away from vital organ areas and genital cutting.

L

Leather: Material made from the cured skin of animals. Wearing leather is a popular sexual fetish. Leather, especially the wearing of black leather gives the wearer a certain sense of power and is commonly worn in the BDSM scene by the dominant. Used for making floggers. whips, etc

Lesbian: General definition: A female who is sexually attracted only to other women. She may or may not act on their attraction. Religious conservatives: A woman who engages in sexual activity with other women.

Liposuction: Is surgery to improve the contour of your body by removing pockets of excess fat from specific areas of the body. Lipo comes from the Greek word lipos, meaning fat. Other names for liposuction are lipoplasty and suction lipectomy.

Lingam: Sanskrit word for the penis. Loosely translated as wand of light.

Licking: Play involving the licking of various body parts.

Lingerie: Women's intimate apparel. Lace bodices, stockings, bras, panties, etc.

M

Masturbation: Usually refers to any manual self-stimulation of a person's sexual organs. Mutual masturbation involves two or more persons stimulating each other.

Massage: Using the hands (generally) to massage areas of the body. Possibly giving a massage to warm up or — foreplay before play.

Monogamy: An exclusive sexual relationship between two persons.

Mono-sexual: A person who is sexually attracted to persons of only one sex. They may have a heterosexual or a homosexual orientation.

Mummification: A specialized kind of bondage in which the whole body, including the head, if a breathing tube is used, is wrapped tightly to prevent any type of mobilization. Common types of materials are saran wrap, gaffa tape, or cloth or latex bandages. Holes are then sometimes made to allow access to the genital area. This form of play is dangerous, and should always have extra help around in case of an emergency.

N

Nipple clamps: Clamp-type devices placed on the nipples during play to stimulate and stop blood flow to the nipple. One of the general household items to be used are clothespins. Care should be exercised to be sure the material used in clamp, does not stick to the skin, as tearing can occur.

O

Oral Sex: The use of the mouth and/or tongue to stimulate another person's genitals.

Orgasm: Intense excitement resulting in an explosive discharge of neuromuscular tensions at the height of sexual arousal that is usually accompanied by the ejaculation of semen by the male and by vaginal contractions in the woman.

Orgasm Control: When one is forced to release or hold their body's desires to orgasm. Can be used in play or punishment.

P

Pain: In broad terms, pain is the body's warning that something is wrong; however, our pain responses are very complex and it is very easy to produce the effect of pain without doing any real harm to the body. The pain threshold at which a stimulus crosses the boundary between intense sensation and pain is a gray area in terms of our perception. BDSM is associated in most people's minds with potentially painful activities, sometimes referred to as pain games. It is true, however, that some people actually enjoy or at least get some satisfaction out of the intense physical sensation. Some of the satisfaction may be attributed to the release of body chemicals also known as endorphins. Most player's interests are a mixture of physical aspects and the psychological dynamics of domination and submission, and some play with hardly any physical pain at all. Those for whom the interest in pain is predominant are sometimes referred to sadists and masochists rather than dominants and submissives. After care is needed, and monitoring the one receiving pain, is mandatory. Not for the novice.

Paraphilia: An umbrella term which includes many conditions in which an adult's sexual arousing fantasies involve non-human objects, the infliction of pain, non-adults, or other non-consenting persons. Some examples are: ephebophila, exhibitionism, hebephilia, fetishism, frotteurism, paedophilia, sexual m asochism, sexual sadism, transves tite behaviour, and voyeurism. It is derived from two Greek words: para means beyond and philia means love for. They may or may not act on their attraction. Some religious and social conservatives link the 25 or so recognized paraphilias with the three generally accepted sexual orientations (homosexuality, bisexuality and heterosexuality) and transgenderism to produce 30 classifications that they define as sexual orientations. There is a near consensus among people who are not religious and social conservatives that there are only the three sexual orientations.

Phone sex: Play which involves having simulated sex over the telephone.

Some phone companies deem this illegal.

Penis ring: Rubber, metal, or leather type ring used to strap around the base of the penis and balls when soft. Increases blood flow to the genital area during self stimulation and sex. When released, causes minor pain during recurring blood flow.

Penis & Ball Torture (PBT): Any form of restraint or orgasm control to a male's genitals. Can be used for play or punishment. Not for the novice, as this can be dangerous.

Pheromones: Is a substance that acts as a molecular messenger, transmitting information from one member of a species to another member of the same species. Pheromones among animals are largely transported through the sense of smell; in mammals and reptiles, pheromones may be detected by the vomeronasal organ, or Jacobson's organ, which lies between the nose and mouth, although some are detected by regular olfactory (nasal) membranes.

Piercing: Piercing of the body with a thin, sharp object such as a needle. There are two types of play, temporary and permanent. Temporary piercing is done with a smaller, thinner needle which can be removed without permanent scarring after the session is completed i.e. nipple, ear and genital piercing). Permanent piercing is done with a thicker needle which enables jewelry to be easily inserted. Mostly done to enhance the sensual areas of the skin, piercing should be done by a professional.

Play therapy: A working definition might be a form of counselling or psychotherapy that therapeutically engages the power of play to communicate with and help people, especially children, to engender optimal integration and individuation.

Psychotherapy: The Treatment of emotional, behavioural, personality, and psychiatric disorders based primarily on verbal or nonverbal communication and interventions with the patient, in contrast to treatments using chemical and physical measures.

R

Rape: A criminal act involving sexual activity without the informed consent of the other person. This may happen because of coercion, or because the other person in not fully capable of granting consent or is underage.

Rope bondage: There are many styles of rope work from simple to very intricate. Study of knots is important to anyone wishing to attempt this play as it can be very dangerous if blood flow is disrupted. Not for the novice.

Rubber / Latex Clothing: Besides leather, this type of clothing is the next best thing. One example may be a rubber hood. Some bondage items are made out of latex sheeting, and as with leather, black seems to be the most popular colour by far.

S

Safe sex: Sexual activity that is completely free of risk for STD. It is non-existent.

Safer sex: Sexual activity in which the risk for STD has been greatly reduced to an acceptable level.

Saint Andrew's cross: This is a cross made in an X formation. It is generally angled and self-supporting. Some are suspended from ceilings, or mounted directly to a wall. The cross has leather restraints for arms, legs and body, Some have hooks along the edges for a person to be —laced to the cross. Used for sexual play, or punishment, can be administered while attached to the cross.

Sensory deprivation: Play which involves depriving the submissive of certain sensory perceptions. May include blindfolds, bondage, gags, etc.

Sensate focus or sensate focusing: Is a term usually associated with a set of specific sexual exercises for couples or for individuals. The term was introduced by Masters and Johnson,[1] and was aimed at increasing personal and interpersonal awareness of self and the other's needs. Each participant is encouraged to focus on their own varied sense experience, rather than to see orgasm as the sole goal of sex.

Sex: Two meanings (1) the definition of a person as male or female, based on their physical appearance and/or primary sexual characteristics. In almost all people, their sex and their gender are the same. For a minority, they differ. To engage in a sexual act.

Sexual act: This is not a well defined term. Most would define it as including all oral, anal, vaginal, and manual activity which has as its goal of arousing a person. Many teens do not include oral sex as a sexual act. Thus, they might consider themselves to be abstinent, even though they engage in oral sex.

Sexual orientation: Some religious and social Christian conservatives define as many as 30 different sexual orientations. The rest of the world has reached a near consensus that there are three sexual orientations: heterosexuality, bisexuality and homosexuality.

Sharing: When used in a sexual sense: multiple couples while together in the same area who perform sexual acts with their own spouses.

Shibari: The art of intricate Japanese rope bondage. Bondage patterns are intricate, and artistically pleasing.

Spanking: involves striking someone with the palm of the hand or other object (paddle, hairbrush, pig slapper, riding crop, etc.) on the buttocks as a form of punishment / humiliation. Mild spanking can be very erotic and when done correctly can push the submissive into subspace releasing endorphins which in turn creates a sense of euphoria.

Spandex: A form-fitting, stretchy type material that clings to the body (i.e., most women's pantyhose are made of spandex). When worn can be quite comfortable and look extremely sexy when worn on tight bodies.

Spreader bar: A bar type device used to spread apart arms/legs of the submissive. Bars can be made of common, inexpensive materials such as dowel rods, pvc pipe, broomsticks, etc.

STD: Any disease transmitted by bacterium, fungus, parasite or virus primarily during sexual intercourse.

Strap-on: A fastening type strap most commonly used to hold a dildo in place. Commonly used in lesbian scening.

Submissive: One who gives freely of themselves for the pleasures of another. A subordinate with negotiated limits.

Switch: One who switches between dominant / submissive roles, from scene-to-scene or within a scene. Some switches may submit to one dominant, and dominate others, etc.

T

Tattoo: A permanent form of scarring to the body in the form of various types of pictures or drawings or names, etc. A permanent form of marking the submissive as property.

Teasing: The act of teasing to enhance erotic play or pleasure. Teasing the partner in such a way as to stimulate sexual pleasure.

TENS Unit: Term meaning Transcutaneous Electrical Neural Stimulation unit. A machine designed to apply electrical impulses to the body at a safe level. **Note:** As with any type of electrical play, safety pre-cautions should be observed as this form of play is very dangerous.

U

Uniform: Play which involves the submissive wearing a uniform. Such uniforms could include cheerleader uniform, maid uniform, etc. Commonly used in role-playing scenes.

V

Vibrator: A dildo type device made in varying shapes and sizes and powered by either battery or plug-in electrical type. Used as a form of genital stimulation most commonly for women to promote orgasm.

Videos: Pre-recorded movies of a sexual nature. Can be watching others or being recorded.

Voyeurism: Term meaning the act of watching, peeping. In BDSM play, means to watch someone engage in sex or other forms of sensual / erotic play.

W

Water torture: A form of torture involving water. After care is extremely important. Example: Laying the submissive face up while dripping water on the forehead for extended periods of time. Derived from the Chinese (i.e., Chinese water torture).

Waxing: Using warmed wax as a form of erotic sensation. Common areas of waxing are the buttocks, breast area, back, etc. The process of using hot wax in scening. The wax most commonly used are candles. Note: Some types of wax, beeswax for instance, have a tendency to become extremely hot during burning and should always be done carefully to prevent permanent burning/scarring of the skin.

Y

Yoni: Sanskrit for sacred space or sacred temple. Refers to a woman's vagina.

www.ingramcontent.com/pod-product-compliance
Lightning Source LLC
Chambersburg PA
CBHW050124170426
43197CB00011B/1703